Economic Growth, Efficiency and Inequality

A collection of essays by experts in economic theory, this book analyses institutions and policies from the perspectives of growth, efficiency and inequality. Original and rigorous, the volume deals with themes such as income distribution, intersectoral disparities, growth cycles, crises, bargaining, increasing returns, non-traded goods, distributional judgements, auctions, games and liability rules. It will be useful to researchers and scholars of economic theory, Indian economy and public policy, and to social scientists interested in issues of growth, efficiency and inequality.

Satish K. Jain is Professor at the Centre for Economic Studies and Planning (CESP), Jawaharlal Nehru University (JNU). He was a member of the faculty at CESP during 1978–2013 and held the Reserve Bank of India Chair during 2011–13. He has authored *Economic Analysis of Liability Rules* (2015) and has edited *Law and Economics* (2010). His areas of research interest are social choice theory, and law and economics.

Anjan Mukherji is Professor Emeritus at JNU and was member of faculty at CESP during 1973–2010. He was Reserve Bank of India Chair Professor during 2005–10 and was awarded the Jawaharlal Nehru National Fellowship by the Indian Council of Social Science Research (2011–13). Since 2011 he has been Honorary Visiting Professor at the National Institute of Public Finance and Policy. He has authored *Walrasian and Non-Walrasian Equilibria: An Introduction to General Equilibrium Analysis* (1990) and co-authored *Mathematical Methods and Economic Theory* (2011).

"This is a valuable book on an engaging theme that seeks to analyze the functioning of institutions to assess outcomes in terms of their impact on growth, efficiency and inequality. It demonstrates how economic theory can be used to improve our understanding of the real world and change it for the better."

Deepak Nayyar
Professor Emeritus
Jawaharlal Nehru University

"*Economic Growth, Efficiency and Inequality* is a major contribution to theory with bearing on economic policy. This well-researched and insightful volume will be a major reference work for students of economics and policy makers alike."

M. Govinda Rao
Member
Fourteenth Finance Commission

"This volume encompasses perfectly clearly written essays that reflect some of the driving themes in economics. It is a presentation for a wide set of readers."

Satya R. Chakravarty
Professor
Indian Statistical Institute

Economic Growth, Efficiency and Inequality

Edited by

**Satish K. Jain
Anjan Mukherji**

Routledge
Taylor & Francis Group

LONDON AND NEW YORK

First published 2015
by Routledge

2 Park Square, Milton Park, Abingdon, Oxfordshire OX14 4RN
711 Third Avenue, New York, NY 10017

Routledge is an imprint of the Taylor & Francis Group, an informa business

First issued in paperback 2017

British Library Cataloguing-in-Publication Data
A catalogue record for this book is available from the British Library

Library of Congress Cataloging-in-Publication Data
A catalog record has been requested for this book.

ISBN: 978-1-138-89046-6 (hbk)
ISBN: 978-0-8153-7330-8 (pbk)

Typeset in ITC Garamond
by SunRise Media

Contents

Figures

Tables

Contributors

Amitava Bose studied at Presidency College, Calcutta, Delhi School of Economics and the University of Rochester. He was a member of the faculty at Indian Institute of Management Calcutta (IIMC), Kolkata, from 1974 to 2013. He was the director of IIMC from 1997 to 2002. He is an economist with specialization in theory, especially general equilibrium theory and macroeconomics. His main papers are in the area of dynamic optimization and overlapping generations. In recent years, his contributions have focused on macroeconomic problems of developing countries, especially the problem of unbalanced growth.

Brati Sankar Chakraborty teaches economics at the Indian Statistical Institute, Kolkata. He has earlier taught at Visva Bharati University, Santiniketan, and at Jadavpur University, Kolkata. His research interest is in the area of international trade, primarily trade theory with imperfectly competitive markets and increasing returns to scale. He has published articles in international journals such as the *Journal of Development Economics and Economica*. He was the recipient of EXIM Bank International Economic Research Award in 2002 for his PhD thesis titled 'Essays on Trade in Goods and Factor Movements under Increasing Returns to Scale'.

Rittwik Chatterjee is an assistant professor in economics at the Centre for Studies in Social Sciences Calcutta, Kolkata. He has a PhD in economics in 2010 from Jawaharlal Nehru University, New Delhi. His research interests include theories of auctions and mechanism design.

Srobonti Chattopadhyay is a post-doctoral research fellow at IIMC, Kolkata. She has a PhD in economics from Jawaharlal Nehru University, New Delhi, in 2012. Her research interests primarily revolve around auction theory and game theoretic modelling involving auctions and imperfectly competitive market structures.

Sugato Dasgupta is a professor at the Centre for Economic Studies and Planning, Jawaharlal Nehru University, New Delhi. He teaches courses in applied econometrics, statistics and political economics. His research agenda has two distinct strands. First, combining data from India with econometric methods, he has studied the various institutional constraints and incentives that condition the behaviour of policy makers (political parties and politicians). Second, using experimental methods, he has documented the extent to which subject behaviour in the laboratory deviates from the predictions of traditional game-theoretic models, which are based on the twin principles of optimization and rational expectations.

Soumya Datta is currently an assistant professor in the faculty of economics at South Asian University, New Delhi. Previously, he was a faculty member at Shyam Lal College (Evening), University of Delhi. His broad research interests are in the areas of macroeconomic theory, non-linear dynamics and complex systems. He completed his PhD at the Centre for Economic Studies and Planning, Jawaharlal Nehru University, New Delhi, in 2011. His PhD thesis explored the applications of the Lotka-Volterra class of models in the macrodynamics of fnancing investment. Currently, his work focuses on growth cycles, asset price bubbles and optimal exchange rate regimes.

Sanmitra Ghosh is an assistant professor at the Department of Economics, Jadavpur University, Kolkata. Previously, he taught at St. Paul's College, Kolkata. His research interests include political economy, experimental and behavioural economics, and social and economic networks.

Rajendra P. Kundu is an assistant professor at the Centre for Economic Studies and Planning, Jawaharlal Nehru University, New Delhi. He has also taught at Delhi School of Economics and Jadavpur University. His research interests include law and economics, social choice theory, social and economic networks, and experimental and behavioural economics. He has published in various journals and edited volumes.

Amarjyoti Mahanta is an assistant professor at the Centre for Development Studies, Thiruvananthapuram. He did his PhD at Jawaharlal Nehru University, New Delhi. His research interest lies in economic theory, particularly in the areas of applied game theory and dynamic economics. He has worked on price adjustment processes, oligopolistic market structures and auctions.

Abhirup Sarkar is a professor of economics at the Indian Statistical Institute, Kolkata, where he has taught for 30 years. He has also taught and researched in various other universities and institutions in the USA, Canada and Europe. His research interests are in international trade, economic development and political economy. He is the chairman of the State Finance Commission of West Bengal, a body which is entrusted with the task of advising the Government of West Bengal on the devolution of funds to its rural and urban local bodies. He is also chairman of West Bengal Infrastructure Development Finance Corporation, a member of the Planning Board of the Government of West Bengal and a past member of the Group of Advisors to the Union Minister of Finance, Government of India, on G20 matters.

S. Subramanian is an Indian Council of Social Science Research (ICSSR) national fellow affliated with the Madras Institute of Development Studies, Chennai. He has research interests in the felds of social and economic measurement, development economics and collective choice theory. His research has appeared in journals such as *Social Choice and Welfare, Theory and Decision, Mathematical Social Sciences, Economics and Philosophy, Journal of Development Economics, Journal of Development Studies* and *Journal of Human Development and Capability*. He is the author of *Rights, Deprivation, and Disparity: Essays in Concepts and Measurement* (Oxford University Press, New Delhi, 2006), *The Poverty Line* (Oxford University Press, New Delhi, 2012), *Economic Offences* (Oxford University Press, New Delhi, 2013) and *Poverty, Inequality, and Population: Essays in Development and Applied Measurement* (co-authored with D. Jayaraj, Oxford University Press, Delhi, 2010).

Gogol Mitra Thakur is a doctoral student at the Centre for Economic Studies and Planning, Jawaharlal Nehru University, New Delhi. He holds MA and MPhil degrees in economics from Jawaharlal Nehru University. His research interests include macroeconomic theory and structural change in developing economies.

Introduction

Satish K. Jain and Anjan Mukherji

An important way to analyse institutions, rules and policies is to ask what kind of outcomes can be expected under them if purposive and self-regarding individuals are constrained to act within their framework. Such an analysis can be used for positive as well as normative purposes. If one is interested in explaining the raison d'être of a particular institution, rule or policy, then one possible approach is to look at the characteristics of the outcomes which are obtained under it as a result of interaction of rational individuals. If it turns out that the outcomes under the institution, rule or policy in question have certain desirable characteristics, then these could constitute a possible explanation why the particular institution, rule or policy exists. The same analysis could of course be used for normative purposes. If one is interested in a particular normative criterion, one could ask whether the fulfilment of the criterion could be expected under the institution, rule or policy in question. If the answer to the question is in the affirmative, then the institution, rule or policy would be found satisfactory; if not, a case could be made for a change. The essays in this volume are in the main concerned with the relationship between institutions, rules and policies, on the one hand, and growth, efficiency and inequality, on the other. As growth, efficiency and lessening of inequality are among the most important objectives of the economic domain, the essays have both positive and normative implications of relevance.

In Chapter 1 ('Intersectoral Disparities and Growth'), Amitava Bose is concerned with the dynamics of growth disparities within the framework of dual economy models of development. Among other questions, the essay explores as to which variable holds the key to explaining the dynamics of growth disparities in dual economy models; whether the growth rates of different sectors converge over time or whether disparities persist; and whether growth in the 'advanced' sector pulls up the 'backward' sector, that is, whether the growth trickles down.

In view of the fact that in recent times the composition of India's GDP has changed significantly and continues to do so, the concerns of the essay are of particular relevance to the country.

Chapter 2 ('Cycles and Crises in a Model of Debt-Financed Investment-Led Growth') by Soumya Datta investigates whether the macrodynamics of debt-financing investment can provide an endogenous explanation for emergence of growth cycles in demand-constrained closed economies. The essay demonstrates possibilities of both convergence to the steady state and emergence of stable growth cycles around it in a simple macrodynamic model of debt-financed investment-led growth. The growth cycles are robust and are generated endogenously. The emergence of multiple limit cycles is also observed under certain conditions. The possibility of a deterioration of financial variables during a boom with the resulting financial crisis providing an endogenous ceiling to a business cycle is examined in this context.

In Chapter 3 ('Policy-Induced Changes in Income Distribution and Profit-Led Growth in a Developing Economy'), Gogol Mitra Thakur is concerned with the following problem. Over the last three decades most of the developing countries have adopted in varying degrees the neoliberal policies. As these policies aim at liberating the market from government intervention so as to achieve allocative efficiency, particular significance is attached to restricting the size of the budget deficit. Assuming that this has resulted in worsening of income inequality in these countries, the post-Keynesian/Kaleckian growth literature then would seem to suggest that these economies would stagnate unless they managed to continuously increase their trade surplus. However, some of these economies have put up very decent growth performance in the face of decreasing budget deficits; and at the same time failing to consistently maintain trade surplus and even experiencing increasing trade deficit. The post-1991 Indian growth experience, particularly of the last decade, being a standout example. The author shows that a developing country can experience a positive equilibrium growth rate of investment and surplus as long as investment in the economy is responsive to the aspirations of the richer section of the population to match the consumption level of the developed world and imitation of foreign production technology is not very expensive. Also, the growth process can be stable under certain conditions. Moreover, worsening of income distribution is not required to sustain this kind of growth process; a sufficiently unequal initial distribution of income is enough to propel it. But the technologically dynamic sector producing for the rich is incapable of generating much employment.

Chapter 4 ('A Simple Dynamic Bargaining Model'), by Amarjyoti Mahanta is concerned with the problem of division of a cake between two persons or players. The importance of the problem arises from its applicability to bargaining over a surplus, the bargaining over surplus being quite common in transactions. Bargaining takes place whenever agents think that they can influence the end outcome in their favour. Mahanta represents the process of bargaining through a dynamic system. The players announce their plans simultaneously and continuously until they agree upon a division. He shows that the outcome depends on the initial claims as well as on the rates of adjustment. If the range over which each player can choose his rate of adjustment is the same, then the outcome is division with equal shares. If the players' capacities to wait or levels of patience are not similar, then the outcome is division with unequal shares. The player with a higher level of patience or capacity to wait gets the higher share.

In Chapter 5 ('Increasing Returns, Non-traded Goods and Wage Inequality'), Brati Sankar Chakraborty and Abhirup Sarkar are concerned with the phenomenon of increasing wage inequality. The phenomenon of the rising wage gap between skilled and unskilled labour is being observed in different parts of the world. The increase in wage dispersion has been most pronounced in the United States where the skill premium has been consistently increasing since the late 1970s. For other Organisation for Economic Co-operation and Development (OECD) countries, there has either been a fall in the relative wage of the unskilled or an increase in their rate of unemployment or both, though the degree has varied from country to country. However, the evidence on rising wage inequality is somewhat mixed for developing countries. Chakraborty and Sarkar provide a theoretical explanation of the rising wage premium in terms of trade liberalization. The essay makes the point that in a world of increasing returns, productivity of skilled labour can be enhanced through trade by expanding the size of the market in all countries participating in world trade. Three models in succession are built to provide an explanation for the trade-driven rise in wage inequality for the trading partners.

In Chapter 6 ('Equality, Priority and Distributional Judgments'), S. Subramanian undertakes an assessment of the substantive significance of Derek Parfit's distinction between Prioritarianism and Egalitarianism. The essay considers issues relating to the 'levelling down objection', the 'Divided World example', and the distinction between 'absolute' and 'relative' valuations of individual benefit. The author argues that 'levelling down' presents a difficulty only for 'pure telic egalitarianism' , not for 'pluralist telic egalitarianism'; that one can have an egalitarian rationalization for favouring equality in the distribution of a smaller sum of well-being over inequality in the distribution of a larger sum even in a 'Divided World'; and that, while a particular 'absolute'/'relative' dichotomy is relevant for a particular 'distribution-invariance'/'distribution-sensitivity' dichotomy, the resulting distinction is useful for differentiating two types of Egalitarianism rather than for differentiating a non-Egalitarian principle such as Prioritarianism from Egalitarianism.

In Chapter 7 ('Contest under Interdependent Valuations'), Rittwik Chatterjee looks at contests when valuations are independent. Valuations are interdependent if the valuation of any contestant not only depends on one's own type but also on the types of all the other contestants. The author discusses whether it is optimal for the contest designer to give a single 'winner take all' first prize or multiple prizes. The author concludes that it may be the case that even with linear cost and performance functions, offering multiple prizes is optimal. This stands in contrast to the private value case.

In Chapter 8 ('Auctions with Synergy'), Srobonti Chattopadhyay and Rittwik Chatterjee discuss auctions in the presence of synergies. There is positive synergy if values are superadditive, i.e., when having objects together yields a value greater than the sum of individual values. There is negative synergy if values are subadditive, that is, when having objects together yields a value less than the sum of individual values. The essay analyses Vickrey auction separately for positive and negative synergies involving two bidders and two units of a homogeneous commodity. Assuming the valuations of each bidder for a single unit to be distributed uniformly over the unit interval and the synergy parameters for both the bidders to be the same, they compare the expected revenues from a Vickrey auction, discriminatory auction and uniform price auction for the case of positive synergy. For the case considered, the uniform price auction fetches the highest expected revenue, while the Vickrey auction fetches the lowest expected revenue, and the discriminatory auction ranks in between. Next they consider the case when the valuation of each bidder for a single unit is distributed uniformly over the unit interval and the synergy parameters are different for the two bidders. They compare the expected revenue, from a second-price sealed bid auction for the package consisting of both the units with that from a Vickrey auction, separately for positive and negative synergies. The results suggest that for positive synergy, the second-price sealed bid package auction yields a higher expected revenue than the Vickrey auction. For negative synergy, other than for values of the synergy parameter very close to 1, the package auction yields a higher expected revenue than the Vickrey auction.

Chapter 9 ('Negligence as Existence of a Cost-Justified Untaken Precaution and the Efficiency of Liability Rules'), by Satish K. Jain investigates the efficiency of liability rules with a particular notion of negligence. Courts employ the notion of negligence in at least two different senses. At times, the courts hold a party to be negligent because its care level falls short of what the courts deem to be the due care for that party; and at times, they hold a party to be negligent on account of its failure to take some cost-justified precaution. Thus, one way to define the idea of negligence is to declare a party to be negligent if and only if its care level is less than the due care specified by the courts for the party in question. Another way to define negligence is to deem a party to be negligent if and only if there exists a precaution which the party could have taken but did not, and which would have cost less than the reduction in expected loss that it would have brought about. If negligence is defined as failure to take at least the due care, then the efficient liability rules are characterized by the condition of negligence liability. However, if negligence is defined as existence of a cost-justified untaken precaution, then there is no liability rule which is efficient. The essay investigates the robustness of this impossibility theorem. The way the proof of the impossibility theorem has been constructed, complementarity in the care levels of the parties seems to play an important role in rendering liability rules inefficient when the notion of negligence is defined in terms of cost-justified untaken pre-cautions. Thus, an interesting question that arises is whether there are any liability rules which are efficient if we rule out complementarity in care levels. It is shown in the essay that even when complementarities are ruled out, there are no liability rules which are efficient, given that negligence is defined as existence of a cost-justified untaken precau-tion. Thus, the impossibility theorem regarding efficient liability rules when negligence is defined as existence of a cost-justified untaken precaution is quite robust.

In Chapter 10 ('The 11–20 Money Request Game and the Level-k Model: Some Experimental Results'), Sugato Dasgupta, Sanmitra Ghosh and Rajendra P. Kundu present and discuss their experimental results on the 11–20 money game introduced by Arad and Rubinstein.[1] The 11–20 is a simultaneous-move two-player game. Each player requests an amount of money, where the amount is restricted to be an inte-ger between 11 and 20 units. A player receives the amount that he requests; furthermore, a bonus of 20 units is received if he asks for exactly one unit less than the other player. The game has a unique Nash equilibrium. In equilibrium, players randomize over the numbers 15 to 20, with probability weights that are weakly decreasing as the numbers increase. The experimental findings of Arad and Rubinstein, however, could not be explained in terms of the Nash equilibrium. Arad and Rubinstein rationalize the behaviour of the subjects in their ex-periment by an appeal to the level-k model. The experimental results ob-tained by the authors confirm the robustness of the results obtained by

---

[1]Arad, Ayala and Ariel Rubinstein. 2012. 'The 11–20 Money Request Game: Evalu-ating the Upper Bound of k-level Reasoning', *American Economic Review*, 102(7): 3561–73.

Arad and Rubinstein. They also discuss whether the level-k model can be used to explain subjects' behaviour. They find that a subject's Cognitive Reflection Test score, viewed as a measure of cognitive ability, predicts his behaviour in their experiment. Specifically, subjects with high Cognitive Reflection Test scores ask for less money and are classified as higher level-k types than subjects with low Cognitive Reflection Test scores. This then provides an independent justification for using the level-k model to rationalize subjects' behaviour in the 11–20 game. The authors also recorded for each subject, both the money amount requested and the time taken to submit the request. They found that subjects asking for the maximal amount of 20 units (deemed to be the most instinctive action according to the level-k model) have higher mean and median response times than the subjects with money requests in the 17–19 range. Thus, the level-k model fails a decisive test. The authors, therefore, advocate caution in using the level-k model to interpret subjects' behaviour in the 11–20 game.

CHAPTER 1

Intersectoral Disparities and Growth

Amitava Bose[*]

Development is associated with changes in the sectoral composition of output. Such changes are driven by disparities in sectoral rates of growth. The dynamics of growth disparities raise a number of analytical questions that can be dealt with in different ways using alternative frameworks. This essay is confined to a particular framework—the framework of dual economy models of development. The objective of the essay is to find out what these models have to say on intersectoral disparities in rates of growth. In particular, it engages with the following issues:

1. What is the variable that holds the key to explaining the dynamics of growth disparities in dual economy models?
2. Do sectoral growth rates converge over time or do disparities persist?
3. A widely debated question in development economics is whether growth in the 'advanced' sector pulls up the 'backward' sector. If it does, growth is said to 'trickle down'. Does the answer depend on whether growth rates converge over time or diverge?

The recent growth experience of the Indian economy has brought these questions to the fore. Two facts stand out. First, the composition of India's gross domestic product (GDP) has changed significantly and continues to do so. In the course of the last two decades, the share of agriculture has fallen from around 35 per cent to almost 15 per cent,

---

[*] My thanks to Subrata Guha, Mihir Rakshit, Susmita Rakshit, Debraj Ray and Soumyen Sikdar for helpful comments.

1

while the share of the services sector has gone up from around 40 per cent to 55 per cent. Second, news on the growth front has been both exciting and disappointing. The Indian economy has been registering high rates of GDP growth in recent years—India is one of the fastest-growing economies of the world—yet employment growth has been low, sometimes negative, especially of unskilled labour. Clearly, growth has not been 'inclusive'. What structural features could be responsible for this? If the different sectors are interlinked, why do disparities persist?

Classical development models yield balanced growth in the long run (convergence), but they can be used to shed some light on intersectoral disparity as well (as part of transitional dynamics). Most macro-models of development are dual economy models characterized by dynamism in one part of the economy and stagnation in the other. The central question—whether dualism will persist or not—depends on the manner in which the two parts are linked to each other. Some linkages are related to resource flows, such as the flow of surplus unskilled labour from the stagnant part to the dynamic part. Other linkages belong to the product side—the flow of food from the rural to the urban sector and the flow of industrial goods in the reverse direction. While recognizing the existence of surplus unskilled labour, demand-side linkages on the product side are emphasized here.

Resources and goods are moved from one part of the economy to the other to take advantage of opportunities for exchange. An exchange equilibrium can be brought about in different ways. This essay focuses on models in which the equilibrating variable is the intersectoral terms of trade (or relative price) between goods of the agriculture sector and goods of the industry-cum-services sector.[1]

Examples of flexible price dual economy models abound in the literature. These models are brought under one umbrella here, using a reduced form model with a very spare frame. This reduced form model can be fitted up to yield either convergence (to the balanced growth equilibrium) or persistent disparity. In the second section, the model is used to generate convergence to balanced growth. There are several elaborate models that can be reduced to this convergent version of the reduced form model, characterized here as the Lewis–Ricardo model.[2] On the other hand, the third section emphasizes various

---

[1] In an alternative class of models that I deal with elsewhere, the link variable is production in the non-agriculture sector; see Bhaduri and Skarstein (2003).
[2] One example of this model is detailed in the Appendix.

contrary possibilities that lead to perpetual uneven growth. In the fourth section, the basic model and its variants are used to comment on the issue of 'trickle-down' and its relation to the existence of perpetual disparity. The fifth section works out an example of a parametric form that covers all possibilities.

The exposition is heuristic and relies entirely on a pair of cross diagrams. We know of no existing model that fits the depiction of persistent growth disparity that is provided in the third and fourth sections, though the issue is of some contemporary relevance.[3]

Disparity and Convergence in the Benchmark L–R Model[4]

There are two sectors: (*a*) agriculture and (*b*) non-agriculture (including manufacturing and services).The relative price of agricultural products in terms of non-agricultural products is denoted as p. The two growth rates are x for agriculture and g for non-agriculture. There is one market for exchange of products. The focus will be on the supply and demand for the agricultural surplus. The supply is denoted X and the demand denoted D. The former is the net exports of agriculture and the latter the net imports of the non-agriculture sector.

Growth Gap

The analysis begins by isolating the variable responsible for differences between the growth rates of the two sectors. Here the variable is taken to be the terms of trade p. Two simple relations are postulated:

1. *An increase in* p *reduces the growth rate* g *of the non-agriculture capital stock* K. This postulate is expressed in terms of a function g = g(p) that yields a downward sloping curve.

$$g = g(p), g'(p) < 0 \qquad (1.1)$$

2. *The agricultural growth rate* x *is given:* $x = \bar{x}$. (This can be changed to x being an increasing function of p without affecting anything of significance.) Here x is the rate of growth of the marketable

---

[3] For a very nice introduction to uneven growth, see Ray (2010).

[4] For details, the reader may consult the Appendix in which a special case has been explicitly worked out. See Basu (1997), Cardoso (1981), Dutt (1992) and Kalecki (1976) for similar models.

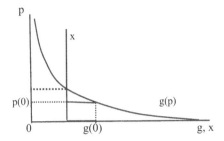

FIGURE 1.1 Determination of Growth Rates

surplus (net exports) of the agricultural sector X.

$$x = \bar{x}, \text{ given} \tag{1.2}$$

It follows that the growth gap [g–x] depends on p. The dependence can be characterized by referring to the 'balanced growth terms of trade' $\bar{p}$ that equalizes the growth rates.[5] The size of the gap is then related to the difference between p and $\bar{p}$.

There is $\bar{p}$ such that

$$g\left(\bar{p}\right) = \bar{x}; \quad g\left(p\right) > \bar{x} \quad \text{for} \quad p < \bar{p}; \quad g\left(p\right) < \bar{x} \quad \text{for} \quad p > \bar{p}. \tag{1.3}$$

Figure 1.1, showing sectoral growth rates as functions of p, is referred to as the Kaldor diagram. It is important to emphasize that Figure 1.1 is *not* about how the market clearing price p(t) is determined at a particular date t. *Given* p(t), Figure 1.1 tells us how sectoral growth rates and the size of the growth gap are determined at that t.

Figure 1.1 also helps identify the balanced growth point. But there is no presumption that p(t) = $\bar{p}$. Moreover, nothing so far suggests that p(t) converges to $\bar{p}$ and there is balanced growth g $(\bar{p})$ = $\bar{x}$ in the long-run (that is, steady state). One needs more than Figure 1.1 to obtain the dynamics of p(t).

The starting point of the dynamics is this. Consider an initial p(0) such that p(0) < $\bar{p}$. Then to start with, the non-agriculture sector grows more rapidly than the agriculture sector: g $\left(p\left(0\right)\right)$ > g $(\bar{p})$ = $\bar{x}$. As a result, the ratio of the agricultural surplus X to the non-agriculture capital stock K decreases. The opposite happens if p(0) lies above $\bar{p}$. To

---

[5] The usual technical details necessary for establishing the existence of $\bar{p}$ are assumed to be fulfilled.

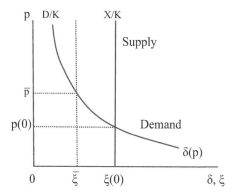

FIGURE 1.2 Determination of the Relative Price: Short-run Equilibrium

investigate the dynamics further, we have to examine how such changes in (X/K) affect p. To do so, one needs a theory about what determines p.

Determination of the Intersectoral Relative Price in the Short Run

We invoke supply and demand curves at a point of time for the (normalized) marketable surplus $\xi = (X/K)$. It is assumed that X(t) and K(t) do not depend on p(t): supplies are price inelastic.

On the demand side, it is stipulated that an increase in p—an increase in the prices of agriproducts relative to non-agriculture products—reduces the non-agriculture sector's demand for agriproducts.[6] The (normalized) demand $\delta = D/K$ is assumed to be a decreasing function of p:$\delta = \delta$ (p) traces out a downward sloping curve.[7]

At any given point in time t, $\xi(t)$ is historically given and determines the market clearing price p(t) at that date: p = p(t) solves

$$\delta(p) = \xi(t). \tag{1.4}$$

Starting at t = 0 with a historically given X/K = $\xi(0)$, the initial price is determined at p(0) as shown earlier. For p < p(0), there will be excess demand. The usual assumption, which will be maintained here,

---

[6] This may be justified in several different ways—one particular justification is given in the Appendix.

[7] Example: Y = Kf(l(p)), where l = (L/K) depends on w, which depends on p. Generally the demand for agricultural goods would be D = D(p, Y). Homogeneity assumptions are used to get D = δ (p)K. See the next section for more on this.

is that this will lead to a rise in p *within the stipulated short period*. On the other hand, the movement of p *over time*, that is, over successive short periods, concerns changes in the market clearing price from one period to another. Changes in p reflect *equilibrium dynamics*.

There is no presumption that one gets $p(0) = \bar{p}$: given $\xi = \xi(0)$, there will be excess demand (positive or negative) if one were to set $p(0) = \bar{p}$. It is clear that $p(0)$ depends on $\xi(0)$. For balanced growth the supply ratio ξ has to be appropriate: $\bar{p} = P\left(\bar{\xi}\right)$, where $P(\cdot) = \delta^{-1}(\cdot)$ solves (1.4).

Equilibrium Dynamics

The dynamics of the market clearing p is very evident and can be read off by combining the two figures (1.1 and 1.2). If, as in Figure 1.2, $p(0) < \bar{p}$, then $\xi(0) > \bar{\xi}$. Then from Figure 1.1, it follows that $g(p(0)) > \bar{x}$. As a result, $\xi=(X/K)$ falls. Going back to Figure 1.2, it is seen that this implies that ξ gets closer to $\bar{\xi}$ and p gets closer to $\bar{p}$.

In the long run, ξ converges monotonically to $\bar{\xi}$ and p converges monotonically to $\bar{p}$.

The heuristics of convergence could be described verbally as follows. Initially the agriculture sector is large and the non-agriculture sector is small. This leads to a low relative price of agriproducts. As a result wages are low and profits are high in the non-agriculture sector since wages would be linked to the price of food. The saving of high profits leads to a high growth rate in the non-agriculture sector, outstripping the growth rate of the agricultural surplus. As a result, the relative abundance of the agricultural surplus falls over time and the relative price of agriproducts rises. This increase in the relative price dampens non-agricultural growth. Growth disparity is thereby reduced. The process continues until the growth rates are equalized.

Figure 1.3 puts the two figures side by side. Starting with a historically determined stocks ratio $\xi(0)$, the initial market clearing price $p(0)$ gets fixed from Figure 1.3(a). This $p(0)$ is then fed into Figure 1.3(b) to get the 'growth gap' $[g(0)-\bar{x}]$. If the gap is positive, then K grows faster than X, so $\xi = (X/K)$ falls. Using this information in Figure 1.3(a), one observes that p goes up, and so on. It follows that p and ξ inch closer to their respective long-term levels $\bar{p}$ and $\bar{\xi}$.

What Makes for Convergence in the L–R Model?

The aforementioned is a brief account of what may be called the Lewis–Ricardo (in short the 'L–R') model. It is useful to isolate those features

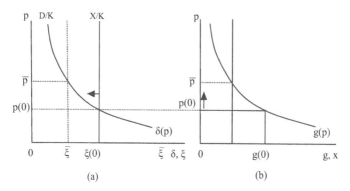

FIGURE 1.3 Convergence to Balanced Growth

in the L–R model that are responsible for the orderly manner in which the growth process self-corrects departures from the balanced growth equilibrium. Some of these are micro details that lie behind the assumed shapes of the curves. It is trivial to observe that had the shapes been different, the results would have been different also. Consider the following alternative response of g to p. As p goes up, there is an increase in agricultural incomes. Suppose this induces greater investment of these incomes in the non-agriculture sector. If this response is sharp enough, g may well go up; at least, there may well be a range over which $g'(p) > 0$. Suppose this is so in the neighbourhood of $\bar{p}$. This destroys the local stability of the balanced growth equilibrium and messes up convergence.

The next section picks on the two homogeneity assumptions that were slipped in while writing the demand function for non-agriculture goods as $D = K\delta(p)$. The demand function can be deduced from the following two relations:

1. The basic demand relation is actually something like $D = Yh(p)$. This means that, given p, the *level* of Y has no impact on (D/Y)—a special assumption.
2. The other relation is something like $Y = Kf(\ell)$ which reflects constant returns to scale. Now from profit maximization, ℓ will depend on the product wage w, and it can be assumed that $w = pv$, where v is the fixed real wage rate. Therefore, $Y = Kf(\ell(p))$. Combining the two relations, $D = [h(p) f (\ell (p))]K = \delta(p)K$.

First consider the demand side. Writing something like $D = h(p)Y$ is to assume unitary income elasticity of demand. This is a strong assumption. The consumption basket of the rich is very different from that of the poor. The income elasticity of demand can hardly be assumed to be independent of the level of income. Changes in Y typically do affect h(p) and thereby δ(p). This will have a major impact on the analysis of the dynamics of growth disparities.

Second, the relation between Y and K could be important. In the preceding derivation, we have assumed constant returns to scale. It has also been assumed that employment is determined by K (since L has been eliminated). This suggests a horizontal labour supply curve—Lewis's unlimited supplies of labour. One could either assume a constant real wage rate or fixed coefficients such as underlying the 'AK'-production function Y = AK. These assumptions too could come under question.

The L–R model can be used to capture an initial phase of industrialization where the main complementary resources are heavy machinery (K) and the unskilled labour supplied by the backward sector. Incremental non-agriculture output (Y) is powered by increases in the real wage bill (vL). Much or all of these additional wages are spent on primary products ('food') obtained from the backward sector (X). For a given p, take the share of wages to be constant, and this suggests a proportional relation between increases in D and increases in Y.

However, the recent growth experience of the Indian economy suggests 'leapfrogging' into the era of services-led growth. The increase in Y does not depend on increases in unskilled labour L but on increases in unskilled labour (say, H) that are not drawn from the backward hinterland. H is scarce and, therefore, better paid; increases in H's income will increasingly *not* be directed to the products of the backward sector (for instance, unprocessed food).

The model of the next section is designed to capture what has been described as the 'services-led' phase of development. Accordingly, the model of the next section is referred to as the S-model.

Services-Led Growth: The S-Model

Structural changes within the non-agriculture sector have important effects on demand curves—both the level demand curve D(.) and the growth demand curve g(.). Consider the Indian case. The rapid increase in the share of the services sector has reduced the dependence of the non-agriculture sector on the resources and the product of the agriculture sector. In particular, the incremental demand for unskilled labour—available in plenty from the overpopulated rural hinterland—has sharply fallen as there is little use for such labour for growth of services. This has, of course, been accompanied by an increase in the demand for certain well-defined skills, particularly in the fast-modernizing parts of manufacturing (for example, cars) and services industries (for example, information technology [IT] and banking). However, increased production of these skills requires little of either the surplus unskilled labour or the output of the agriculture sector. It may be assumed that the non-agriculture sector is self-sufficient in the production of such skills.[8]

If one assumes that growth is accompanied by increases in the share of the better-paid skilled labour vis-à-vis the low-wage unskilled labour, then it is reasonable to suppose that non-agriculture growth has little impact on the demand for food. This calls for a different specification of the (D/K) function.

A Zero Income Elasticity of Demand for Food

Two alternative demand functions for food will be considered. The first formulation is the following one:

$$D(p) = a + h(p) \text{ with } h'(p) < 0 \text{ and asymptotic to the axes} \quad (1.5)$$

The market clearing price at date t, p(t), is that p for which

$$h(p) = X - a, \quad (1.6)$$

given $X = X(t)$ where $X(t) = X(0) e^{xt}$.

Assume, as before, that there is balanced growth equilibrium for $p = \bar{p}$ with $g(\bar{p}) = x$.

Suppose $p < \bar{p}$, so that $g(p) > x$. What is the effect of this growth gap on p? Actually p depends on X and is independent of (X/K), the variable that is affected by the growth gap [g−x]. In fact, since $x > 0$, X will increase and that will cause p to decline. If $h(p) \to \infty$ requires $p \to 0$, then over time p(t) will become vanishingly small. This persistent decline in p will increase the growth gap perpetually.

Therefore, in contrast to the L–R model, here there is no convergence. The non-agriculture growth rate increases without limit.

We can sum up the contrast as follows:

---

[8] In the last decade, 'communications' has grown at more than 20 per cent per annum and much of this growth has been skill intensive.

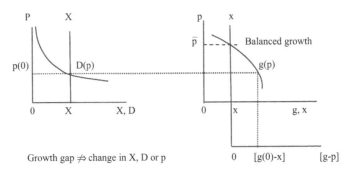

FIGURE 1.4 Growth Gap Blows Up

L–R model: Large share of agriculture sector $\Rightarrow$ low price of food $\Rightarrow$ high profits in industry $\Rightarrow$ high industrial growth $\Rightarrow$ fall in share of agriculture sector + increased demand for food $\Rightarrow$ rise in p $\Rightarrow$ fall in growth. Thus in L–R, a growth gap cannot persist *ad infinitum*: high $g \Rightarrow g$ will fall.

S–model: High growth in non-agriculture output $\nRightarrow$ increase in p. Hence, high g $\nRightarrow$ squeezing of profits and thereby reduction of g. In other words, high g $\nRightarrow$ g will fall. Conclusion: A growth gap can persist ad infinitum.

Positive but Low Income Elasticity of Demand for Food

It is rather extreme to assume that, beyond a point, the demand for food has zero elasticity with respect to increases in non-agriculture incomes, especially when one considers the 'luxury' demand for processed food. I now move to the considerably milder assumption that the relevant income elasticity is positive but less than unity. Assume that

$$D = K^{\sigma} m(p), 0 < \sigma < 1, m'(p) < 0. \qquad (1.7)$$

Therefore, the short-run equilibrium condition reduces to

$$m(p) = XK^{-\sigma}. \qquad (1.8)$$

Let $\eta = XK^{-\sigma}$. Then the rate of growth of η is $[x - \sigma g]$. Now consider p such that there is balanced growth $x = g(p)$, that is, $p = \bar{p}$. *The problem is that balanced growth is not sustainable.* This is because with $x = g$ the rate of growth of η is $(1 - \sigma)x$, and this is positive given $x > 0$ and $\sigma < 1$. Therefore, $XK^{-\sigma}$ will increase, starting with $x = g$. Since $m'(p) < 0$, this implies that p will fall. Market clearing will take the economy

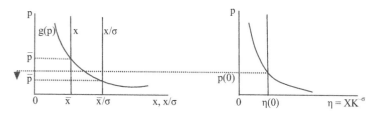

FIGURE 1.5 Perpetual Disparity in the Long Run

away from balanced growth. Clearly the long-run equilibrium—the limit of the market clearing trajectory—is a growth situation with $x = \sigma g < g$. Thus, in this model too the rate of growth of the non-agriculture sector outstrips that of the agriculture sector in perpetuity—if one insists on balanced growth, there is bound to be excess supply of agricultural goods. However, the non-agriculture rate of growth g does not blow up; it converges to some $g > x$.

It is easy to tell the story of the dynamics of growth disparity in pictures.

Figure 1.5 is analogous to Figure 1.3 once x is replaced by (x/σ) and ξ is replaced by η. The dynamics unfolds in exactly the same manner. The outcome is convergence of g—not to x but to $(x/\sigma) > x$. The long-run equilibrium price is $\hat{p} < \bar{p}$. There are two cases that can be considered. (*a*) If the initial relative size of the agriculture sector is large, $p(0) < \hat{p}$ is likely. In that case, p will rise and the growth gap will dwindle over time. (*b*) If the relative size of the agriculture sector is not that large to begin with, as in Figure 1.5, then p will fall over time, and the growth gap will keep getting bigger.

To proceed further along this path would require fleshing out the model in terms of micro details.

Increasing Returns

The possibility of increasing returns to capital—a cornerstone of endogenous growth theory—is also damaging to the convergence conclusions of the L–R model. Taking one thing at a time, let us reintroduce homogeneity of demand as follows:

$$D = Yz(p) \qquad (1.9)$$

However, assume that $Y = K^{\varphi}$, with $\varphi > 1$. Then $D = K^{\varphi} z(p)$, which is the same form as in the previous sub-section except that the exponent of K is now strictly greater than unity. Therefore, the conclusions get reversed. Start with x = g. This would lead to a fall in X $K^{-\varphi}$ and push p up. As p goes up, g falls. The long run is a situation in which x= φg with $\varphi > 1$. Thus, in the long-run equilibrium, x > g; somewhat surprisingly, increasing returns to capital makes for a negative growth gap in the longrun.

The diagrammatic depiction of the dynamics is identical to that shown in Figure 1.5 except that the relevant vertical to which g adjusts will now be to the left of $\bar{x}$ rather than to the right.

The following two observations are important:

1. We may allow for both demand non-homogeneity D = $Y^\sigma z(p)$ with $\sigma < 1$ and increasing returns Y = K^φ with $\varphi > 1$. Combine the two yields D = $K^\theta z(p)$ with $\theta = \sigma\varphi$. There are two possibilities. If demand inelasticity dominates ($\sigma < 1/\varphi$), then $\theta < 1$ and one obtains g > x in the limit with a low p. On the other hand, if increasing returns dominate ($\varphi > 1/\sigma$), then $\theta > 1$ and g < x in the limit with a high p.

2. Note that with $\sigma = 1$ and $\varphi > 1$, even though g < x in the limit, in terms of the rate of growth of *output* G = $\dot{Y}/Y$, there is no growth gap in the limit: $\left(\dot{Y}/Y\right) = \varphi$ g = x. Thus, the long-run behaviour of output, growth is determined by the nature of the demand function D(p,Y) rather than by the nature of the production function Y = F(K). It follows that *a persistent growth gap in outputs reflects non-homogeneity on the demand side.*

Autonomous Investment and Trickle-Down

So far it was assumed that g depends on the saving ratio. An increase in p will raise agricultural incomes. In classical theory, the accompanying redistribution of profits from industrialists to landlords is assumed to reduce the saving ratio. This is the chief reason for a negative association between g and p.

However, there are reasons to dispute this relationship also. To say that g is driven by the saving ratio is to submit to reasoning that has been termed 'pre-Keynesian' by Joan Robinson. In India the S-phase— or service-led-growth—has also been accompanied by increasing opening up of the economy to the rest of the world. The opening up of the capital accounts makes it possible for investments to be less dependent on the availability of domestic saving. If that is so, then g will tend to be independent of p; possibly g will be a function of expected growth in external markets.

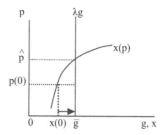

FIGURE 1.6 Laggard Growth Being Pulled Up

Second, it is perhaps better to view the non-agriculture sector as a self-contained one-sector model without a (unskilled) labour constraint and with a comparative-advantage-driven incentive to unify with the rest of the world. This will typically make the non-agriculture sector less constrained by the domestic agriculture sector for demand as well as resources and this, of course, will weaken the intersectoral linkage.

All this tends to give g(p) a near vertical shape. This puts at peril the existence of balanced growth equilibrium if we stick to the assumption that x is given. In a class of models,[9] the assumption instead is $x = x(p)$, $x'(p) > 0$. The broad idea is that a movement of the terms of trade in favour of agricultural products—other than those caused by temporary fluctuations—will be accompanied by improvements in the returns to investment in the agriculture sector. This should stimulate investment and growth in the agriculture sector. Therefore, the following alternative model can be considered:

$$g = \bar{g} \tag{1.10}$$

$$x = x(p), x'(p) > 0 \tag{1.11}$$

First consider homogeneous demand and production so that the exchange equilibrium is given by (1.4): $\delta\left(p\right) = \xi$. For the dynamic cross diagram, only a small change is required.

The same Figure 1.6 can be used to portray long-run equilibrium for three cases (*a*) $\lambda = 1$: the homogeneous case that leads to convergence to balanced growth; (*b*) $\lambda < 1$: the case of income inelasticity of demand leading to perpetual excess of g over x; and (*c*)$\lambda > 1$: the case of increasing returns to capital leading to perpetual excess of x over g. It is always the case that p converges to $\hat{p}$.

---

[9] See, for instance, Dutt (1992).

It follows that 'trickle-down' (faster-growing sector pulls up the rest) occurs in each of these cases provided $p(0) < \hat{p}$ regardless of the fact that disparities may be permanent. Thus, it is, strictly speaking, not the case that 'uneven growth' destroys trickle down.

Trickle-down is mostly discussed when $g > x$ in the shortrun. In the previous parts of the essay, it was assumed that x is given and $g'(p) < 0$. Consider now the case of convergence to balanced growth. Obviously, this can only involve a downward adjustment of g to x. In growth terms, this is hardly a trickle down.[10] However, in the alternative model of Figure 1.6, convergence to balanced growth, starting with $g > x$, does involve a pulling up of the backward rural sector's growth rate to equality with the growth rate of the non-agriculture sector. However, the point is that the issue is unrelated to balanced or unbalanced growth. Trickle-down only occurs when the laggard sector's growth rate responds to the economic incentive of relative price movements.

Example of a General Dual Growth Model Using Simple Parametric Forms

For quick reference, an example that covers all versions of the model is worked out here.

Demand for agricultural goods from the non-agriculture sector is as follows:

$$D(t) = [Y(t)]^{\sigma}[p(t)]^{-\varepsilon}, \qquad (1.12)$$

where $\sigma \le 1$ and $0 < \varepsilon < 1$ are constants.

Production of non-agriculture output Y depends on that sector's capital stock K:

$$Y(t) = [K(t)]^{\alpha} 1 \le \alpha, \qquad (1.13)$$

where α is a constant.

Combining (1.12) and (1.13), we get

$$D(t) = [K(t)]^{\theta}[p(t)]^{-\varepsilon}. \qquad (1.14)$$

---

[10] Trickle-down involves more than growth rates. Note that an increase in p redistributes income in favour of the agriculture sector. To the extent that poorer farmers are net sellers of food, there would be an income gain for them in the transition to long-run equilibrium. So there could be some trickle-down even though agricultural growth rate is given.

Market clearing at date t is

$$X(t) = D(t). \tag{1.16}$$

Substituting for D and suppressing t, we get

$$XK^{-\theta} = p^{-\varepsilon}. \tag{1.17}$$

On logarithmic differentiation with respect to t:

$$\frac{\dot{X}}{X} - \theta \frac{\dot{K}}{K} = -\varepsilon \frac{\dot{p}}{p}. \tag{1.18}$$

Define g and x as growth rates:

$$gK = \dot{K}; x = \dot{x}. \tag{1.19}$$

(1.18) reduces to

$$\varepsilon\dot{p} = p(\theta g - x). \tag{1.20}$$

The growth rates as functions of p are as follows:

$$g = 1/p \tag{1.21}$$

$$x = 1 - (1/p) \tag{1.22}$$

Inserting in (1.20),

$$\dot{p}(t) = a = bp(t), \text{ where } a/(1+\theta)/\varepsilon, \ b = 1/\varepsilon. \tag{1.23}$$

This has the solution

$$p(t) = \hat{p} + [p(0) - \hat{p}]e^{-bt} \text{ where } \hat{p} = \frac{a}{b} = (1+\theta). \tag{1.24}$$

Therefore,

$$\lim_{t\to\infty} p(t) = \hat{p}; \quad \lim_{t\to\infty} g(t) = 1/(1+\theta); \quad \lim_{t\to\infty} x(t) = \theta/(1+\theta) \tag{1.26}$$

$$\lim_{t\to\infty} [g(t) - x(t)] = (1-\theta)/(1+\theta). \tag{1.27}$$

The following cases can be generated:

Assumption	Conclusion
Homogeneity: $\theta = 1$:	convergence to balanced growth
Increasing returns dominate: $\theta > 1$:	convergence to $[x > g]$
Income inelasticity dominates: $0 < \theta < 1$:	convergence to $[g > x]$
Zero income elasticity: $\theta = 0$:	$p \to 1; g \to 1; x \to 0$

Appendix: Behind the L–R Model—A Lewis–Ricardo Model with Real Wage Constancy

Agriculture sector

X: marketed surplus of agriproducts
x: rate of growth of marketed surplus
p: relative price of agriproducts

Non-agriculture sector

Y: non-agriculture output
L: non-agri employment
K: non-agri capital stock
$Y = L^\alpha K^{1-\alpha} = K\ell^\alpha$; $\ell = (L/K)$
w: product wage; $v = (w/p)$: real wage
Profit maximizing condition: MPL = w
or, $\alpha\ell^{\alpha-1} = vp$ or $\ell = [\alpha/vp]^{1/1-\alpha} \equiv \ell(p)$
g: rate of growth of K
Assume $g = (Y - wL)/K$, that is, saving = profits
Hence, $g = (1 - \alpha)\ell^\alpha = (1-\alpha)[\alpha/vp]^{\alpha/1-\alpha} = Ap^{-\beta}$, where $\beta = [\alpha/(1 - \alpha)]$

Market Clearing

wL = pX or vL = X.
Dividing both sides by K,
$v\ell = \xi$ where $\xi = (X/K)$

Dynamics

$$\dot{\ell} = \ell\left(x-g\right)$$

From profit maximization, $(1^{-\alpha})\ell^{\alpha-1} = vp$ hence $p\ell^{1-\alpha} = (1 - \alpha)v$. Therefore, $\frac{\dot{\ell}}{\ell} = -\frac{\dot{p}}{p}/(1 - \alpha) = x - Ap^{-\beta}$ or $\dot{p} = p(1 - \alpha)[Ap^{-\beta} - x]$. This has the solution $p(t)^\beta = \frac{(1-\alpha)A}{\bar{x}} + \left[p(0)^\beta - \frac{(1-\alpha)A}{\bar{x}}\right]e^{-\beta\bar{x}t}$.
Clearly, $p(t) \to \bar{p} = (1 - \alpha)/\bar{x}^{1/\beta}$ monotonically as $t \to \infty$.
Thus, $\dot{p} > 0 \Leftrightarrow p < \bar{p} \Leftrightarrow \xi = (X/K) > \bar{\xi} = v\ell(\bar{p})$. The terms of trade will keep moving in favour of agriproducts if and only if initially the size of the non-agricultural capital stock is too low relative to the marketed surplus of agriproducts.

References

Basu, K. 1997. *Analytical Development Economics: The Less Developed Economy Revisited*. Cambridge, Mass.: MIT Press, chapter 4.

Bhaduri, A. and R. Skarstein. 2003. 'Effective Demand and the Terms of Trade in a Dual Economy: A Kaldorian Perspective', *Cambridge Journal of Economics*, 27(4):583–95.

Cardoso, E. 1981. 'Food Supply and Inflation', *Journal of Development Economics*, 8(3):269–84.

Dutt, A. K. 1992. 'A Kaldorian Model of Growth and Development Revisited: A Comment on Thirlwall', *Oxford Economic Papers*, 44(1):156–68.

Kalecki, M. 1976. 'The Problem of Financing Development', in his *Essays on Developing Economies*. Brighton, UK: Harvester Press. Reprinted in vol. V of J. Osiatynski (ed.). 1993. *The Collected Works of M. Kalecki*. Oxford: Oxford University Press.

Ray, D. 2010. 'Uneven Growth: A Framework for Research in Development Economics', *Journal of Economic Perspectives*, 24(3): 45–60.

CHAPTER 2

Cycles and Crises in a Model of Debt-Financed Investment-Led Growth*

Soumya Datta

The primary objective of this study is to investigate whether the macro-dynamics of debt-financing investment can provide an endogenous explanation for the emergence of growth cycles in demand-constrained closed economies. In addition, we also attempt to examine the possibilities of economic crises, especially of financial origins, emerging as a by-product of such growth cycles.

The basic motivation for this study comes from our observation of a two-way causality between the real and the financial sector. A simple interaction between the multiplier and the accelerator in a demand-constrained closed economy might lead to a monotonic movement of output and investment. Such models, therefore, would require exogenous ceilings and floors to stay bounded. In the presence of financial factors, however, an expansion of output and investment (or the rates of growth thereof) might, under certain conditions, lead

* The essay draws extensively from the author's Ph.D. thesis, titled 'Macrodynamics of Financing Investment: Applications of Lotka–Volterra Class of Models', completed at the Centre for Economic Studies and Planning (CESP), Jawaharlal Nehru University (JNU), New Delhi under the supervision of Prof. Anjan Mukherji in 2011. The author is grateful to the referee and the participants of the 5th Economic Theory and Policy Conference at NIPFP for their comments. Usual disclaimer applies.

to deterioration of certain financial variables. This, in turn, might lead to creation of conditions under which the initial increase in investment might be depressed. If suitably modelled, this might provide us with an endogenous explanation of growth cycles, with the real and the financial variables chasing each other.

One area of particular interest in this story of growth cycles is the possibility of complications arising from the borrowers defaulting on their payment commitments. A substantial literature in this area suggests that the lenders, when faced with the possibility of the borrowers defaulting under conditions of market imperfections like incomplete and asymmetric information, might adopt non-market clearing methods like redlining and rationing credit and, thus, discriminate between various borrowers based on some assessment of their creditworthiness.[1]

There is also a substantial literature, influenced by the contributions of Fisher (1932, 1933) and Minsky (1975, 1982, 1986, 1994), which argues that there is a general tendency for expansion of credit to lead to a deterioration of the financial variables in the economy during periods of boom and prosperity. A financial crisis follows, which is then followed with a contraction of the real sector as well, putting an end to the boom phase. The interaction between the real and the financial sector, therefore, leads us to an endogenous explanation for bounded systems and growth as well as financial cycles. Minsky's contribution, in particular, has influenced a huge literature on debt-deflation and financial crisis. Kindleberger's interesting and influential account of financial cycles, for instance, is influenced by Minsky's financial instability hypothesis. Similarly, there is a vast literature of economic models on financial fragility, which originates in an attempt to model at least some aspect of Minsky's descriptive account.[2] However, the popularity and huge interest in Minsky's work notwithstanding, a critical component of Minsky's story, consisting of uncertainties regarding realization of profits and its

---

[1] See, for instance, Catt (1965), Hodgman (1960), Jaffee and Russell (1976), Jaffee and Stiglitz (1990), Keynes (1930), and Stiglitz and Weiss (1981, 1983, 1992).

[2] See, for instance, Andresen (1996, 1999), Arena and Raybaut (2001), Asada (2001), Charles (2008a, 2008b), Chiarella et al. (2001), Datta (2005), Downe (1987), Fazzari et al. (2001, 2008), Foley (1987, 2003), Franke and Semmler (1989), Gatti and Gallegati (2001), Greenwald and Stiglitz (1993), Guilmi et al. (2009), Keen (1995, 1996), Lagunoff and Schreft (2001), Lavoie (1986–87), Lima and Meirelles (2007), Meirelles and Lima (2006), Palley (1994), Semmler (1987), Setterfield (2004), Skott (1994, 1995), Taylor and O'Connell (1985), Taylor and van Arnim (2008), and Vercelli (2000).

consequent impact on repayment of debt commitments, is described at the microeconomic level. In a demand-constrained economy, a higher investment translates to a higher level of macroeconomic profits through the operation of the multiplier. Hence, there is no straightforward way to aggregate the afore mentioned story of problems arising out of uncertainties faced by individual firms over realization of profits from investment to the macroeconomic level. An alternative story is required, therefore, to explain why during a prolonged boom, there is a steady shift among firms from hedge towards speculative and ponzi financial postures, increasing the overall indebtedness and leverage in the economy and eventually leading to a financial crisis, putting an end to the boom. This is one of the questions which we attempt to address in this essay.

We begin by introducing the model in the second section and then proceed to discuss some of the preliminary results in the third section. In the fourth section, we explore cyclical possibilities. The main economic interpretations of these results are provided in the fifth section. Finally we reconsider the Fisher–Minsky hypothesis in light of these results in the last section.

The Basic Model

Goods Market

We consider a simple continuous time model of a closed economy, consisting of the firm and the household sector. The household sector consists of two kinds of households—type 1 households consisting of workers, deriving income from wages, and type 2 and 3 households, deriving their income from two kinds of financial assets, debt and equities respectively. The aggregate demand at time t, $AD(t)$, is composed of the total expenditure on investment and consumption made by the firms and the households respectively, that is, $AD(t) = C(t) + I(t)$. A firm finances its investment either internally out of retained earnings or externally by issuing debt and equity instruments. The national income, Y, might be measured by the income method as the sum of wages, W, and profits, P, that is, $Y(t) = W(t) + P(t)$. In terms of various sectors in the economy, the total income might also be represented as $Y(t) = Y_f(t) + Y_{h1}(t) + Y_{h2}(t) + Y_{h3}(t)$, where Y_f, Y_{h1}, Y_{h2} and Y_{h3} is the income to firms (profits after paying outstanding debt commitments and dividends) and type 1, type 2 and type 3 households respectively. In other words, $Y_f(t) = \sigma P(t)$, where σ is the fraction of profits retained by firms, whereas $Y_{h1}(t) = W(t)$, where W represents the wages, so that $Y_{b2}(t) = (1 - \sigma)P(t) - Y_{b3}(t)$, with Y_{b2} and Y_{b3} being the part of profits representing return to financial assets (debt and equities). If s_1, s_2 and s_3 represent the fraction of the respective incomes saved by type 1, 2 and 3 households respectively, with $s_1 < s_2 = s_3$, then we have

$$C(t) = (1 - s_1)W(t) + (1 - s_2)(1 - \sigma)P(t). \tag{2.1}$$

Assuming a regime of mark-up pricing, where the price per unit is obtained by adding a fixed mark-up over the wage costs of production, we have

$$P(t) = \psi Y(t), \tag{2.2}$$

where ψ is the share of profits in national income. Following a simple algebraic manipulation, the consumption by the household sector can now be represented as $C(t) = (1 - s)Y(t)$, where $s = 1 - \{(1 - s_1)(1 - \psi) + (1 - s_2)(1 - \sigma)\psi\}$ is the propensity to save out of national income.

Let the potential output or the rate of capacity utilization of production in the economy, Y^*, be defined as the maximum output that can possibly be produced, given the existing constraints of factors and a given technology. Assuming the availability of capital as the binding constraint on production, we have $Y^*(t) = \beta K(t)$, where β is the output–capital ratio determined by the existing technology. The actual level of output or the national income, Y, can now be represented as $Y(t) = \min(AD(t), Y^*(t))$. In other words, for all $AD \leq Y^*$, aggregate demand acts as the main constraint on the level of production and the output is determined by the aggregate demand.

At the goods market equilibrium, the level of output measured by the income method equals the aggregate demand, that is, $Y(t) = AD(t)$ so that $W(t) + P(t) = C(t) + I(t)$. Substituting the value of C from (2.1), we have

$$Y(t) = \frac{1}{s}I(t). \tag{2.3}$$

Let the rate of capacity utilization be defined as the ratio of actual to potential output, that is, $u(t) = Y(t)/Y^*(t)$. We define the rate of investment as

$$g(t) \equiv \frac{I(t)}{K(t)}. \tag{2.4}$$

From the definition of u, Y^* and g, and the goods market equilibrium condition given in (2.3), we have

$$g(t) = s\beta u(t), \tag{2.5}$$

with a feasibility condition $0 \le u \le 1 \Leftrightarrow 0 \le g \le g_{max}$, where $g_{max} \equiv s\beta$ represents the rate of investment corresponding to full capacity utilization.

Let $g^\star$, the desired rate of investment, depend directly and linearly on the rate of capacity utilization, that is, $g^\star(t) = \bar{\gamma} + \gamma(t)u(t)$. Substituting from (2.5), we have

$$g^\star(t) = \bar{\gamma} + \frac{\gamma(t)g(t)}{s\beta}, \qquad (2.6)$$

where γ is the 'financial accelerator' or the sensitivity of the desired rate of investment, $g^\star$, to the rate of capacity utilization, u, and is determined by financial factors. $\bar{\gamma}$, on the other hand, due to reasons given by Duménil and Lévy (1999: 686), comprises the exogenous component of investment. Next, we turn our attention to the financial sector.

Dynamics of Debt

Consider a simple model of debt dynamics. The total stock of outstanding debt commitment in any given period, t, is given by a history of borrowing, B, at a rate of interest, r, and repayment, R. If the rate of interest, r, as mentioned above, is given exogenously by the central bank, then the stock of debt in period t is given by

$$D(t) = \int_{\tau=0}^{t} (B(\tau) - R(\tau)) e^{r(t-\tau)} d\tau, \qquad (2.7)$$

which, with simple algebraic manipulation and differentiation with respect to t, reduces to

$$\dot{D}(t) = B(t) - R(t) + rD(t). \qquad (2.8)$$

Equation (2.8) provides us with the basic accounting identity describing the growth in stock of debt. Next, we proceed to construct a macroeconomic index of financial fragility or gearing ratio, in the form of a ratio of the level of indebtedness to the ability to pay for all the debtors, that is, the firm sector together.

In any time period, t, the firm sector's total payment commitment consists of principal and interest commitments. However, since the debt stock is accumulated over a period of time, the debtors are expected to pay only a part of the total principal in a given period. For each borrower, the minimum part of principal that is expected to be paid back in each period would differ and would, among other things, depend on a credit rating of the borrower by the lenders. A borrower who is considered relatively safe (that is, less likely to default) by the lenders would be expected to pay a smaller fraction of the principal in each period than a borrower who is considered relatively unsafe. In other words, borrowers with higher credit ratings will have access to loans with longer terms, resulting in a proportionally smaller minimum repayment requirements each period.

At the macroeconomic level, however, the lenders as a whole expect, in each time period, an exogenously given minimum fraction of the total debt stock as repayment towards the principal. Let this fraction be q of the total outstanding debt commitments. The interest commitments, on the other hand, are accumulated within the time period and, hence, are expected to be fully paid. In any given period t, therefore, the total minimum payment commitment of debtors is given by $(q + r) D(t)$, where $qD(t)$ and $rD(t)$ are the principal and interest component respectively. These payments are to be paid by the debtors out of their current retained profits or the internal finance. The macroeconomic index of financial fragility or gearing ratio can now be represented as

$$\lambda(t) = \frac{(q + r) D(t)}{\sigma P(t)}. \tag{2.9}$$

We define

$$d(t) \equiv \frac{D(t)}{K(t)} \tag{2.10}$$

as the stock of debt in intensive form. Substituting from (2.2), (2.3), (2.4) and (2.10) into (2.9), we have

$$\lambda(t) = \frac{(q + r) sd(t)}{\sigma \psi g(t)}. \tag{2.11}$$

The actual repayment in period t, denoted by $R(t)$, however, is independent of $(q + r) D(t)$. It might either exceed or fall short of it, depending on the profile of the borrowers and repayment by individual borrowers. Let us consider a situation where a fraction $\phi(t)$ of the total outstanding debt stock is repaid in period t, that is,

$$R(t) = \phi(t) D(t). \tag{2.12}$$

This fraction, $\phi(t)$ depends on the following:

1. The ability of the firms to repay, given by the ratio of retained profits to the capital stock, $\sigma P/K$. A higher ratio of retained profits to capital stock would enable the borrowers to repay a larger fraction of the outstanding debt commitments without altering its capital structure (that is, without taking recourse to additional external finance).
2. The level of the index of financial fragility, λ. A higher level of λ is associated with a borrower profile where firms, in general, have higher gearing ratios and, hence, are forced to repay back a higher fraction of outstanding debt stock. Thus, in aggregate, a higher fraction of outstanding debt stock will actually be repaid.

Based on these considerations, we suggest the following functional form for $\phi(t)$:

$$\phi(t) = \phi\left(\frac{\sigma P(t)}{K(t)}, \lambda(t)\right); \qquad \phi_{\sigma P/K} > 0, \ \phi_\lambda > 0, \qquad (2.13)$$

which, taking a multiplicative form, might be expressed as

$$\phi(t) = m\frac{\sigma P(t)}{K(t)}\lambda(t),$$

where m is constant. Substituting for the value of $P(t)$ from (2.2) and (2.3), and for the value of $\lambda(t)$ from (2.9), we have $\phi(t) = m(q+r)(D(t)/K(t))$ or

$$\phi(t) = m(q+r)d(t). \qquad (2.14)$$

Next, we turn to the borrowing function, $B(t)$. In any given period t, let a fraction $a(t)$ of the total investment made by the firm sector be financed by fresh borrowing, that is,

$$B(t) = a(t)I(t). \qquad (2.15)$$

The fraction, $a(t)$, will be determined by the financial structure of the firms, that is, the manner in which the firms decide to finance fresh investments. To arrive at a particular level of $a(t)$ the firms need to take two kinds of decisions: (a) the decision on distribution of the cost of investment between internal (that is, retained profits) and external (debt and outside equities) sources of finance, and (b) the decision on how to distribute the proportion of investment costs marked for external source between debt and equity financing. We first note the following:

Proposition 1. *For a given level of profits, a higher rate of investment would necessarily mean a higher level of outside sources of finance.*

Proof: Following a flow of funds approach, we note that the firm sector receives its funds from retained profits, borrowing and equity financing, and uses these funds in making planned investment, paying out outstanding debt commitments and unplanned accumulation of inventories, that is, $\sigma P(t) + B(t) + E(t) \equiv I(t) + R(t) + \Delta N(t)$, where $\Delta N(t)$ represents the unplanned accumulation of inventories by the firm sector in period t. Substituting from (2.2), (2.3), (2.12) and (2.14), we have

$$B(t) + E(t) \equiv \left(1 - \frac{\sigma\psi}{s}\right) I(t) + m\left(q + r\right) \{d(t)\}^2 K(t) + \Delta N$$

(2.16)

$$\Rightarrow \frac{\partial(B(t) + E(t))}{\partial I(t)} \equiv \left(1 - \frac{\sigma\psi}{s}\right) > 0.$$

(2.17)

In other words, for a given level of profits, higher the level of investment higher would be the use of outside sources of finance like debt and outside equities.

Further, though a detailed analysis of equity financing is beyond the scope of our analysis, we note the following:

Remark 1. *Between two sources of external finance, there might be an increasing preference for debt as the rate of investment increases.*

Remark 1 could be explained by the following:

1. The main difference between debt and equities is with regard to the resulting payment commitments. While the payment commitments arising out of debt commitments, consisting of the principal and the interest, is independent of profits, the payment commitments arising out of equity financing, consisting of dividends, $(1 - \sigma)P(t)$, depend directly on profits. Hence, in periods of prosperity, characterized by a high rate of both investment and profits (related through the multiplier from (2.3)), the cost of equity financing would be higher. In other words, any increase in investment would increase the cost of equity financing faster than the cost of debt financing.
2. Further, as increases in investment lead to increased recourse to external financing from proposition 1, the managers of the firms might be averse to continue increasing the dilution of

shareholding from equity financing. Since a dilution of shareholding, by changing the ownership structure, increases the threat of hostile takeovers and change in corporate controls (provided, of course, such markets exist), managers might prefer debt financing when the requirement of external financing is higher.

It should be pointed out that proposition 1 and remark 1, taken together, establishes a direct relationship between the fraction of investment cost in any period, $a(t)$, financed by debt, $B(t)$. In addition, we also note the following:

Remark 2.   *An increase in the level of financial fragility, λ, might necessitate financing a higher proportion of the cost of investment through debt.*

We should note that remark 2 is motivated by the relationship implied in (2.13). A higher level of financial fragility, λ, from (2.13), will imply that a higher fraction outstanding debt commitments will have to be repaid in the current period. This will require a higher level of borrowing, to be used not only towards meeting the cost of investment but also repaying outstanding debt commitments.

From proposition 1, and remarks 1 and 2, we suggest the following functional form for $a(t)$:

$$a(t) = a\left(g(t), \lambda(t)\right); \qquad a_g > 0, \ a_\lambda > 0, \qquad (2.18)$$

which, taking a multiplicative form and substituting from (2.2), (2.3) and (2.11), might be expressed as

$$a(t) = \frac{k(q+r)s}{\sigma\psi}d(t) \qquad (2.19)$$

where k is a constant. Substituting from (2.12), (2.14), (2.15) and (2.19) into (2.8), we have

$$\dot{d}(t) = \left[\left\{\frac{k(q+r)s}{\sigma\psi} - 1\right\}g(t) - m(q+r)d(t) + r\right]d(t) \qquad (2.20)$$

Financial Determinants of Investment

We now turn our attention to the financial determinants of the rate of investment. Consider the process of assessment of loan application by lenders. Any decision on such an application, in the form of an approval or lack of it, would involve a detailed analysis of the creditworthiness of the loan application. While the actual process of an assessment of creditworthiness can be quite complicated,[3] we consider a simple version of this process here. Broadly, the quantitative factors determining the creditworthiness of a loan application might be categorized into two classes: those which remain unchanged across various stages of a business cycle and those which vary as an economy moves through a business cycle. In the first category, which might be considered as a preliminary assessment by the lending institutions, we might include permanent factors like the credit history and reputation of an individual or a group of individuals. Based on these factors, the lending institutions assign a credit rating or score to the borrowers. A borrower might be classified as either *prime* or *sub-prime* through such a process. Once classified, the identity of a borrower does not change across various stages of the business cycle; in other words, a change in the rate of capacity utilization will have no impact on this identity of the borrower. However, the final decision on creditworthiness is also likely to consider an additional component that includes current determinants. This would include, for instance, the current income of the loan applicant and an assessment of the expected future income. Assessment of future income might include, among other things, the expected profitability and risk associated with the investment project for which the borrower seeks a loan. As would be evident, these factors would vary across various stages in a business cycle; in particular, it would depend on the current rate of capacity utilization.

We begin by attempting to formalize the first, that is, the fixed component of creditworthiness. As we have already noted, this depends on an individual credit rating of each borrower. Consequently, consider the portfolio of a lender; this portfolio will be characterized by a certain spread of prime or safe and sub-prime or risky borrowers. This might be formalized by introducing η, an indicator of the proportion of borrowers with high perceived risk of default in the overall debt portfolio, such that $\eta \in [0, 1]$. A higher value of η would imply a greater proportion of borrowers with high perceived risk of default in the macroeconomic distribution of debt.

Here we recall that one of the main arguments made in the Fisher–Minsky story described earlier was that periods of relative prosperity

---

[3] See, for instance, Abrahams and Zhang (2009) and Kalapodas and Thomson (2006), for a discussion of the process of credit risk assessment.

might be accompanied with a gradual worsening of the profile of borrowers, leading to inclusion of borrowers with higher perceived risk of
default (that is, the sub-prime borrowers). This inclusion of sub-prime
borrowers would be quite evident if the prudential norms followed by
the lenders are fixed at an absolute level. For instance, if having access to a particular value of loan requires furnishing a fixed amount
of collateral, it is clear that a greater number of potential borrowers
would be able to provide the required collaterals and, hence, have access to loan in periods of prosperity. In other words, those excluded by
the debt market during periods with lower levels of economic activity
would be included during periods of prosperity. The prudential norms,
however, typically do not remain fixed but, in fact, are relaxed during
periods of prosperity because of optimistic expectations. Apart from a
direct relaxation, financial innovation and predatory lending practices
by organized lenders during a boom and emergence of new financial
instruments might aid such relaxation of prudential norms during periods of prosperity.[4] This reinforces the impact of a phase of prosperity
in increasing the proportion of risky borrowers in the macroeconomic
distribution of debt.

Next, we formalize the aforementioned argument. Since the period
of prosperity, as defined throughout our analysis, is characterized by an
increase in u, Y and g, we suggest the following functional formulation
for the proportion of risky borrowers, η in the portfolio:

$$\eta(t) = \eta_g g(t), \tag{2.21}$$

where η_g is a constant such that $\eta_g \in \left[0, \frac{1}{g_{max}}\right]$.

We now construct a cumulative index of risk of default by including
the impact of η, as defined in (2.21), and the macroeconomic indicator
of financial fragility, λ, as defined in (2.9), as follows:

$$\Lambda(t) = \Lambda_\eta \eta(t) + \Lambda_\lambda \lambda(t), \tag{2.22}$$

where Λ_η and Λ_λ represent the sensitivity of the cumulative index of
risk of default to η and λ respectively.

One should note that the cumulative index of risk of default, Λ,
consists of two separate risk components. These two components might
be interpreted as emerging from two different kinds of risks involved in

---

[4] See, for instance, Abrahams and Zhang (2009), Akerlof and Shiller (2010),
Kregel (2008), Reinhart and Rogoff (2009) and Shiller (2008).

credit expansion. The first, or the proportion of risky borrowers in the macroeconomic distribution of debt or η, might be considered an indicator of risk involved in credit widening, that is, inclusion of new borrowers, some of whom might be considered subprime. The second, the macroeconomic indicator of financial fragility or λ, on the other hand, might be considered a more conventional financial ratio that takes into account both credit deepening and credit widening. Hence, taken together, Λ might be considered a more comprehensive macroeconomic indicator of risk of default than some of the conventional indicators, since it takes into account both credit deepening and credit widening.

There are two ways the rate of investment might be affected by the risk of default. First, as we have argued before, the managers are concerned with the risk of default, since in the case of a default, a firm might face a hostile takeover, leading to a change in corporate control threatening the jobs of the managers. Hence, an increase in Λ might prompt the managers to respond by reducing the sensitivity of the rate of investment to the capacity utilization, that is, the accelerator. Second, the lenders are concerned with the risk of default. An increase in a macroeconomic indicator of the risk of default like Λ is likely to make them more cautious about lending. In light of a substantial literature in this area,[5] we might note that a rationing and redlining of credit might be one of the possible responses from the lenders under such a situation. While such a rationing and redlining will directly affect only a section of borrowers, all borrowers are likely to take steps to reduce the possibility of being rationed and redlined. Since individual or firm-level gearing ratio is one of the deciding factors on which firms are rationed or redlined, an increase in Λ is likely to induce individual firms to respond by trying to reduce their gearing ratios. Since this logic applies to all the firms, an increase in Λ will have a negative impact on the accelerator of the investment function. We formalize this argument by introducing the following formulation for the accelerator:

$$\gamma(t) = \bar{\mu} - \hat{\mu}\Lambda(t), \qquad (2.23)$$

where $\hat{\mu}$ is the sensitivity of the accelerator to the cumulative risk of default, and $\bar{\mu}$ represents the maximum possible level of the accelerator when there is no risk of default. Substituting the values of $\lambda(t)$ and $\eta(t)$ from (2.11) and (2.21) into (2.22), and then substituting the resultant

---

[5] See, for instance, Catt (1965), Hodgman (1960), Jaffee and Stiglitz (1990), Kalecki (1937), and Stiglitz and Weiss (1981, 1983, 1992).

expression into (2.23), we have

$$\gamma(t) = \bar{\mu} - \hat{\mu}\Lambda_\eta \eta_g g(t) - \frac{\hat{\mu}\Lambda_\lambda (q+r) s}{\sigma\psi} \frac{d(t)}{g(t)}. \tag{2.24}$$

Substituting the value of accelerator, $\gamma(t)$, from (2.24) into the investment function in (2.6), we have

$$g^\star(t) = \frac{\bar{\mu}}{s\beta} g(t) - \frac{\hat{\mu}\Lambda_\eta \eta_g}{s\beta} \{g(t)\}^2 - \frac{\hat{\mu}\Lambda_\lambda (q+r)}{\sigma\psi\beta} d(t) + \bar{\gamma}. \tag{2.25}$$

Let the rate of investment be continuously adjusted so as to meet a fraction, h, of the gap between the actual and the desired rate of investment, that is,

$$\frac{\dot{g}(t)}{g(t)} = h\left(g^\star(t) - g(t)\right), \tag{2.26}$$

subject to the feasibility condition $0 \le g \le g_{max}$, where h represents the speed of adjustment of the actual investment to the desired level by the investors. Substituting the value of $g^\star(t)$ from (2.25) into (2.26), we have the following equation of motion to represent the dynamics of the rate of investment:

$$\dot{g}(t) = \left[\left(\frac{\bar{\mu}}{s\beta} - 1\right) g(t) - \frac{\hat{\mu}\Lambda_\eta \eta_g}{s\beta} \{g(t)\}^2 - \frac{\hat{\mu}\Lambda_\lambda (q+r)}{\sigma\psi\beta} d(t) + \bar{\gamma}\right] hg(t), \tag{2.27}$$

subject to the feasibility condition, $0 \le g(t) \le g_{max}$.

Complete Model

From (2.27) and (2.20), we get the following **2 × 2** dynamical system:

$$\dot{g}(t) = \left[\left(\frac{\bar{\mu}}{s\beta} - 1\right) g(t) - \frac{\hat{\mu}\Lambda_\eta \eta_g}{s\beta} \{g(t)\}^2 - \frac{\hat{\mu}\Lambda_\lambda (q+r)}{\sigma\psi\beta} d(t) + \bar{\gamma}\right] hg(t)$$

$$\dot{d}(t) = \left[\left\{\frac{k(q+r) s}{\sigma\psi} - 1\right\} g(t) - m(q+r) d(t) + r\right] d(t) \tag{2.28}$$

which we rewrite as follows:

$$\dot{g}(t) = \left[a_1 g(t) - a_2 \{g(t)\}^2 - a_3 d(t) + a_4\right] hg(t)$$
$$\dot{d}(t) = \left[b_1 g(t) - b_2 d(t) + b_3\right] d(t) \tag{2.29}$$

where $a_1 \equiv \frac{\bar{\mu}}{s\beta} - 1$, $a_2 \equiv \frac{\bar{\mu}\Lambda_\eta \eta_g}{s\beta}$, $a_3 \equiv \frac{\bar{\mu}\Lambda_\lambda(q+r)}{\sigma\psi\beta}$, $a_4 \equiv \bar{\gamma}$, $b_1 \equiv \frac{k(q+r)s}{\sigma\psi} - 1$, $b_2 \equiv m\left(q+r\right)$, $b_3 \equiv r$, with $a_1, a_2, a_3, a_4, b_1, b_2, b_3 \in]0, \infty[$. It might be noted that the dynamics in (2.29) resembles that of the generalized predator–prey or Kolmogorov–Lotka–Volterra class of models. The debt–capital ratio, d, is the predator that feeds on the rate of investment, g. We should point out here that (2.29) contains at least two financial dampeners to mitigate the positive impact of the accelerator on the rate of investment, g, or the prey: first, the debt–capital ratio, which works through the indicator of financial fragility, λ; and second, the rate of investment itself for all $g > a_1/2a_2$, which works through the index of risk of default. We should also note that the rate of investment here plays a dual role: on the one hand, it has a positive role on itself through the accelerator and, on the other hand, it has a self-limiting negative role on itself through the risk of default. The self-limiting role originates in the arguments found in the Fisher–Minsky hypothesis described in the first section. Solving for the steady state of the dynamical system (2.29), we have the following:

$$E_1 : \left(\bar{g}_1, \bar{d}_1\right) = (0, 0) \tag{2.30a}$$

$$E_2 : \left(\bar{g}_2, \bar{d}_2\right) = \left(-\frac{\sqrt{4a_2 a_4 + a_1^2} - a_1}{2a_2}, 0\right) \tag{2.30b}$$

$$E_3 : \left(\bar{g}_3, \bar{d}_3\right) = \left(\frac{\sqrt{4a_2 a_4 + a_1^2} + a_1}{2a_2}, 0\right) \tag{2.30c}$$

$$E_4 : \left(\bar{g}_4, \bar{d}_4\right) = \left(0, \frac{b_3}{b_2}\right) \tag{2.30d}$$

$$E_5 : \left(\bar{g}_5, \bar{d}_5\right) = \left(-\frac{\sqrt{4a_2 b_2^2 a_4 - 4a_2 b_2 a_3 b_3 + b_1^2 a_3^2 - 2a_1 b_1 b_2 a_3 + a_1^2 b_2^2} + b_1 a_3 - a_1 b_2}{2a_2 b_2},\right.$$

$$\left. -\frac{b_1 \sqrt{4a_2 b_2^2 a_4 - 4a_2 b_2 a_3 b_3 + b_1^2 a_3^2 - 2a_1 b_1 b_2 a_3 + a_1^2 b_2^2} - 2a_2 b_2 b_3 + b_1^2 a_3 - a_1 b_1 b_2}{2a_2 b_2^2}\right) \tag{2.30e}$$

$$E_6 : \left(\bar{g}_6, \bar{d}_6\right) = \left(\frac{\sqrt{4a_2 b_2^2 a_4 - 4a_2 b_2 a_3 b_3 + b_1^2 a_3^2 - 2a_1 b_1 b_2 a_3 + a_1^2 b_2^2} - b_1 a_3 + a_1 b_2}{2a_2 b_2},\right.$$

$$\left. \frac{b_1 \sqrt{4a_2 b_2^2 a_4 - 4a_2 b_2 a_3 b_3 + b_1^2 a_3^2 - 2a_1 b_1 b_2 a_3 + a_1^2 b_2^2} + 2a_2 b_2 b_3 - b_1^2 a_3 + a_1 b_1 b_2}{2a_2 b_2^2}\right) \tag{2.30f}$$

It would be evident that $E_2 \notin \mathfrak{R}^2_{++}$ since $\bar{g}_2 < 0$. Hence, we do not discuss E_2 any further in the following sections. Further, E_3 and E_4 are non-negative, and lie on the g and d axis respectively. Regarding E_5 and E_6, we note the following:

Remark 3. *Whenever E_5 and E_6 are real and distinct, $\dot{d}/d = 0$ must intersect $\dot{g}/g = 0$ from above at E_5 and from below at E_6. If E_5 and E_6 are not distinct, then $\dot{d}/d = 0$ is a tangent to $\dot{g}/g = 0$ at the point representing the unique non-trivial steady state.*

Remark 4. *$a_3 b_3 < a_4 b_2$ is a sufficient (though not necessary) condition for the non-trivial steady state E_6 to be inside the real positive orthant, $\mathfrak{R}^2_{++}$.*

Remark 5. *For $g(t) \geq \bar{g}_3$, we have $\dot{g}(t) \leq 0$ for all $d(t) \in \mathfrak{R}^+$; in other words, if $\bar{g}_3 \leq g_{max}$, then the feasibility condition $0 \leq g(t) \leq g_{max}$ is always satisfied.*

For any $(g^\circ, d^\circ) \in \text{int } \mathfrak{R}^2_{++}$ as the initial point, let the solution to (2.29) be represented by $\Theta(t) = (g(t), d(t); g^\circ, d^\circ)$. From (2.29), we can conclude the following about the behaviour of trajectories in case the initial point is on one of the axes:

1. $\dot{g} > 0, \ \dot{d} = 0 \ \forall \ \{(g^\circ, d^\circ) : g^\circ \in \ ]0, \bar{g}_3[, \ d^\circ = 0\}$
as the initial point.

2. $\dot{g} < 0, \ \dot{d} = 0 \ \forall \ \{(g^\circ, d^\circ) : g^\circ \in \ ]\bar{g}_3, \infty[, \ d^\circ = 0\}$
as the initial point.

3. $\dot{g} = 0, \ \dot{d} > 0 \ \forall \ \{(g^\circ, d^\circ) : g^\circ = 0, \ d^\circ \in \ ]0, \bar{d}_4[\}$ (2.31)
as the initial point.

4. $\dot{g} = 0, \ \dot{d} < 0 \ \forall \ \{(g^\circ, d^\circ) : g^\circ = 0, \ d^\circ \in \ ]\bar{d}_4, \infty[\}$
as the initial point.

Therefore, both the g axis and the d axis are trajectories. Since trajectories cannot cross each other, this would make the real positive orthant invariant, that is, trajectories starting from an initial point in the real positive orthant will always remain within it. Given that only dynamics strictly within the real positive orthant are economically meaningful, we focus our attention on only such trajectories and ignore other trajectories in the rest of our discussion. In other words, among the steady states listed in (2.30), we only consider E_5 and E_6 for discussion, and do not discuss the other steady states in the rest of this study.

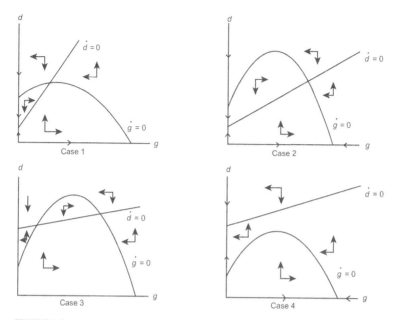

FIGURE 2.1 Phase Diagram of (2.29): Four Cases

Next we turn our attention to the trajectories starting from an initial point inside the real positive orthant. For $g, d \neq 0$, from (2.29) we have

$$\dot{g}(t) \lesseqgtr 0 \Leftrightarrow d(t) \gtreqless \frac{a_1}{a_3} g(t) - \frac{a_2}{a_3} \{g(t)\}^2 + \frac{a_4}{a_3}$$

$$\dot{d}(t) \lesseqgtr 0 \Leftrightarrow d(t) \gtreqless \frac{b_1}{b_2} g(t) + \frac{b_3}{b_2}. \tag{2.32}$$

Depending on the configuration of parameters, we can list four different possibilities exhibiting qualitatively different dynamics (see Figure 2.1):

1. Case 1: Here, $a_4 b_2 - a_3 b_3 > 0$, that is, intercept of $\dot{g}/g = 0$ is greater than that of $\dot{d}/d = 0$; $b_1/b_2 > (a_1 - 2a_2 \bar{g}_6)/a_3 > 0$, that is, $\dot{d}/d = 0$ intersects $\dot{g}/g = 0$ from below in the positively sloped section of the latter curve. $E_6 \in \text{int}\mathfrak{R}_{++}^2$ is the only steady state in this case inside the real positive orthant.

2. Case 2: Here, $a_4 b_2 - a_3 b_3 > 0$, that is, intercept of $\dot{g}/g = 0$ is greater than that of $\dot{d}/d = 0$, but unlike case 1 $(a_1 - 2a_2 \bar{g}_6)/a_3 < 0 < b_1/b_2$, that is, $\dot{d}/d = 0$ intersects $\dot{g}/g = 0$ from below in the

negatively sloped section of the latter curve. $E_6 \in \text{int}\mathfrak{R}^2_{++}$ is the unique steady state inside the real positive orthant.

3. Case 3: Here, $a_4b_2 - a_3b_3 < 0$, that is, intercept of $\dot{g}/g = 0$ is less than that of $\dot{d}/d = 0$; $(a_1 - 2a_2\bar{g}_5)/a_3 > b_1/b_2 > 0 > (a_1 - 2a_2\bar{g}_6)/a_3$, that is, $\dot{g}/g = 0$ intersects $\dot{d}/d = 0$ from below at E_5 when the former is sloping upward and from above at E_6 when the former is sloping downward. In this case, $E_5, E_6 \in \text{int}\mathfrak{R}^2_{++}$, that is, $\dot{d}/d = 0$ intersects $\dot{g}/g = 0$ twice in the interior of the real positive orthant.

4. Case 4: Here, $a_4b_2 - a_3b_3 < 0$, that is, intercept of $\dot{g}/g = 0$ is less than that of $\dot{d}/d = 0$ and, unlike case 3, $E_5, E_6 \notin \text{int}\mathfrak{R}^2_{++}$ so that there does not exist any steady state in the interior of the real positive orthant. Since we are interested in only the real positive orthant, we do not consider case 4 any further in the rest of our discussion.

Further, performing the Routh–Hurwitz test for local stability on the two economically meaningful steady states, E_5 and E_6, we note that (a) *whenever the non-trivial steady state solution, E_5, exists and is distinct from E_6, and lies in the interior of real positive orthant, it is a saddle-point;* (b) *depending on the configuration of the parameters, the non-trivial steady state solution, E_6, whenever it exists and is distinct from E_5, and lies within the interior of the real positive orthant, is either a source or a sink.* We further note that E_6 is always a sink in case 2 and 3.

Possibilities of Cyclical Behaviour

Next, we investigate possibilities of growth cycles emerging from an interaction between the investment function and debt dynamics. For this purpose, we restrict our attention to case 1 of Figure 2.1 since, from above, this is the only case where cyclical possibilities exist. We recall that this is the case where E_6 is the unique steady state in the interior of positive orthant, and at E_6, the positive impact of g on $\dot{g}/g$ outweighs its negative impact.

Cyclical possibilities in dynamical systems of the type represented by (2.28) or (2.29) have been investigated extensively in Datta (2012). Here we present a summary of these results:

1. For the dynamical system represented by (2.28) or (2.29), we define a critical value of the parameter b given by $\hat{b}$, where b

represents the rate of adjustment of the actual rate of investment to its desired rate by the private investors and $\hat{h}$ is defined as follows:

$$\hat{h} = \frac{b_2 \bar{d}_6}{\left(a_1 - 2a_2 \bar{g}_6\right) \bar{g}_6} > 0, \tag{2.33}$$

which, by substituting the values of $\bar{g}_6$ and $\bar{d}_6$ from (2.30), might be expanded as

$$\hat{h} = \frac{b_1 \, b_2 \, \sqrt{4 \, a_2 \, b_2^2 \, a_4 - 4 \, a_2 \, b_2 \, a_3 \, b_3 + b_1^2 \, a_3^2 - 2 \, a_1 \, b_1 \, b_2 \, a_3 + a_1^2 \, b_2^2} + 2 \, a_2 \, b_2^2 \, b_3 - b_1^2 \, b_2 \, a_3 + a_1 \, b_1 \, b_2^2}{(2 b_1 a_3 - a_1 \, b_2) \sqrt{4 a_2 \, b_2^2 \, a_4 - 4 \, a_2 \, b_2 \, a_3 \, b_3 + b_1^2 \, a_3^2 - 2 \, a_1 \, b_1 \, b_2 \, a_3 + a_1^2 \, b_2^2} - 4 \, a_2 \, b_2^2 \, a_4 + 4 \, a_2 \, b_2 \, a_3 \, b_3 - 2 \, b_1^2 \, a_3^2 + 3 \, a_1 \, b_1 \, b_2 \, a_3 - a_1^2 \, b_2^2} \tag{2.34}$$

At $h = \hat{h}$, we have a point of the non-degenerate Andronov–Hopf bifurcation, leading to emergence of limit cycles.

2. Depending on the values of various parameters, the Andronov–Hopf bifurcation is either supercritical or subcritical, leading to the emergence of either stable or unstable limit cycles respectively. Whether the Andronov–Hopf bifurcation is stable or unstable can be determined if we are provided with information on the values of various parameters.[6]

3. In case the limit cycle emerging from the Andronov–Hopf bifurcation is unstable, we have another stable limit cycle enclosing the unstable limit cycle.

4. For $h > \hat{h}$, we have a stable limit cycle from an application of the Poincaré–Bendixson theorem.

In other words, there exists a unique stable limit cycle for all $h \geq \hat{h}$.

---

[6] For instance, if the parameters have values as follows:

$s = 0.3$, $\sigma = 0.4$, $\psi = 0.3$, $r = 0.1$, $q = 0.6$, $m = 0.6$, $k = 0.7$,

$\beta = 0.8$, $\bar{\mu} = 0.3$, $\hat{\mu} = 0.4$, $\eta_g = 0.1$, $\Lambda_\eta = 0.1$, $\Lambda_\lambda = 0.63$, $\bar{\gamma} = 0.5$, then at

the non-trivial steady state, E_6, the rate of investment, $\bar{g}_6$, is at 8.49 per cent and the debt–capital ratio is at 28.36 per cent. The Poincaré–Andronov–Hopf bifurcation for this steady state occurs at $h = 5.67$, leading to the emergence of limit cycles. The first lyapunov exponent at this point can be calculated to be -1.02×10^{-5}, which is negative; hence, the Andronov–Hopf bifurcation is supercritical and the limit cycles are stable.

We should further note, given that the limit cycle is to be interpreted as a growth cycle in the rate of investment, g, and the debt–capital ratio, d, we have a robust result for the existence of a growth cycle. The growth cycle emerges under a wide range of conditions, that is, for all $b \geq \hat{b}$, irrespective of the values of other parameters, and for a very wide range of initial conditions.

We next turn to the implication of this result, by looking closely at some of the properties of this growth cycle.

Business and Financial Cycles

We noticed in the earlier section a variety of cyclical possibilities. We now turn our attention to the behaviour of the economy through various stages of a business cycle.

Business Cycles

STAGE 1: PERIOD OF HIGH GROWTH

In this stage, there is an increase in both the rate of investment, g, and the debt–capital ratio, d. Following a recent history of a high growth phase (Figure 2.2), this phase is also accompanied with all-round optimistic expectations. However, this phase also contains conditions for a worsening of financial variables in the following ways:

1. An increase in d, ceteris paribus, leads to an increase in financial fragility, λ. This leads to an increase in the cumulative index of risk of default, Λ.
2. An increase in g, as argued earlier, will lead to an increased inclusion of risky or subprime borrowers, resulting in a fall in the profile of borrowers. In our model, this is captured by an increase in the proportion of risky borrowers, η. This will further put an upward pressure on the cumulative risk of default, Λ.

As we have argued earlier, an increase in Λ creates a negative impact on the rate of investment, g, in our model. This negative impact occurs because of two sets of reasons. First, the managers are concerned with the risk of default, since in case of a default, a firm might face a hostile takeover, leading to a change in corporate control threatening the job of the managers. Hence, an increase in Λ might prompt the managers to respond by reducing the sensitivity of the rate of investment to the capacity utilization, that is, the accelerator. Second, the lenders are concerned with the risk of default. An increase in a macroeconomic

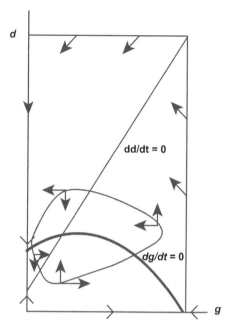

FIGURE 2.2 An Economic Cycle

indicator of the risk of default like Λ is likely to make them more cautious about lending, possibly leading to a rationing and redlining of credit. While such a rationing and redlining will directly affect only a section of borrowers, all borrowers are likely to take steps to reduce the possibility of being rationed and redlined. Since individual or firm-level gearing ratio is one of the deciding factors on which firms are rationed or redlined, an increase in Λ is likely to induce individual firms to respond by trying to reduce their gearing ratios. Since this logic applies to all the firms, an increase in Λ will have a negative impact on the accelerator of the investment function.

The negative impact, however, will be offset in this stage by the positive impact of an increase in g. Primarily this will operate through an increased demand having a positive impact on investment through a combination of the multiplier and the accelerator. There will also be an indirect positive impact: an increase in g, by increasing retained earnings, ceteris paribus, will have a negative impact on financial fragility and risk of default, which, in turn, will have a positive impact on the rate of investment, g.

STAGE 2: ONSET OF A FINANCIAL CRISIS   This stage begins when the negative factor discussed earlier starts dominating the positive factors, resulting in a fall in the rate of investment, g. A fall in g would lead to a reduction in borrowing, imparting a negative impact on the debt–capital ratio, d. The negative impact on d will be further reinforced by an increase in λ forcing an increase in repayment of debt. However, the negative impact on d will lead to an actual decrease in d only with a lag. Till that happens, the economy will be characterized by classic features of onset of an economic crisis: a fall in the rate of investment along with an increase in debt–capital ratio.

STAGE 3: FULL-BLOWN RECESSION   In this stage, g continues to fall. The negative factors on d discussed earlier finally result in a fall in d. In other words, both the rate of investment and the debt–capital ratio falls in this stage. Conditions for a turnaround and recovery, however, are also created in this stage. This would primarily operate through an improvement in financial variables in the following manner:

1. A decrease in d, ceteris paribus, leads to a decrease in the financial fragility, captured by λ. This leads to a reduction in the cumulative index of risk of default, Λ.
2. A decrease in g, implying a recession, will lead to fall in the proportion of risky or subprime borrowers, leading to a fall in η. This would primarily operate through a process of exclusion from the debt market. In other words, recession would lead to exclusion of those borrowers who might have had access to loans during better times. This would lead to a fall in the cumulative index of risk of default, Λ.

One should expect a fall in Λ to have a positive impact on the rate of investment, g. Such an expectation should follow from a straightforward and symmetric application of the logic provided in our discussion of stage 1. First, a decrease in the risk of default would reduce fear of defaults and takeover for the managers of the firms, allowing them to invest more aggressively. Second, the lenders, faced with a reduced risk of default, might eventually reduce credit rationing and redlining, allowing the firms to borrow and invest more.

The positive impact on g, however, is offset by the negative impact of a decrease in g. This will primarily operate through a situation of reduced demand having a negative impact through multiplier and the accelerator. Further, a fall in g, by reducing profits and retained earnings, will also tend to increase the financial fragility, λ (where g appears in the denominator), which, through the investment function, will have a further negative impact on g. The negative effect will dominate in this stage.

One also needs to exercise a bit of caution here in a symmetric application of the logic provided in stage 1. Unlike the process of inclusion of risky borrowers in stage 1 (which leads to an immediate impact), their exclusion is not as straightforward. This is because despite their exclusion from fresh borrowing, the risky borrowers who have already borrowed will still remain in the market. Further, unlike the process of inclusion, the process of exclusion might also lead to these borrowers facing a payment crisis, leading to various complications beyond the scope of analysis of our model. In other words, there is an element of asymmetry in an increase and a decrease in η—a fact which is not captured in our model.

STAGE 4: RECOVERY This stage begins when the factors that have a positive impact on g, as discussed earlier, start dominating, leading to an increase in g. The debt–capital ratio, d, however, will continue to fall. An increase in g, by increasing borrowing, will have a positive impact on d. This will be further reinforced by a fall in d reducing λ and, hence, repayments. However, these effects will lead to an actual increase in d only with a lag. Till that happens, the economy will be in a purely recovery path, with the rate of investment, g, increasing along with a continuing fall in the debt–capital ratio, d. Once there is a turnaround in d, the economy leaves stage 4 and re-enters stage 1.

The dynamics of g and d through various stages of cycle are shown below in Figure 2.3 and 2.4 respectively.

Financial Cycles

It would be evident from the preceding discussion that the financial sector in the form of debt market plays an important role in the business cycle. Hence, we would expect a financial cycle to accompany the business cycle. However, we show below that the financial cycle is not synchronized with the business cycle (that is, the cycle in g) but, in fact, precedes the latter. This is best captured by the index of financial fragility, λ, in our model. We recall from (2.11) that the index of financial fragility, λ, is given by

$$\lambda = \frac{k\left(q + r\right)sd}{\sigma\psi g}.$$

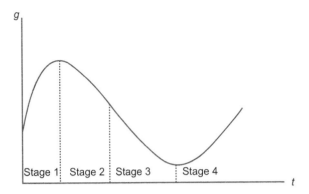

FIGURE 2.3 The Rate of Investment through a Business Cycle

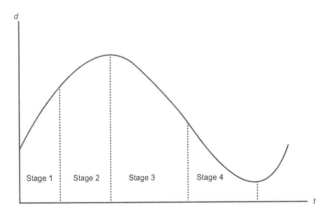

FIGURE 2.4 The Debt-Capital Ratio through a Business Cycle

Taking logarithmic differentiation of both sides, we have

$$\frac{\dot{\lambda}}{\lambda} = \frac{\dot{d}}{d} - \frac{\dot{g}}{g}. \tag{2.35}$$

From (2.35), it would be clear that λ starts stage 1 by decreasing till it reaches a trough, and then starts increasing within stage 1. It continues to increase through stage 2 and the beginning of stage 3. Within stage 3, it reaches a peak and then starts declining. This decline in λ continues through stage 4 into stage 1. This is shown in Figure 2.5.

It would be clear that the cycle in λ precedes the cycle in g. For instance, in stage 1, the turnaround in λ occurs when it starts increasing

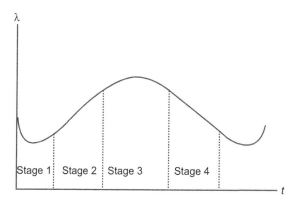

FIGURE 2.5 A Financial Cycle

in the middle of stage 1. However, the turnaround in *g* occurs only at the
end of stage 1 when *g* starts falling. Similarly, while the next turnaround
in λ occurs in the middle of stage 3 when it starts falling, the turnaround
in *g* occurs only at the end of stage 3. The lag between two cycles is
shown in Figure 2.6, where both the business and the financial cycles
are superimposed on each other. This also seems to fit in well with the
general observation that a financial crisis typically works as a precursor
to a general economic crisis.

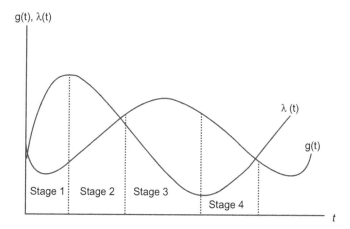

FIGURE 2.6 Lag between Financial and Business Cycles

Concluding Remarks: A Reconsideration of Fisher–Minsky Hypothesis

The model developed in this study includes the primary contention of the Fisher–Minsky hypothesis that there is a deterioration of financial variables during a boom, captured by an increase in Λ. In addition, it also offers a macroeconomic mechanism by which this deterioration of financial variables might put an end to the boom. We find that such a macroeconomic mechanism, in addition to providing endogenous bounds, also leads to growth cycles, involving cyclical behaviour in the rate of investment and the debt–capital ratio. Further, we find that a financial cycle would typically precede cycles in the rate of investment and output. Thus, our model offers an endogenous explanation for turnarounds in business cycles driven by financial factors and, hence, preceded by a financial cycle. A boom will end, for instance, when a deterioration in financial variables will induce a cutback in the rate of investment. The end to the boom, therefore, will be preceded by a financial crisis. In this sense, we might offer our model as providing a more complete story of finance-led growth cycles than the existing literature around the Fisher–Minsky hypothesis. Since it explains some of the missing links without resorting to some of the less than convincing routes often found in some of the literature, we might consider this as a substantial contribution to the literature in this area.

We should, however, exercise a bit of caution while drawing conclusions from the model we have developed. First, we should note that while in our model the turnaround at the peak and the trough of the growth cycle is treated in a symmetric manner, in the real world, a number of complications might make such a symmetric treatment unwarranted. As we have noted earlier, the exclusion of subprime borrowers, unlike their inclusion, often involves a time lag. While the lenders might exclude new borrowers from having access to fresh borrowing, existing subprime borrowers can be excluded only with a time lag, that is, only after the existing debt contracts have expired. Further, exclusion of these borrowers might trigger off an all-round payment crisis in the economy, creating further complications. Thus, typically in a real world economy, while the end to the boom might occur endogenously, the end to a recession often requires state intervention in the form of writing off existing loans or playing the role of lender-of-last-resort. Second, the model does not include income distribution considerations and the role of expectations leading to changes in asset prices. In light of a substantial literature in this area, we should note that such considerations might play a significant role in these growth cycles. This is an area we reserve for future research.

In other words, the model presented in this essay should primarily be looked upon as an investigation into the nature of macroeconomic feedback mechanism between an investment function and debt dynamics. Such a feedback mechanism is able to provide an endogenous bound to the rate of investment and, in this sense, fills a gap in the existing literature attempting to model the Fisher–Minsky hypothesis.

References

Abrahams, C. and M. Zhang. 2009. *Credit Risk Assessment: The New Lending System for Borrowers, Lenders and Investors*. Hoboken, New Jersey: John Wiley and Sons, Inc.

Akerlof, G. A. and R. J. Shiller. 2010. *Animal Spirits: How Human Psychology Drives the Economy, and Why It Matters for Global Capitalism*. Princeton, New Jersey: Princeton University Press.

Andresen, T. 1996. 'Economic Black Holes', *Économies et Sociétés, Série Monnaie et Production*, 30(2/3):83–116.

———. 1999. 'The Dynamics of Long-Range Financial Accumulation and Crisis', *Nonlinear Dynamics, Psychology and Life Sciences*, 3(2):161–96.

Arena, R. and A. Raybaut. 2001. 'On the Foundations of Minsky's Business Cycle Theory: An Interpretation', in R. Bellofiore and P. Ferri (eds), *Financial Fragility and Investment in the Capitalist Economy*, Vol. II of The Economic Legacy of Hyman Minsky. Cheltenham, UK: Edward Elgar Publishing Limited, pp. 113–32.

Asada, T. 2001. 'Non-linear Dynamics of Debt and Capital: A Post-Keynesian Analysis', in Y. Aruka (ed.), *Evolutionary Controversies in Economics*. Tokyo: Springer-Verlag.

Catt, A. 1965. 'Credit Rationing and Keynesian Model', *The Economic Journal*, 75(298):358–72.

Charles, S. 2008a. 'A Post-Keynesian Model of Accumulation with Minsky an Financial Structure', *Review of Political Economy*, 20(3):319–31.

———. 2008b. 'Corporate Debt, Variable Retention Rate and the Appearance of Financial Fragility', *Cambridge Journal of Economics*, 32(5):781–95.

Chiarella, C., P. Flaschel and W. Semmler. 2001. 'The Macrodynamics of Debt Deflation', in R. Bellofiore and P. Ferri (eds), *Financial Fragility and Investment in the Capitalist Economy*, Vol. II of The Economic Legacy of Hyman Minsky. Cheltenham, UK: Edward Elgar Publishing Limited, pp. 133–84.

Datta, S. 2005. 'Chaotic Dynamics of Financing Investment', *Metroeconomica*, 56(1):58–84.

———. 2012. 'Robustness and Stability of Limit Cycles in a Class of Planar Dynamical Systems', MPRA Paper 56970, University Library of Munich, Germany. Available at http://mpra.uni-muenchen.de/id/eprint/56970.

Downe, E. A. 1987. 'Minsky's Model of Financial Fragility: A Suggested Addition', *Journal of Post Keynesian Economics*, 9(3):440–54.

Duménil, G. and D. Lévy. 1999. 'Being Keynesian in the Short Term and Classical in the Long Term: The Traverse to Classical Long-Term Equilibrium', *The Manchester School*, 67(6):684–716.

Fazzari, S. M., P. Ferri and E. Greenberg. 2001. 'The Macroeconomics of Minsky's Investment Theory', in R. Bellofiore and P. Ferri (eds), *Financial Fragility and Investment in the Capitalist Economy*, Vol. II of The Economic Legacy of Hyman Minsky. Cheltenham, UK: Edward Elgar Publishing Limited, pp. 99–112.

———. 2008. 'Cash Flow, Investment and Keynes-Minsky Cycles', *Journal of Economic Behaviour and Organization*, 65(3–4):555–72.

Fisher, I. 1932. *Booms and Depressions: Some First Principles*. New York: Adelphi.

———. 1933. 'The Debt-Deflation Theory of Great Depressions', *Econometrica*, 1:337–57.

Foley, D. K. 1987. 'Liquidity-Profit Rate Cycles in a Capitalist Economy', *Journal of Economic Behaviour and Organization*, 8(3):363–76.

———. 2003. 'Financial Fragility in Developing Economies', in A. K. Dutt and J. Ros (eds), *Development Economics and Structuralist Macroeconomics*. Aldershot, UK: Edward Elgar, pp. 157–68.

Franke, R. and W. Semmler. 1989. 'Debt-Financing of Firms, Stability and Cycles in a Dynamic Macroeconomic Growth Model', in W. Semmler (ed.), *Financial Dynamics and Business*

Cycles: New Perspectives. Armonk, New York: M. E. Sharpe, Inc, pp. 38–64.

Gatti, D. D. and M. Gallegati. 2001. 'Financial Instability Revisited: Aggregate Fluctuations due to Changing Financial Conditions of Heterogeneous Firms', in R. Bellofiore and P. Ferri (eds), *Financial Fragility and Investment in the Capitalist Economy*, Vol. II of The Economic Legacy of Hyman Minsky. Cheltenham, UK: Edward Elgar Publishing Limited, pp. 185–200.

Greenwald, B. and J. E. Stiglitz. 1993. 'Financial Market Imperfections and Business Cycles', *Quarterly Journal of Economics*, 108(1):77–114.

Guilmi, C. D., M. Gallegati and S. Landini. 2009. 'Financial Fragility, Mean-Field Interaction and Macroeconomic Dynamics: A Stochastic Model'., in N. Salvadori (ed.), *Institutional and Social Dynamics of Growth and Distribution*. Cheltenham, UK: Edward Elgar Publishing Inc., pp. 319–53.

Hodgman, D. R. 1960. 'Credit Risk and Credit Rationing', *The Quarterly Journal of Economics*, 74(2):258–78.

Jaffee, D. and T. Russell. 1976. 'Imperfect Information, Uncertainty and Credit Rationing', *Quarterly Journal of Economics*, 90(4):651–66.

Jaffee, D. and J. E. Stiglitz. 1990. 'Credit Rationing', in B. Friedman and F. Hahn (eds), *Handbook of Monetary Economics*, Vol. II. North-Holland, Amsterdam: Elsevier Science Publishers B.V., Chapter 16.

Kalapodas, E. and M. E. Thomson. 2006.'Credit Risk Assessment: A Challenge for Financial Institutions', *IMA Journal of Management Mathematics*, 17(1):25–46.

Kalecki, M. 1937. 'The Principle of Increasing Risk', *Economica*, New Series, 4(16): 440–47.

———. 1971. *Selected Essays on the Dynamics of Capitalist Economy.* Cambridge: Cambridge University Press.

Keen, S. 1995. 'Finance and Economic Breakdown: Modeling Minsky's Financial Instability Hypothesis', *Journal of Post-Keynesian Economics*, 17(4):607–35.

———. 1996. 'The Chaos of Finance: The Chaotic and Marxian Foundations of Minsky's Financial Instability Hypothesis', *Economies et Sociétés, Monnaie et Production, Série M.P.*, 10(2–3):55–82.

Keynes, J. M. 1930. *A Treatise on Money*. London: Macmillan.

Kindleberger, C. P. 1978. *Manias, Panics and Crashes: A History of Financial Crisis*. New York: Basic Books Inc.

Kregel, J. 2008. 'Minsky's Cushions of Safety Systemic Risk and the Crisis in the U.S. Subprime Mortgage Market', Economics Public Policy Brief Archive, The Levy Economics Institute.

Lagunoff, R. and S. L. Schreft. (2001), 'A Model of Financial Fragility', *Journal of Economic Theory*, 99(1–2):220–64.

Lavoie, M. 1986–87. 'Systemic Financial Fragility: A Simplified View', *Journal of Post Keynesian Economics*, 9(2):258–66.

Lima, G. T. and A. J. Meirelles. 2007. 'Macrodynamics of Debt Regimes, Financial Instability and Growth', *Cambridge Journal of Economics*, 31(4):563–80.

Meirelles, A. J. and G. T. Lima. 2006. 'Debt, Financial Fragility, and Economic Growth: A Post Keynesian Macromodel', *Journal of Post Keynesian Economics*, 29(1):93–115.

Minsky, H. P. 1975. *John Maynard Keynes*. New York: Columbia University Press.

———. 1982. *Inflation, Recession and Economic Policy*. New York: M. E. Sharpe Inc.

———. 1986. *Stabilizing the Unstable Economy*. New Haven: Yale University Press.

———. 1994. 'Financial Instability Hypothesis', in P. Arestis and M. Sawyer (eds), *Elgar Companion to Radical Political Economy*. Vermont, USA: Edward Elgar Publishing Limited, pp. 153–58.

Palley, T. I. 1994. 'Debt, Aggregate Demand, and the Business Cycle: An Analysis in the Spirit of Kaldor and Minsky', *Journal of Post Keynesian Economics*, 16(3):371–90.

Reinhart, C. M. and K. S. Rogoff. 2009. *This Time is Different: Eight Centuries of Financial Folly*. Princeton, New Jersey: Princeton University Press.

Semmler, W. 1987. 'A Macroeconomic Limit Cycle with Financial Perturbations', *Journal of Economic Behavior and Organization*, 8(3):469–95.

Setterfield, M. 2004. 'Financial Fragility, Effective Demand and the Business Cycle', *Review of Radical Political Economics*, 16(2):207–23.

Shiller, R. J. 2008. *The Subprime Solution: How Today's Global Financial Crisis Happened, and What To Do About It*. Princeton, New Jersey: Princeton University Press.

Skott, P. 1994. 'On the Modelling of Systemic Financial Fragility', in A. K. Dutt (ed.), *New Directions in Analytical Political Economy*. Cheltenham, UK: Edward Elgar, pp. 49–76.

———. 1995. 'Financial Innovations, Deregulation and Minsky Cycles', in G. Epstein and H. Gintis (eds), *Macroeconomic Policy after the Conservative Era*. Cambridge, Massachussets, Cambridge University Press, pp. 255–73.

Stiglitz, J. E. and A. Weiss. 1981. 'Credit Rationing in Markets with Imperfect Information', *American Economic Review*, 71(3):393–410.

———. 1983. 'Incentive Effects of Terminations: Applications to the Credit and Labor Markets', *American Economic Review*, 73:912–27.

———. 1992. 'Asymmetric Information in Credit Markets and Its Implications for Macroeconomics', *Oxford Economic Papers*, 44(4):694–724.

Taylor, L. and S. A. O'Connell. 1985. 'A Minsky Crisis', *Quarterly Journal of Economics*, 100(Supplement):871–85.

Taylor, L. and C. R. von Arnim. 2008. 'Debt-Equity Cycles in the Twentieth Century: Empirical Evidence and a Dynamic Keynesian Model', in P. Flaschel and M. Landesmann (eds), *Mathematical Economics and the Dynamics of Capitalism: Goodwin's Legacy Continued*. London: Routledge, pp. 145–62.

Vercelli, A. 2000. 'Structural Financial Instability and Cyclical Fluctuations', *Structural Change and Economic Dynamics*, 11(1–2):139–56.

CHAPTER 3

Policy-Induced Changes in Income Distribution and Profit-Led Growth in a Developing Economy

Gogol Mitra Thakur*

The post-Keynesian/Kaleckian growth literature places the central emphasis, while examining the growth process of an economy, in the generation of aggregate demand. Aggregate demand in the economy is the sum of consumption, investment, budget deficit and trade surplus. In the absence of budget deficit and trade surplus, dynamics of consumption and investment explain the growth path of the economy. Consumption is described by the classical savings assumption wherein the entire wage income is consumed and a fixed proportion of the profit is saved, wage and profit being the only income categories. On the other hand, investment is assumed to be a function of demand in the economy.

In this set-up, a worsening of income distribution is expected to cause stagnation in the economy. This is because, according to Kalecki (1971), investment in any given period depends on decisions taken in

* This essay formed my MPhil dissertation. I am extremely grateful to my supervisor Dr Subrata Guha for his guidance, without which the essay was almost impossible. Comments and suggestions from Prof. Amit Bhaduri, Dr Debarshi Das and Kumar Rishabh greatly helped the work to take its present shape. I would also like to thank Dr Soumya Datta for his valuable suggestions on the final draft. However, I am solely responsible for all the shortcomings of the essay.

previous periods and these decisions depend on the level of demand in the previous periods. Since the entire wage income is consumed, investment generates savings out of profit equal to itself in the equilibrium. If profit share is fixed by the 'degree of monopoly', then the fixed level of investment determines the level of output. If income distribution worsens due to an increase in the 'degree of monopoly', then in the equilibrium, output level would be less than what it would be in case there is no change in the income distribution. Since the output is less than what it would be without worsening of distribution, investment in the next period would be less too.

Bhaduri and Marglin (1990) pointed out that the profit rate can be decomposed into the profit share and capacity utilization, where the latter indicates the level of demand. They proposed that the investment rate in the economy is a function of both profit share and capacity utilization. In the case where the sensitivity of the investment rate to profit share is greater than that of the savings rate, capacity utilization in the economy increases with increase in the profit share. They term this as the *exhilarationist* regime contrary to the *stagnationist* regime where the opposite happens. However, as pointed out by Rowthorn (1982) and Dutt (1984), if income distribution is fixed, we will expect that an exogenous increase in the profit share will decrease the growth rate due to the resulting fall in consumption out of wages. Moreover, Blecker (2002), using linear and Cobb–Douglas specifications for Bhaduri and Marglin's investment function, has pointed out that *exhilarationism* either does not arise or arises only under the extreme elasticity assumption on the investment function.

Over the last three decades, most of the developing countries have adopted a more or less universal set of economic policies, often known as the neoliberal policies. These policies aim at liberating the market from government intervention so as to achieve allocative efficiency. Therefore, a particular significance is attached to restricting the size of budget deficit. Many economists have argued that this has resulted in a worsening of income inequality in these countries. Assuming this to be true, the post–Keynesian/Kaleckian growth literature seems to suggest that these economies should stagnate unless they manage to continuously increase their trade surplus. However, some of these economies have put up a decent growth performance in the face of decreasing budget deficits. At the same time, they have failed to consistently maintain a trade surplus and have even experienced an increasing trade deficit. The post-1991 Indian growth experience, particularly most of the last decade, is a standout example.

Kalecki (1971) argued that technological innovation is one major factor which can sustain the growth process. Technological innovation not only leads to obsolescence of old machinery and plants leading to their replacement by new ones but also provides a strong stimulus for investment by opening up new investment opportunities. In fact, Kalecki argued that the impact of a steady stream of innovations on investment is comparable with the impact of a steady increase in profit because both give rise to 'certain additional investment decisions' (Kalecki 1969: 58). He also emphasized that despite the demand-stimulating nature of technological innovation, there is no guarantee that the degree of utilization of resources stays at a constant level.

Patnaik (2007) has argued that in developing countries, the richer section of the population aspires to match the consumption standards of the developed countries. As income distribution worsens, this section is in a position to afford more and more of goods consumed in the developed countries. With an increase in demand for goods consumed in developed countries, the incentive of firms to produce such goods, by imitating foreign production techniques, also increases. Thus, Patnaik argues that growth and technological change in the developing countries are induced by the demand of the richer section of the population for goods available in the advanced countries, which increases with increase in inequality. Patnaik terms this process as a 'structural-cum-technological' change. He, however, concludes that though it is possible for such developing countries to experience high rates of growth, the growth process is highly unstable and any sufficiently strong negative shock to investment can take the economy to a state of stagnation.

In this essay, we first show that a developing country can experience a positive equilibrium growth rate of investment and surplus as long as investment in the economy is responsive to the aspirations of the richer section of the population to match the consumption level of the developed world through an imitation of foreign production technology which is not very expensive. Unlike Patnaik (2007), the growth process need not be unstable but can be stable under certain conditions. Moreover, worsening of income distribution is not required to sustain this kind of growth process, but a sufficiently unequal initial distribution of income, is enough to propel it. Next, we show that the technologically dynamic sector producing for the rich is incapable in generating much employment. If the process is accompanied by no change in the distribution of income, then the employment share of the the technologically stagnant sector producing for the poor increases at the cost of a declining growth rate of real wage. In case the growth process is accompanied by an exogenous change in the distribution of income induced by shifts in the economic policy regime, then the positive and stable equilibrium growth rate of investment is associated with an increasing growth rate of output, though more is gained in terms of increase in output growth when income distribution improves rather than worsens. On the other hand, growth rate of employment for the entire economy might decline.

As for the structure of the essay, in the next section we describe the major assumptions of our model. In the third and fourth sections, we discuss the existence and local stability of a positive equilibrium growth rate of investment respectively. In the fifth section, we consider change in income distribution caused by changes or shifts in the economic policy paradigm/regime, for example, the government adopting neoliberal reforms or becoming more mindful of equity considerations. We consider regime changes which either worsen (by increasing the profit share) or improve (by decreasing the profit share) over a period of time. We discuss the impact of such a change in the distribution of income on the growth rate of output along the equilibrium growth path of investment. In the sixth section, we discuss the implications for growth rates of employment and labour productivity in the economy. The final section contains concluding remarks where we summarise and discuss the results.

Model

Consider a closed economy model with no government budget. This economy is neatly divided into two classes—capitalists and workers. The capitalists own all the means of production, that is, capital. They carry out production by combining their capital with hired labour in order to earn profit. The workers have only labour which they sell to the capitalists in return for wages. The capitalists and the workers consume entirely different goods. The workers consume a subsistence good, whereas the capitalists consume a variety of luxury goods but not the subsistence good. Luxury goods are defined to be goods which have been developed in the advanced countries and are initially available for consumption only in these economies. These luxury goods are substitutes to each other in the sense that as new luxury goods are introduced in the market, the old tend to disappear because their demand falls. We assume that luxury goods are made available in this economy only through imitation of foreign production technologies.

There are two sectors in the economy: the luxury sector and the non-luxury sector. In the luxury sector, luxury goods for the capitalists and investment goods required to produce luxury goods are produced. Similarly, in the non-luxury sector, the subsistence good for the workers and the investment goods required to produce the subsistence good are produced. There is no technological progress in the non-luxury sector. On the other hand, following Patnaik (2007), we assume that the production technology associated with new luxury goods are more labour saving. Over time, goods with more sophisticated technologies and higher labour productivity are introduced in the advanced countries.[1] We will assume that there exists a ranking of the luxury goods, which are introduced in the economy under consideration such that the production techniques of newer luxury goods are associated with higher labour productivity.

Consumption and Savings

The workers spend all their wages on the consumption of the subsistence good. The capitalists consume a part of their profit and save the rest. We assume that the level of consumption out of profit increases not only when the level of profit increases but also when, given a level of profit, more and more new luxury goods make their way into the market. In other words, we assume that consumption out of profit is directly related to both the level of profit and the rate at which new luxury goods are introduced in the market.

We will assume that the faster the rate at which new luxury goods are introduced in this economy, the higher the rate of change in the labour productivity of the luxury goods sector, $\dot{a}$. This is because if at any point of time, new luxury goods are introduced at a faster rate, then at that point of time the proportion of new luxury goods demanded and produced would be greater as compared to a situation where there is a slower rate of introduction of luxury goods. Labour productivity of the luxury goods sector, a, will increase at a higher rate because, one, a faster rate of introduction means that more new luxury goods with higher labour productivities are produced and, two, since the luxury goods are substitutes in the sense described earlier, the output share of old luxury goods is smaller when new luxury goods are introduced at a

---

[1] Labour productivity is defined as value of output per unit labour. Values are expressed in terms of the subsistence good, which is assumed to be the numeraire.

faster rate as compared to a slow rate. Thus, we use the rate of change in the labour productivity of the luxury goods sector to proxy the rate at which new luxury goods are introduced in the market.

We can, therefore, describe consumption out of profit, C, by the following function,

$$C = C(\Pi, \dot{a}), \qquad (3.1)$$

with $0 < C_\Pi < 1$ and $C_{\dot{a}} > 0$, where Π is the level of profit, $\dot{a}$ is that rate of change in the labour productivity of the luxury sector which proxies for the rate of introduction of new luxury goods. Since workers do not save, savings for the economy is given by

$$S = \Pi - C(\Pi, \dot{a}) = S(\Pi, \dot{a}), \qquad (3.2)$$

with $0 < S_\Pi < 1$ and $S_{\dot{a}} < 0$.

Investment

Net investment in this economy is assumed to depend on the current level of profit and the rate at which new luxury goods are introduced in the market. A high current level of profit is the predictor of a high future level of demand in the economy, and also a high level of profit eases the financing constraints on the capitalists' decision to invest Kalecki (1969). Therefore, we assume investment in the economy to positively depend on the current level of profit.

The relationship between the rate at which new luxury goods are introduced and investment is ambiguous and depends on the ease with which firms can imitate the production techniques of the new goods.[2] Given our assumptions about consumption demand out of profit, a higher rate of introduction of new luxury goods into the market is associated with more opportunities to invest for the firms, and all firms would like to invest at a higher rate in the production of new luxury goods.

On the other hand, if cost of imitation is very high, say, due to strict enforcement of intellectual property rights, then at any point of time only a few firms will invest in the production of new luxury goods. Since we have assumed that as new luxury goods are introduced in the market, older ones tend to disappear, firms producing old luxury goods, unable to get access to production techniques of the relatively new luxury goods, will hold back new investment on their existing

---

[2] Henceforth, by investment we mean net investment.

plants and let their capital stock depreciate. Moreover, if some of the old luxury goods are forced out of the market as new luxury goods are introduced, firms producing these goods will have to shut down in case they can not imitate the production technology of new luxury goods.

Thus, investment in the economy, I, is given by the following function,

$$I = I(\Pi, \dot{a}), \tag{3.3}$$

with $I_\Pi > 0$ and $I_{\dot{a}}$ either positive or negative. $\dot{a}$ in (3.3) is again the proxy for the rate of introduction of new luxury goods.

Technological Change in the Luxury Goods Sector

Technological change in the luxury goods sector is endogenously driven by the growth of profit in the economy. Any increase in the growth rate of profit in the economy impacts both the demand and supply of luxury goods. On the one hand, increase in the growth rate of profit increases the incomes of the profit earners at a faster rate. Thus, their ability to consume at the high end of the goods available in the developed world increases at a faster rate (Patnaik 2007). On the other hand, the ability of the firms to meet the cost of imitation also increases at a faster rate as the growth rate of profit increases. Therefore, when the growth rate of profit increases, it becomes profitable to introduce more of the high-end goods available in the developed world. The high-end goods in the developed world are associated with higher labour productivities than the existing luxury goods in this economy. This, combined with our assumption that the old luxury goods tend to disappear from the market with the introduction of the new luxury goods, implies that the labour productivity of the luxury goods sector tends to increase at higher rates.

The current technological capabilities of firms in the economy are commensurate with the technological requirements of the existing luxury goods being produced within the economy. It is reasonable to assume that as one moves up the hierarchy of goods being produced in the advanced countries, technological requirements of production become more sophisticated compared to the current technological capabilities of firms in the economy. Thus, as more and more new luxury goods are introduced in the economy at a point in time, the actual cost of imitation and introduction of additional new luxury goods increases. Therefore, we assume that at any point of time, the rate of growth of labour productivity of the luxury goods sector in this economy increases with an increase in the growth rate of profit but at a decreasing rate. This relationship between the growth rate of labour productivity in the luxury goods sector, g_a, and the growth rate of profit is given by the following equation:

$$g_a = \phi(g_\Pi), \tag{3.4}$$

with $\phi(0) = 0$ and for all $g_\Pi \in (0, \infty)$, $\phi(g_\Pi) \geq 0$, $\phi'(g_\Pi) > 0$ and $\phi''(g_\Pi) < 0.$[3]

Demand-Induced Changes in the Growth Rate of Profit

Whenever investment in the economy is greater than savings, either price adjustment happens which raises the share of profit in output leaving the aggregate output level constant or the level of aggregate output increases leaving the share of profit in the aggregate output unchanged, or both the adjustments happen simultaneously. In any case, whenever investment is more than savings, the level of profit will rise. Similarly, when investment is less than savings, the level of profit will fall, and when investment is equal to savings, the level of profit will remain unchanged. This process of change in the level of profit due to mismatch between investment and savings is conveniently captured by the following equation:

$$(\ln \dot\Pi) = \alpha[\ln(\frac{I}{S})] = \alpha(\ln I - \ln S), \tag{3.5}$$

where α is a positive constant.

Differentiating equation (3.5) with respect to time, we get

$$\dot{g}_\Pi = \alpha(g_I - g_S), \tag{3.6}$$

---

[3] Patnaik (2007) assumes that the growth rate of labour productivity is an increasing convex function of the growth rate of investment, which, in turn, is an increasing function of the growth rate of profit. It is argued that in a developing economy where technology is just imitated from abroad, there is no given set of knowledge to be progressively used up, but with increasing investment, more investments in new projects will be taken up. This we feel implicitly assumes that as the economy moves up the hierarchy of goods in the developed economies at any point of time, the cost of moving from one step to the next in the hierarchy goes down. Since at any given point in time, the technological capabilities in the economy are fixed, it is difficult to believe that at the margin the cost of introducing new luxury goods will go down. Therefore, we think $\phi''(g_\Pi) < 0$ to be a more plausible assumption than $\phi''(g_\Pi) > 0$.

where $\alpha > 0$ and $\dot{g}_\Pi$ is the rate of change in g_Π (the growth rate of profit), g_I is the rate of growth of investment and g_S is the rate of growth of savings.[4] From (3.2) and (3.3), growth rates of savings and investment are

$$g_S = \sigma_{S,\Pi} g_\Pi + \sigma_{S,\dot{a}} \frac{1}{\dot{a}} \frac{d\dot{a}}{dt} \tag{3.7}$$

and

$$g_I = \sigma_{I,\Pi} g_\Pi + \sigma_{I,\dot{a}} \frac{1}{\dot{a}} \frac{d\dot{a}}{dt} \tag{3.8}$$

respectively. $\sigma_{i,j}$ is elasticity of i with respect to j, where $i = I, S$ and $j = \Pi, \dot{a}$. $\sigma_{S,\Pi} > 0$, $\sigma_{S,\dot{a}} < 0$ for $\dot{a} > 0$ and $\sigma_{I,\Pi} > 0$. $\sigma_{i,j}$s are assumed to be constant throughout.

Substituting for g_I and g_S from (3.7) and (3.8) in equation (3.6), we obtain

$$\dot{g}_\Pi = \alpha(\sigma_{I,\Pi} - \sigma_{S,\Pi}) g_\Pi + \alpha(\sigma_{I,\dot{a}} - \sigma_{S,\dot{a}}) \frac{1}{\dot{a}} \frac{d\dot{a}}{dt}. \tag{3.9}$$

From equation (3.4), using the definition of growth rate and logarithmic differentiation, we obtain

$$\frac{1}{\dot{a}} \frac{d\dot{a}}{dt} = \phi(g_\Pi) + \rho \frac{\dot{g}_\Pi}{g_\Pi}, \tag{3.10}$$

where $\rho = \frac{g_\Pi}{\phi(g_\Pi)} \phi'(g_\Pi)$ is the elasticity of the growth rate of labour productivity in the luxury goods sector with respect to the growth rate of profit and $\rho > 0$ as $\phi' > 0$. We assume that ρ is a constant.

---

[4] Bhaduri (2006) uses a general form function, instead of the natural logarithm function used in our model, to derive an expression for the rate of change in the growth rate of output, $\dot{g}_Y$, similar to equation (3.5), that is, $\dot{g}_Y = \alpha[g_I - g_S]$ with $\alpha > 0$ by assuming that any mismatch between investment and savings gives rise only to output adjustments. However, to get the expression $\dot{g}_Y = \alpha[g_I - g_S]$ from the general form function, it is assumed that any deviation of investment, I, from an initial commodity market clearing equilibrium, $I = S$, stays arbitrarily close to the value of investment at the initial equilibrium. Moreover, it is assumed that whenever $I = S$, output grows at some equilibrium rate, g_Y^*, in contrast to our contention that $\dot{g}_\Pi = 0$ whenever $I = S$. We simply argue that demand-side adjustment in the economy, which is the focus of our model, stops whenever $I = S$.

Substituting for $\frac{1}{\dot{a}}\frac{d\dot{a}}{dt}$ in equation (3.9) from equation (3.10) and then rearranging the terms we obtain

$$\dot{g}_\Pi = \frac{\alpha g_\Pi[(\sigma_{I,\Pi} - \sigma_{S,\Pi})g_\Pi + (\sigma_{I,\dot{a}} - \sigma_{S,\dot{a}})\phi(g_\Pi)]}{[g_\Pi - \alpha(\sigma_{I,\dot{a}} - \sigma_{S,\dot{a}})\rho]}, \qquad (3.11)$$

where $\dot{g}_\Pi$ is not defined for $g_\Pi = \alpha(\sigma_{I,\dot{a}} - \sigma_{S,\dot{a}})\rho$. This implies that $\dot{g}_\Pi$ is not defined when $\phi(\alpha(\sigma_{I,\dot{a}} - \sigma_{S,\dot{a}})\rho) = \alpha(\sigma_{I,\Pi} - \sigma_{S,\Pi})(\sigma_{I,\dot{a}} - \sigma_{S,\dot{a}})\rho$.[5] We will assume that $\phi(\alpha(\sigma_{I,\dot{a}} - \sigma_{S,\dot{a}})\rho) \neq \alpha(\sigma_{I,\Pi} - \sigma_{S,\Pi})(\sigma_{I,\dot{a}} - \sigma_{S,\dot{a}})\rho$.

Equation (3.11) expresses the rate of change of the growth rate of profit, $\dot{g}_\Pi$, as a function of the growth rate of profit, g_Π, in the economy.

Positive Equilibrium Growth Rate of Profit

An equilibrium for equation (3.11), that is, $\dot{g}_\Pi = 0$ implies either $g_\Pi = 0$ or $[(\sigma_{I,\Pi} - \sigma_{S,\Pi})g_\Pi + (\sigma_{I,\dot{a}} - \sigma_{S,\dot{a}})\phi(g_\Pi)] = 0$. Therefore, it is obvious that a positive equilibrium growth rate of profit exists if and only if the equation

$$[(\sigma_{I,\Pi} - \sigma_{S,\Pi})g_\Pi + (\sigma_{I,\dot{a}} - \sigma_{S,\dot{a}})\phi(g_\Pi)] = 0$$

has a positive solution. This implies that $\sigma_{I,\Pi} \neq \sigma_{S,\Pi}$ and $\sigma_{I,\dot{a}} \neq \sigma_{S,\dot{a}}$. Rearranging the previous equation gives us

$$\phi(g_\Pi) = zg_\Pi, \qquad (3.12)$$

where $z = \frac{(\sigma_{S,\Pi} - \sigma_{I,\Pi})}{(\sigma_{I,\dot{a}} - \sigma_{S,\dot{a}})}$, a constant. Notice that the assumptions on the function $\phi(g_\Pi)$, mentioned earlier, ensure a positive solution of equation (3.12) as long as $z > 0$. In Figure 3.1, g_Π^* denotes the positive equilibrium growth rate of profit. Given that profit grows at the positive equilibrium rate g_Π^*, investment and savings in the economy grow at constant positive rates $g_I^* = \sigma_{I,\Pi}g_\Pi^* + \sigma_{I,\dot{a}}\phi(g_\Pi^*)$ and $g_S^* = \sigma_{S,\Pi}g_\Pi^* + \sigma_{S,\dot{a}}\phi(g_\Pi^*)$. Thus, the equilibrium growth rates of investment and savings depend, apart from the equilibrium growth rate of profit, on the responsiveness of investment and savings to profit and the rate of introduction of new luxury goods in the economy, and on the form of the function ϕ. Moreover, from the definition of g_Π^*, we know that in equilibrium, $g_I^* = g_S^*$.

The fact that under certain conditions a positive equilibrium growth path of profit exists in the economy implies that at every instance of

---

[5] By rearranging equation (3.11) we get $\dot{g}_\Pi[g_\Pi - \alpha(\sigma_{I,\dot{a}} - \sigma_{S,\dot{a}})\rho] = \alpha g_\Pi[(\sigma_{I,\Pi} - \sigma_{S,\Pi})g_\Pi + (\sigma_{I,\dot{a}} - \sigma_{S,\dot{a}})\phi(g_\Pi)]$. Substituting $\alpha(\sigma_{I,\dot{a}} - \sigma_{S,\dot{a}})\rho$ for g_Π in the previous expression gives $\phi(\alpha(\sigma_{I,\dot{a}} - \sigma_{S,\dot{a}})\rho) = \alpha(\sigma_{I,\Pi} - \sigma_{S,\Pi})(\sigma_{I,\dot{a}} - \sigma_{S,\dot{a}})\rho$.

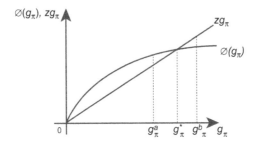

FIGURE 3.1 Positive Equilibrium Growth Rate of Profit

time on it, investment is greater than savings by a fixed proportion. Notice that we can rewrite equation (3.4) as

$$g_\Pi = \alpha[\ln(\frac{I}{S})].$$ (3.13)

Substituting g_Π^* in equation (3.13) and then rearranging it, we get the following.

$$\frac{g_\Pi^*}{\alpha} = \ln(\frac{I}{S})$$ (3.14)

Since $\frac{g_\Pi^*}{\alpha}$ is a positive constant, $\frac{I}{S}$ must be a constant greater than one. The investment savings ratio being a constant greater than one means that the short-run macroeconomic equilibrium characterized by the equality investment and savings in the ex-ante sense is never realized on the equilibrium growth path of profit in the economy. This is because profit growth in our model is fuelled by the excess of investment over savings in the ex-ante sense.

Stability

Local stability of the equilibrium requires that $\frac{dg_\Pi}{dg_\Pi}$ at $g_\Pi = g_\Pi^*$ is less than zero, where g_Π^* is the positive equilibrium growth rate of profit. Differentiating (3.11) with respect to g_Π and then substituting g_Π^* for g_Π, we get

$$\frac{dg_\Pi(g_\Pi^*)}{dg_\Pi} = \frac{\alpha(\sigma_{I,\dot{a}} - \sigma_{S,\dot{a}})g_\Pi^*(\phi'(g_\Pi^*) - z)}{[g_\Pi^* - \alpha(\sigma_{I,\dot{a}} - \sigma_{S,\dot{a}})\rho]},$$ (3.15)

where $\frac{dg_\Pi(g_\Pi^*)}{dg_\Pi}$ is $\frac{dg_\Pi}{dg_\Pi}$ evaluated at $g_\Pi = g_\Pi^*$. Now α and g_Π^* are positive constants. Existence of positive equilibrium growth rate of profit implies that $(\phi'(g_\Pi^*) - z) < 0$. To see this, notice that $\phi(g_\Pi) - zg_\Pi = 0$ at both

$g_\Pi = 0$ and $g_\Pi = g_\Pi^*$. The claim then necessarily follows from Rolle's theorem[6] and the assumption $\phi''(g_\Pi) < 0$. Thus, the necessary and sufficient conditions for local stability of g_Π^* are $g_\Pi^* > \alpha(\sigma_{I,\dot{a}} - \sigma_{S,\dot{a}})\rho$ and $\sigma_{I,\dot{a}} - \sigma_{S,\dot{a}} > 0$.

The first condition, $g_\Pi^* > \alpha(\sigma_{I,\dot{a}} - \sigma_{S,\dot{a}})\rho$, requires that the equilibrium growth rate of profit is sufficiently large. We can rewrite (3.11) as

$$\dot{g}_\Pi = \alpha(\sigma_{I,\dot{a}} - \sigma_{S,\dot{a}})\psi(g_\Pi) + \frac{\alpha(\sigma_{I,\dot{a}} - \sigma_{S,\dot{a}})\rho}{g_\Pi}\dot{g}_\Pi, \qquad (3.16)$$

where $\psi(g_\Pi) = \phi(g_\Pi) - zg_\Pi$. The right-hand side of equation (3.16) is the impact of the excess of growth rate of investment over the growth rate of savings, which for the sake of simplicity let us call the growth rate of the I/S ratio, on the the rate of change in the growth rate of profit. Notice that the first term in this expression is zero when $g_\Pi = 0$, that is, $(\sigma_{I,\dot{a}} - \sigma_{S,\dot{a}})\psi(g_\Pi) = 0$ when $g_\Pi = 0$, while the second term is zero when $\dot{g}_\Pi = 0$, that is, $\frac{(\sigma_{I,\dot{a}} - \sigma_{S,\dot{a}})\rho}{g_\Pi}\dot{g}_\Pi = 0$ when $\dot{g}_\Pi = 0$. Therefore, we can think of $(\sigma_{I,\dot{a}} - \sigma_{S,\dot{a}})\psi(g_\Pi)$ as the component of the growth rate of the I/S ratio explained by g_Π and $\frac{(\sigma_{I,\dot{a}} - \sigma_{S,\dot{a}})\rho}{g_\Pi}\dot{g}_\Pi$ as the component of the growth rate of the I/S ratio explained by $\dot{g}_\Pi$. From equation (3.16), it is clear that the rate of change in the growth rate of profit $(\dot{g}_\Pi)$ has the same sign as the component of the growth rate of the I/S ratio explained by the growth rate of profit, $(\sigma_{I,\dot{a}} - \sigma_{S,\dot{a}})\psi(g_\Pi)$, if and only if $\frac{\alpha(\sigma_{I,\dot{a}} - \sigma_{S,\dot{a}})\rho}{g_\Pi} < 1$. $g_\Pi^* > \alpha(\sigma_{I,\dot{a}} - \sigma_{S,\dot{a}})\rho$ implies that for values of g_Π in a sufficiently small neighbourhood of g_Π^*, $\frac{\alpha(\sigma_{I,\dot{a}} - \sigma_{S,\dot{a}})\rho}{g_\Pi} < 1$.

The second condition, $\sigma_{I,\dot{a}} - \sigma_{S,\dot{a}} > 0$, requires that either investment responds non-negatively to changes in the rate of introduction of new luxury goods or even when it responds negatively, the responsiveness of savings is more than the responsiveness of investment.[7] In either case, the indirect impact of a positive growth rate of profit on its rate of change is always positive, that is, $\alpha(\sigma_{I,\dot{a}} - \sigma_{S,\dot{a}})\phi(g_\Pi) > 0$. Since $z > 0$, $\sigma_{I,\dot{a}} - \sigma_{S,\dot{a}} > 0$ implies that $\sigma_{S,\Pi} - \sigma_{I,\Pi} > 0$. So the direct impact of a positive growth rate of profit on its rate of change is negative, that is, $(\sigma_{I,\Pi} - \sigma_{S,\Pi})g_\Pi < 0$.

---

[6] See, for example (Albrecht and Smith 2003: 106).

[7] Notice that since $\sigma_{S,\dot{a}} < 0$, $\sigma_{I,\dot{a}} - \sigma_{S,\dot{a}} > 0$ implies either $\sigma_{I,\dot{a}} \geq 0$ or $(\sigma_{I,\dot{a}} < 0$ and $|\sigma_{I,\dot{a}}| < |\sigma_{S,\dot{a}}|)$.

Figure 3.1 shows two values of g_Π, g_Π^a and g_Π^b, close to g_Π^*. Let us assume that $g_\Pi^* > \alpha(\sigma_{I,\dot{a}} - \sigma_{S,\dot{a}})\rho$. This means g_Π has the same sign as the component of the growth rate of the I/S ratio explained by g_Π. At g_Π^a, $\phi(g_\Pi^a) > z g_\Pi^a$, thus, $\psi(g_\Pi^a) > 0$. Therefore, from the definition of $\psi(g_\Pi)$, $\alpha(\sigma_{S,\Pi} - \sigma_{I,\Pi})g_\Pi^a < \alpha(\sigma_{I,\dot{a}} - \sigma_{S,\dot{a}})\phi(g_\Pi^a)$. The direct negative impact of the growth rate of profit on its rate of change is less than the indirect positive impact. Thus, the component of the growth rate of the I/S ratio explained by g_Π at g_Π^a is positive, which increases g_Π. Similarly, at g_Π^b, since $\psi(g_\Pi^b) < 0$, we have $\alpha(\sigma_{S,\Pi} - \sigma_{I,\Pi})g_\Pi^b > \alpha(\sigma_{I,\dot{a}} - \sigma_{S,\dot{a}})\phi(g_\Pi^b)$. In this case, the direct negative impact of the growth rate of profit on its rate of change dominates the indirect positive impact. Therefore, g_Π decreases at g_Π^b. Thus, g_Π^* is locally stable.

Changes in Income Distribution and Output Growth

In this and the next section, we will consider change in the distribution of income induced by exogenous shifts in the economic policy regime, and examine its effect on output and employment growth in the economy. When a policy regime changes, many policy measures are adopted that are expected to have an impact on the distribution of income in the economy. For example, let us consider the government going in for neoliberal reforms. In that case, many policy changes like easing the norms for mergers and acquisition, labour reforms, privatization of state-run enterprises and reduction of corporate income tax would take place that tend to increase the 'degree of monopoly' in the economy. As a result, we would expect the profit share to gradually rise over a period of time. On the other hand, suppose the government, under popular pressure, tries to orient its economic policy towards the consideration of equity. In that case, policies like employment guarantee and minimum wages would be adopted which tend to reduce the 'degree of monopoly', and we would expect the profit share to gradually decrease over a period of time.

In the analysis that follows, we consider shifts in the policy regime which either improve or worsen the distribution of income and assume that whenever such shifts in the policy regime happen, the profit share changes continuously at a constant rate over a period of time. Moreover, we assume that such shifts in policy regime do not have any independent effect on investment and savings in the economy but through changes in the level of profit. This implies that the equilibrium growth rate of profit derived in the third section remains unaffected. Nonetheless, there is an impact on the adjustment process because any excess of investment over savings increases profit in order to generate savings. As the share of profit gradually changes due to a shift in the policy regime, it affects the level of profit and also puts pressure on the adjustment required in the level of profit in response to the investment–savings gap.

In order to examine this clearly and also for closing the model, we will assume that the adjustment in the level of profit in response to the investment–savings gap is achieved only through output increase in the absence of any policy-induced increase in the profit share. In periods along the equilibrium growth path of profit, when there is a policy-induced worsening of the income distribution, that is, $\dot{h} > 0$, a part of the increase in profit required due to excess of investment over savings is automatically achieved by the exogenous rise in the profit share, while the rest is achieved through endogenous output increase. On the other, hand in case of an improvement in the distribution of income, that is, $\dot{h} < 0$, decline in profit share will decrease the the level of profit and, thus, the excess of investment over savings will result in a greater endogenous adjustment in the level of output.

By definition $\Pi = Yh$, where Y is the total output of the economy and h is share of profit in output. Therefore, the growth rate of profit is $g_\Pi = g_Y + \frac{\dot{h}}{h}$, where g_Y is the growth rate of output and $\frac{\dot{h}}{h}$ is the growth rate of profit share. On the equilibrium growth path of profit, the growth rate of output is

$$g_Y = g_\Pi^* - \frac{\dot{h}}{h}. \tag{3.17}$$

We will assume that the change in profit share, $\dot{h}$, is an exogenously given policy determined parameter. Thus, output grows at a rate equal to the equilibrium growth rate of profit when income distribution does not change, that is, the $\dot{h} = 0$. When the profit share increases, that is, $\dot{h} > 0$, then $g_Y < g_\Pi^*$, whereas when profit share decreases, that is, $\dot{h} < 0$, $g_Y > g_\Pi^*$.

The growth rate of output, after these aforementioned changes, however, is not constant but increases in both the cases. First, suppose $\dot{h} > 0$, then profit share, h, increases over time. This implies $\frac{\dot{h}}{h}$ decreases as $\dot{h}$ is fixed. Thus, it follows from (3.17) that g_Y increases as $\dot{h} > 0$. Next suppose $\dot{h} < 0$, then the profit share, h, decreases over time. This implies $|\frac{\dot{h}}{h}|$ increases as $\dot{h}$ is fixed. Since $\dot{h} < 0$, it follows again from (3.17) that g_Y increases. Nonetheless, the growth rate of output is always higher in the case of the economic policy regime shifting in favour of the workers than the case where the shift is in favour of the capitalists.

This is because when $\dot{b} > 0$, then the increase in the growth rate follows a discrete drop from g_Π^*, and also the increase must taper off at some point less than g_Π^* as b can never become greater than one. On the other hand, when $\dot{b} < 0$, then the growth rate of output at first jumps above g_Π^* and then keeps on increasing as long as the impact of a shift in the policy regime in favour of the workers on the profit share remains.

Growth of Labour Productivity and Employment

Labour productivity of the entire economy is the weighted average of labour productivities in the luxury goods sector and the non-luxury goods sector with the weights being their respective employment shares. Thus, the labour productivity of the entire economy, x, is given by the following equation:

$$x = al_a + b(1 - l_a), \tag{3.18}$$

where b is a positive constant which is always less than a. a and b are the labour productivities of the luxury goods sector and the non-luxury goods sector respectively. l_a is the employment share of the luxury goods sector. From (3.18), the growth rate of labour productivity in the economy is

$$g_x = \frac{l_a}{x}\{ag_a + (a - b)g_{l_a}\}, \tag{3.19}$$

where g_x, g_a and g_{l_a} are respectively the growth rates of labour productivity for the entire economy, the luxury goods sector and the employment share of the luxury goods sector.

Since only capitalists consume luxury goods, we would expect the share of luxury goods output in the total output to increase as the share of profit in output increases. Therefore, we assume the share of luxury goods output in total output to be an increasing function of the profit share as described subsequently:

$$\frac{Y_a}{Y} = f(b), \tag{3.20}$$

where $0 \leq f(b) \leq 1$ and $f'(b) > 0$. Y_a is the output of the luxury goods sector.

Using the definition of l_a and (3.20) we obtain,

$$l_a = \frac{f(b)x}{a}. \tag{3.21}$$

From (3.21), the growth rate of the employment share of the luxury goods sector is,

$$g_{l_a} = \frac{f'(b)}{f(b)}\dot{b} + g_x - g_a. \tag{3.22}$$

Substituting for l_a and g_{l_a} respectively from equations (3.21) and (3.22) in equation (3.19) and then rearranging the terms, we obtain the following expression for the growth rate of labour productivity in the economy:

$$g_x = \frac{bf(b)g_a + (a-b)f'(b)\dot{b}}{\{1 - f(b)\}a + f(b)b}$$

On the equilibrium growth path of profit $g_a = \phi(g_\Pi^*)$. Therefore, g_x is

$$g_x = \frac{bf(b)\phi(g_\Pi^*) + (a-b)f'(b)\dot{b}}{\{1 - f(b)\}a + f(b)b}. \tag{3.23}$$

Thus, the growth rate of labour productivity in the economy at any instant along the equilibrium growth path of profit depends on the constant growth rate of labour productivity in the luxury goods sector, labour productivities of the two sectors, the share of the luxury goods sector's output in the total output and the exogenously given rate of change in the profit share. Since a grows at a constant rate, g_x is not constant along the equilibrium growth path of profit. In the absence of any exogenous change in the distribution of income, that is, when $\dot{b} = 0$, from equation (3.23), we know that the growth rate of labour productivity in the economy continuously declines over time. The growth rate of employment in the economy on the equilibrium growth path of profit is $g_L = g_\Pi^* - g_x$. As g_x falls over time, the growth rate of employment increases to approach g_Π^*. This is obvious because when income distribution is fixed, then the employment share of the luxury goods sector declines and approaches zero as its labour productivity grows at a constant rate. Since labour productivity in the non-luxury sector is fixed, the growth rate of labour productivity in the economy must decline and approach zero and the growth rate of employment approaches g_Π^*. The entire gain in the employment in the economy comes in the non-luxury sector and, moreover, this decline in g_x gets translated into a decline in the growth rate of the real wage which ultimately become stagnant.

However, in periods when the distribution of income changes ($\dot{b} \neq 0$) due to shifts in the policy regime, then g_x need not always decline but can also increase. Let us consider the case of a period when there is worsening of income distribution. Along the equilibrium growth path of profit, $\dot{b} > 0$. Since now both a and b are not constants but grow over time from (3.23), we can not say whether g_x will decline or increase over time. The increase in labour productivity of the luxury goods sector tends to decrease its employment share, but this is countered by an increasing share of its output due to a worsening of income distribution. When the latter tendency outweighs the former, g_x rises along the equilibrium growth path of profit, leading to a possibility of a declining growth rate of employment. We derive some conditions when g_x declines in periods when $\dot{b} > 0$ in the Appendix. Similarly, in periods when $\dot{b} < 0$ too, the behaviour of g_x and g_L over time is ambiguous.

Conclusion

The basic idea on which this essay is based is that not only the level of demand but also its composition is important while studying economic growth. In the closed economy model presented in the essay, we have shown that in a developing country, the consumption demand of the richer section of the population for goods available in developed countries can sustain a positive and steady growth rate of investment and profit. The consumption demand of the rich for goods available in developed countries is an incentive to the firms for investing in the production of such goods by imitating foreign production techniques. In order to capture the aspirations of the rich in the economy to match the consumption standards in the developed countries, we have postulated that the consumption out of profit is not only an increasing function of the level of profit but also of the rate of introduction of new luxury goods in the economy, which are goods that are already available in developed countries. Since a faster rate of introduction of new luxury goods increases the consumption demand of the richer section of the population, it also provides an incentive to the producers to invest in the production of such goods, which has a tendency to increase net investment. On the other hand, if imitation is very costly, the net investment might also decline because the luxury goods are substitute goods in nature. In fact, one condition for the local stability of equilibrium is that even if investment responds negatively to the rate of introduction of new luxury goods, its responsiveness should be less than that of savings.

Assuming that over time, goods introduced in the developed countries are more sophisticated and are associated with higher labour productivities, we have proxied the rate of introduction of new luxury goods in the model by the rate of change in the labour productivity of the luxury sector, $\dot{a}$. The growth process is associated with a particular kind of technological change such that the labour productivity in the luxury sector grows at a constant rate, whereas, by assumption, there is no technological change in the non-luxury sector. The technological change in the luxury sector is induced by the growth rate of profit which indicates the ability of richer section of the population to afford sophisticated goods available in the developed countries. This is captured by a Kaldor kind of technological progress function given by equation (3.4). The equilibrium growth rate of profit and investment depends upon the responsiveness of investment and savings functions to changes in the level of profit, and the rate of change in the labour productivity of the luxury sector, along with the form of the function ϕ. It is obvious from Figure 3.1 that the equilibrium growth rate of profit (and the growth rate of investment) increases with an exogenous increase in $\sigma_{I,\Pi}$, $\sigma_{I,\dot{a}}$ and $|\sigma_{S,\dot{a}}|$ because they decrease z. On the other hand, any increase in $\sigma_{S,\Pi}$ decreases the equilibrium growth rate of profit (and the growth rate of investment) because it increases z. Similarly, any upward shift in the curve of the function ϕ increases the equilibrium growth rate of profit (and the growth rate of investment).

If income distribution in the economy is fixed, then the growth of output along the equilibrium growth path of profit is constant and equal to the positive equilibrium growth rate of profit. From equation (3.20), it then follows that the growth rate of employment in the luxury sector is $g_{L_a} = (1 - z)g_{\Pi}^*$. Thus, the growth rate of employment in the luxury sector is positive if and only if $z < 1$, that is, $\sigma_{S,\Pi} + \sigma_{S,\dot{a}} < \sigma_{I,\Pi} + \sigma_{I,\dot{a}}$. However, in the previous section, we have seen that along the equilibrium growth path of profit, the employment share of the luxury sector continuously declines and approaches zero because labour productivity in the economy declines, while increasing at a constant rate in the luxury sector. Since labour productivity in the economy declines, the growth rate of employment in the economy increases to approach g_{Π}^*. The gain in employment comes primarily in the non-luxury sector where technology is stagnant. This gain in employment growth comes at the cost of decline in the growth rate of real wage which ultimately becomes stagnant.

In the fifth section, we have considered the impact of shifts in the economic policy regime of the government, which are either in favour of the capitalists or the workers, on the growth rate of output along the equilibrium growth path of profit. Whenever such shifts in the policy regime occur many policy changes occur that tend to gradually increase the income share of the class towards which the regime shift is biased. We have assumed that the profit share changes at a constant rate for a period of time when such regime shifts happen. Assuming that in the absence of changes in the policy regime, only output adjustment takes place, we show, in conformity with the existing post-Kaleckian literature, that the growth rate of output declines when there is an exogenous increase in the profit share and increases when there is a decrease in the profit share. However, in both cases the growth rate of output is not constant but increasing because the impact of the redistribution on the growth rate of profit share diminishes over time. As a result, a shift in the economic policy regime in favour of the capitalists does create a spectacle of increasing the output growth for some time but only after an initial decrease. Nonetheless, much more is to be gained in terms the output growth by a shift of the policy regime in favour of the workers, that is, by improving income distribution rather than worsening it, because not only does the growth rate of output increase immediately when the policy regime shifts in favour of the workers but also the increase is sustained. In the previous section we have seen that in periods when $\dot{b} \neq 0$, labour productivity growth in the economy can increase or decrease. This is because labour productivity in the economy is the weighted average of the labour productivities in the two sectors with the weights being their respective employment share. Any change in the income distribution tends to change the output share of the luxury sector, which might counter the impact on the employment share of the luxury sector due to a continuous increase in its labour productivity. The analysis of the impact of government policy–induced changes in income distribution on the growth process presented in the essay is, however, limited to only those kinds of policy measures which are less likely to have any direct bearing upon investment and savings in the economy. In case the change in income distribution due to shifts in the policy regime has an independent impact on investment and savings, then the entire analysis would change. This and allowing for simultaneous adjustment in the profit share and output in response to the investment–savings gap are on the agenda for future research.

Appendix

The total differential of g_x is

$$dg_x = \frac{\partial g_x}{\partial a} da + \frac{\partial g_x}{\partial b} db, \tag{3.24}$$

where dg_x, da and db are the changes in g_x, a and b respectively with $da > 0$ and $db > 0$; $\frac{\partial g_x}{\partial a}$ and $\frac{\partial g_x}{\partial b}$ are the respective partial derivatives of g_x with respect to a and b.

From equation (3.23) the partial derivative of g_x with respect to a is

$$\frac{\partial g_x}{\partial a} = \frac{f'(b)\dot{b}}{[(1-f(b))a+f(b)b]} - \frac{(1-f(b))\{bf'(b)\phi(g_\Pi^*) + (a-b)f''(b)\dot{b}\}}{[(1-f(b))a+f(b)b]^2}$$

and the partial derivative of g_x with respect to b is

$$\frac{\partial g_x}{\partial b} = \frac{\{bf'(b)\phi(g_\Pi^*) + (a-b)f''(b)\dot{b}\}}{[(1-f(b))a+f(b)b]}$$

$$+ \frac{(a-b)f'(b)\{bf'(b)\phi(g_\Pi^*) + (a-b)f'(b)\dot{b}\}}{[(1-f(b))a+f(b)b]^2}$$

Substituting for $\frac{\partial g_x}{\partial a}$ and $\frac{\partial g_x}{\partial b}$ in equation (3.24) and then rearranging the terms we get

$$dg_x = \frac{f'(b)\dot{b}da}{[(1-f(b))a+f(b)b]} + \frac{[bf'(b)\phi(g_\Pi^*) + (a-b)f''(b)\dot{b}]db}{[(1-f(b))a+f(b)b]}$$

$$+ \frac{[(a-b)f'(b)db - (1-f(b))da][bf'(b)\phi(g_\Pi^*) + (a-b)f'(b)\dot{b}]}{[(1-f(b))a+f(b)b]^2}.$$

Since $\phi(g_\Pi^*)$, $\dot{b}$, a, and b are all positive with $a > b$ and $0 < f(b) < 1$, it follows from the previous equation that if $f''(b) \geq 0$ and $(a-b)f'(b)db - (1-f(b))da \geq 0$ then dg_x is positive. Otherwise, dg_x can be negative. Since $adb > 0$ and $\frac{da}{dt} = \dot{a} = a\phi(g_\Pi^*)$ and $\frac{db}{dt} = \dot{b}$, $(a-b)f'(b)db - (1-f(b))da \geq 0$ implies

$$(a-b)f'(b)\dot{b} \geq a(1-f(b))\phi(g_\Pi^*). \tag{3.25}$$

If we assume that the share of luxury goods output increases at a constant or an increasing rate as the profit share increases, that is, $f''(b) \geq 0$, then in periods when government policy changes result in worsening of income distribution, the growth rate of labour productivity increases as long as the inequality (3.25) is satisfied.

References

Albrecht, A. W. and A. H. Smith. 2003. *Fundamental Concepts of Analysis*. New Delhi: Prentice–Hall of India.

Bhaduri, A. 2006. 'Endogenous Economic Growth: A New Approach', *Cambridge Journal of Economics*, 30(1):69–83.

Bhaduri, A. and S. A. Marglin. 1990. 'Unemployment and the Real Wage: The Economic Basis for Contesting Political Ideologies', *Cambridge Journal of Economics*, 14(4):375–93.

Blecker, R. A. 2002. 'Distribution, Demand and Growth in Neo-Kaleckian Macro Models', in M. Setterfield (ed.), *The Economics of Demand-Led Growth: Challenging the Supply Side Vision of the Long Run*. Cheltenham, UK: Edward Elgar, pp. 129–52.

Dutt, A. K. 1984. 'Stagnation, Income Distribution and Monopoly Power', *Cambridge Journal of Economics*, 8(1):25–40.

Kalecki, M. 1969. *Theory of Economic Dynamics: An Essay on Cyclical and Long-Run Changes in Capitalists Economy*. London: Unwin University Book.

———. 1971. *Selected Essays on the Dynamics of the Capitalist Economy*. London: Cambridge University Press.

Patnaik, P. 2007. 'A Model of Growth of the Contemporary Indian Economy', *Economic and Political Weekly*, 42(22):2077–81.

Rowthorn, R. E. 1982. 'Demand, Real Wages and Economic Growth', *Studi Economici*, 18:3–53.

CHAPTER 4

A Simple Dynamic Bargaining Model*

Amarjyoti Mahanta

In this essay we look at a problem involving the division of a cake between two players. The division of cake problem is studied in economics to analyse the outcome of bargaining over a surplus.[1] Bargaining over a surplus is very common in transactions. Suppose a firm is run by two partners. After paying all dues, they are left with a surplus of, say, 10 in monetary units. In such a situation, a question arises: How should these 10 units be divided between the two partners?

Bargaining takes place whenever agents think they can influence the end outcome in their favour to some extent. Thus, there is always a possibility of conflict among the parties involved in bargaining. How does one resolve this possible conflict? In the literature, various bargaining solutions deal with the ways to resolve this conflict.

The bargaining between players has been studied in terms of both cooperative games and non-cooperative games in the literature. The solutions to the bargaining problem have been studied in axiomatic form and also in strategic form games. In the axiomatic forms, the actual

* This essay is a chapter of my PhD thesis. I am thankful to Prof. Anjan Mukherji and Prof. Krishnendu Ghosh Dastidar, my PhD supervisors for their helpful comments and inputs. I thank Dr Subrata Guha for his comments in the presentation done at the Centre for Economic Studies and Planning (CESP), Jawaharlal Nehru University (JNU), New Delhi. I am grateful to Dr Soumya Dutta, Prof. Satish K. Jain, Dr Uday Bhanu Sinha, Prof. P.G. Babu and an anonymous referee for their valuable comments. The usual disclaimer applies.
[1] This motivation of studying division of cake problem in economics is given in Binmore (1992:91).

process of negotiation between the players has been abstracted from the bargaining problem. In some of the strategic forms, the process has been defined to say explicitly how the players will go about negotiating among themselves to reach an agreement.

We consider first a brief literature review on complete information bargaining theory in the next section, at the end of which we provide the motivation for a dynamic bargaining process. In the following section, we build a model which shows the dynamics of a bargaining process and how we reach an agreement. Within this section, we show that the dynamic system is stable. We also endogenize the choice of rate of adjustment and the initial demand, and analyse the nature of equilibrium.

Literature Review

Nash (1950) puts forward the first axiomatic solution to the bargaining problem. The Nash (1950) bargaining solution is that under the axioms of Pareto optimality, symmetry, invariance of equivalent pay-off representation and independence of irrelevant alternatives, the maximization of the product of the utility function of the players give a unique solution.

Prior to Nash, Zeuthen[2] developed a model of a bargaining process which may be described as follows: if the two players reach an agreement A, then they get $U_1(A)$ and $U_2(A)$. If they fail to reach an agreement, then a conflict situation C will arise and both the players will get $U_1(C)$ and $U_2(C)$. The bargaining process is described in stages. At the K+1 stage, each player has three options:

1. Repeat his last proposal
2. Accept his opponents offer
3. Make a new proposal which is more favourable to the opponent

Thus, there arises the possibility of revision. The concessions will be made by the player whose r_i is such that $r_i < r_{-i}, i \neq -i, i = 1, 2$, where $r_i = \dfrac{U_i(A_i) - U_i(A_j)}{U_i(A_i) - U_i(C)}$.

Harsanyi (1956) showed the relation between Zeuthen's bargaining process and the Nash bargaining solution. Assuming $U_i(C) = 0, i = 1, 2$ and putting the expression of $r_i, i = 1, 2$ in the inequality $r_1 < r_2$, we get $U_1(A_1)U_2(A_1) < U_2(A_2)U_1(A_2)$. The process of making concessions

---

[2] A version of Zeuthen's model appeared in Harsayanyi (1977:149–66).

by each player would increase the value of the product $U_1()U_2()$. At the end, the two players would arrive at the term that maximizes the value of this product, which is the Nash bargaining solution.

Harsanyi (1963) has extended the Nash bargaining solution to n persons where bargaining between the players takes place pairwise. Luce and Raiffa (1957) have argued that the Nash solution to the bargaining problem is an arbitration scheme. Arbitration scheme is a function or rule which associates to each conflict between two players in a non-strictly competitive game, a unique pay-off to the players. In this sense, the Nash solution has been considered by some as a fair solution which is invoked through axiom of symmetry.

The property of independence of irrelevant alternative has been criticized in the literature mainly because if the possibility of a player is truncated, the outcome is not changed. The level of aspiration does not affect the bargaining outcome in a Nash solution. To get away with the axiom of independence of irrelevant alternatives, Kalai and Smorodinsky (1975) introduced another axiom called the axiom of individual monotonicity. Because of the axiom of individual monotonicity, there is a utopian point. The intersection of the Pareto frontier and the line joining the disagreement point and the utopian point gives the Raiffa–Kalai–Smorodinsky solution. Lensberg and Thomson (1988) also have a similar kind of bargaining solution where if a solution is acceptable for a group, then that solution should give the bargaining solution for a subgroup of that group.

Cross (1965) developed a process of bargaining that can lead to an agreement in the division of a cake between two players. When the players are similar or symmetric, that is, the expected rate of concession of each player about the other player is same and the cost of bargaining in utility terms is same for each player, the agreement point is the Nash bargaining solution.

Another way of analysing the bargaining problem is through strategic behaviour of the players. Rubinstein (1982) proved the existence of a solution in a bargaining between two players over a pie of size 1. Each player makes a proposal alternatively till it is accepted. The accepted proposal is a perfect equilibrium.

Binmore et al. (1986) have noted that agreement in a bargaining game depends on two important factors (*a*) impatience to enjoy the fruit of an agreement and (*b*) the fear that if the players prolong the negotiation, there might be a breakdown in the negotiation and no agreement may be reached at all. Rubinstein et al. (1992) have shown that the limit of the solution to the time preference model and the model with uncertain termination of bargaining is the Nash solution when the time between the subsequent periods tends to zero.

Shaked and Sutton (1984) have shown the existence of a unique subgame perfect Nash equilibrium in an alternating-offer bargaining game when the bargaining can continue till some exogenously given finite number of times.

The negotiation in the bargaining has also been studied through commitment and non-commitment strategies. According to Schelling (1956) the bargaining process is a struggle between players to commit themselves, that is, to convince their opponents that they will not retreat from an advantageous bargain. The players make a demand, and it is costly for them to back out from their demand. This also explains the occurrence of an impasse in the bargaining because of the possibility of mutually incompatible commitments. Crawford (1982) has shown the possibility of an impasse in bargaining because of uncertainty and irreversibility of commitment, and not because of irrationality.

Sutton (1986) has shown that in an alternating-offer bargaining model, there is no unique subgame perfect Nash equilibrium when the number of players are more than two.

In many instances, we see that there lies a trial and error process through which the players arrive at some agreement. We propose to study a process through which some agreement point is reached when the two players are bargaining to divide a cake. It is not necessary that players will reach an agreement point instantaneously always. Suppose this does not happen, how will they reach the agreement point? If they are out of an equilibrium situation or initially not in equilibrium,[3] will they reach the equilibrium position? In the example given in the beginning, we saw that the two partners negotiate to divide the surplus of 10. One of the partners may demand 7 and the other may demand 6. In such a situation, the division is not feasible. One way to get out of this impasse is that each of them reconsider their demands and make adjustments. While making adjustments, each player will contemplate how much the rival player is going to adjust. This adjustment will continue till an agreement point is reached. Thus, there may be processes through which the conflict in the bargaining is resolved. We have tried to represent this process of bargaining through a dynamic system. The equilibrium points of the system gives us the agreement points of the negotiation.

---

[3] These two phrases mean that the sum of demands of each individual is not feasible.

Model

We are considering a problem which involves the division of a cake. The division takes place through a process of bargaining. Suppose there are two players, 1 and 2, who are bargaining to divide a cake of size M. Both players quote their demand simultaneously and continuously till they agree upon a share. Consequently, we need to specify what the players do when they do not agree on any particular share.

Suppose the demand made by the player 1 is x_1 and the demand made by player 2 is x_2. In case $x_1 + x_2 = M$, we assume that players have reached an agreement. If $x_1 + x_2 \neq M$, then both the players make some adjustments, since both the players prefer an agreement to a no-agreement situation. It may happen that only one of the players makes large adjustments and the other does not. The question is whether these adjustments have a bearing on the outcome. Thus, we will get a class of adjustment processes. We define a dynamic system in the following way:

$$\dot{x}_1 = \lambda_1(M - x_1 - x_2)$$
$$\dot{x}_2 = \lambda_2(M - x_1 - x_2) \dots \text{ system A}$$

where $\lambda_i > 0$, constant, $i = 1, 2$.
λ_i = rate of adjustment, that is, the rate at which demand made by player i is changing.

$$\Rightarrow \dot{x}_1 = \lambda_1(M - x_1 - x_2)$$
$$\Rightarrow \dot{x}_2 = \lambda_2(M - x_1 - x_2)$$
$$\Rightarrow \frac{\dot{x}_2}{\dot{x}_1} = \frac{\lambda_2}{\lambda_1}$$
$$\Rightarrow \frac{x_2}{\lambda_2} = \frac{x_1}{\lambda_1} + \bar{c}, \quad \text{by integration,}$$
$$\Rightarrow \frac{x_2}{x_1} = \frac{\lambda_2}{\lambda_1} + \frac{\lambda_2 \bar{c}}{x_1}, \text{ the solution of system A.}$$

The equilibrium points of the system A are given by the line $x_1 + x_2 = M$.

For initial values $x^o = (x_1^o, x_2^o)$, we get
$$\frac{x_2^o}{x_1^o} = \frac{\lambda_2}{\lambda_1} + \frac{\lambda_2 \bar{c}}{x_1^o}.$$
Thus, we get three different cases:

1. $\dfrac{x_2^o}{x_1^o} = \dfrac{\lambda_2}{\lambda_1}, \quad \Rightarrow \bar{c} = 0$

2. $\dfrac{x_2^o}{x_1^o} > \dfrac{\lambda_2}{\lambda_1}, \quad \Rightarrow \bar{c} > 0$

3. $\quad \dfrac{x_2^o}{x_1^o} < \dfrac{\lambda_2}{\lambda_1}, \quad \Rightarrow \bar{c} < 0.$

The Nature of Dynamics and Stability of System A

We have three different cases based on the initial point and the rate of adjustment. We will look at the effect of the initial point and the rate of adjustment on the trajectories and its limit. The phase diagrams of case 1, case 2 and case 3 are shown in Figures 4.1, 4.2 and 4.3 respectively. From the phase diagrams, it is clear that if the trajectories hit the line $x_1 + x_2 = M$, it will not cross the line $x_1 + x_2 = M$. So we have analysed the situations when the initial point (x_1^o, x_2^o) is $x_1^o + x_2^o > M$ and $x_1^o + x_2^o < M$.

The solution of the system A is:

$\dfrac{x_2(t)}{\lambda_2} = \dfrac{x_1(t)}{\lambda_1} + \bar{c}$, for an initial point (x_1^o, x_2^o).

$\Rightarrow \dfrac{x_2(t)}{x_1(t)} = \dfrac{\lambda_2}{\lambda_1} + \dfrac{\lambda_2 \bar{c}}{x_1(t)}$. Note $\dfrac{d}{dt}\left(\dfrac{x_2(t)}{x_1(t)}\right) = \dfrac{d}{dt}\left(\dfrac{\lambda_2}{\lambda_1} + \dfrac{\lambda_2 \bar{c}}{x_1}\right)$, substituting from the solution.

$= \lambda_2 \bar{c} \dfrac{\dot{x}_1}{x_1^2}.$

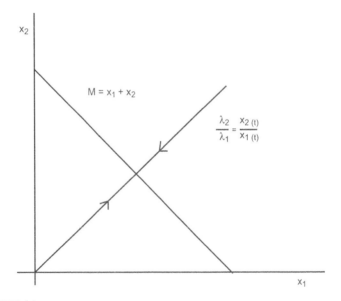

FIGURE 4.1 Case 1

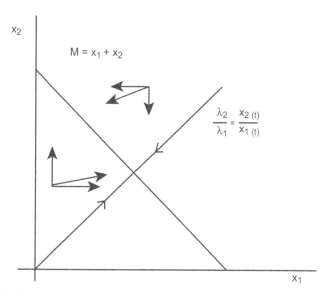

FIGURE 4.2 Case 2

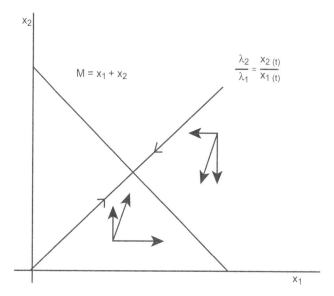

FIGURE 4.3 Case 3

$$= \lambda_2 \bar{c} \frac{\lambda_1 (M - x_1 - x_2)}{x_1^2}.$$

$$= -\frac{\bar{c} \lambda_2 \lambda_1 [M - x_1 - x_2]}{x_1^2}.$$

For $\bar{c} > 0$, $\frac{d}{dt}(\frac{x_2(t)}{x_1(t)})$ is either always positive or negative, if $(M - x_1 - x_2) > 0$ or $(M - x_1 - x_2) < 0$ respectively. For $\bar{c} < 0$, the sign of $\frac{d}{dt}(\frac{x_2(t)}{x_1(t)})$ is opposite of the above.

In case 1, $(\frac{x_2^o}{x_1^o} = \frac{\lambda_2}{\lambda_1})$, we get two subcases: $(a) x_1^o + x_2^o > M$ and (b) $x_1^o + x_2^o < M$. We know that $\bar{c} = 0$ in case 1, so the trajectory is $\frac{x_2(t)}{x_1(t)} = \frac{\lambda_2}{\lambda_1}$ and $\frac{d}{dt}(\frac{x_2(t)}{x_1(t)}) = 0$ in both the subcases. If the trajectories converge, they will converge to a point (x_2^*, x_1^*) of following nature $\frac{x_2^*}{x_1^*} = \frac{\lambda_2}{\lambda_1}$ and $x_2^* + x_1^* = M$.

In case 2, $(\frac{x_2^o}{x_1^o} > \frac{\lambda_2}{\lambda_1})$, we get two subcases: $(a) x_1^o + x_2^o > M$ and (b) $x_1^o + x_2^o < M$. We know that $\bar{c} > 0$, so in subcase (a) $\frac{d}{dt}(\frac{x_2(t)}{x_1(t)}) > 0$, since $x_1(t) + x_1(t) > M$, as long as the trajectory does not hit the line $x_1 + x_2 = M$. This is because the trajectories cannot cross the line $x_1 + x_2 = M$. If the trajectory converges, the point of convergence (x_1^*, x_2^*) will be of the following nature $\frac{x_2^*}{x_1^*} > \frac{x_2^o}{x_1^o} > \frac{\lambda_2}{\lambda_1}$ and $x_1^* + x_2^* = M$. In subcase (b) $\frac{d}{dt}(\frac{x_2(t)}{x_1(t)}) < 0$, since $x_1(t) + x_2(t) < M$. The point of convergence is $\frac{x_2^o}{x_1^o} > \frac{x_2^*}{x_1^*} > \frac{\lambda_2}{\lambda_1}$ and $x_1^* + x_2^* = M$, if the trajectory converges. It cannot be $\frac{x_2^*}{x_1^*} = \frac{\lambda_2}{\lambda_1}$, since $\bar{c} > 0$.

In case 3, $(\frac{x_2^o}{x_1^o} < \frac{\lambda_2}{\lambda_1})$, we get two subcases: (a) $x_1^o + x_2^o > M$ and (b) $x_1^o + x_2^o < M$. We know that $\bar{c} < 0$, so in subcase (a) $\frac{d}{dt}(\frac{x_2(t)}{x_1(t)}) < 0$, since $x_1(t) + x_2(t) < M$, as long as the trajectory does not hit the line $x_1 + x_2 = M$. If the trajectory converges, the point of convergence (x_1^*, x_2^*) will be of the following nature $\frac{x_2^*}{x_1^*} < \frac{x_2^o}{x_1^o} < \frac{\lambda_2}{\lambda_1}$ and $x_2^* + x_1^* = M$. In subcase (b), $\frac{d}{dt}(\frac{x_2(t)}{x_1(t)}) > 0$, since $x_2(t) + x_1(t) < M$ as long as the trajectory does not hit the line $x_1 + x_2 = M$. If the trajectory converges, then the point of convergence (x_1^*, x_2^*) is $\frac{x_2^o}{x_1^o} < \frac{x_2^*}{x_1^*} < \frac{\lambda_2}{\lambda_1}$ and $x_1^* + x_2^* = M$. It cannot be $\frac{x_2^*}{x_1^*} = \frac{\lambda_2}{\lambda_1}$, since $\bar{c} < 0$.

We can show that the system converges to an equilibrium point for a given initial point through the construction of a Lyapunov function. Consider a function $V(x_1(t), x_2(t)) = \lambda_2(x_1(t) - x_1^*)^2 + \lambda_1(x_2(t) - x_2^*)^2$. The function $V(x_1(t), x_2(t)) > 0, \forall x_1(t) \geq 0, x_2(t) \geq 0$ except

$x_1(t) + x_2(t) = M$, at $x_1(t) + x_2(t) = M$, $V(x_1(t), x_2(t)) = 0$.

$\dot{V} = 2(x_1(t) - x_1^*)\lambda_2\dot{x}_1(t) + 2(x_2(t) - x_2^*)\lambda_1\dot{x}_2(t)$

$= 2(x_1(t) - x_1^*)\lambda_2\lambda_1(M - x_1(t) - x_2(t)) + 2(x_2(t) - x_2^*)\lambda_1\lambda_2(M - x_1(t) - x_2(t))$

$= 2(M - x_1(t) - x_2(t))(\lambda_1\lambda_2 x_1(t) - \lambda_1\lambda_2 x_1^* + \lambda_1\lambda_2 x_2(t) - \lambda_1\lambda_2 x_2^*).$

$= 2(M - x_1(t) - x_2(t))\lambda_1\lambda_2(x_1(t) + x_2(t) - M)$

$= -2\lambda_1\lambda_2(M - x_1(t) - x_2(t))^2$

$\dot{V}(x_1(t), x_2(t)) < 0$ for $x_1(t) \geq 0$, $x_2(t) \geq 0$ and $x_1(t) + x_2(t) \neq M$.

$\dot{V}(x_1(t), x_2(t)) = 0$ for $x_1(t) \geq 0$, $x_2(t) \geq 0$ and $x_1(t) + x_2(t) = M$.

Therefore, system A is globally asymptotically stable. The convergence to the equilibrium points can be interpreted as the points of agreement of the negotiation between the two players.

From the foregoing analysis, it is clear that the nature of equilibrium is dependent on the initial demand made by each player and the rate of adjustment. For example, suppose $\frac{\lambda_2}{\lambda_1} = 1$, then for the initial point as defined in case 1, the equilibrium is such that $\frac{x_2^*}{x_1^*} = 1$. For the initial point as defined in case 2, the equilibrium is such that $\frac{x_2^*}{x_1^*} > 1$. For the initial point, as defined in case 3, the equilibrium is such that $\frac{x_2^*}{x_1^*} < 1$.

Choice of Rate of Adjustment and Initial Demand

Suppose the players make adjustments to their demands as defined by the system A. Then, for an initial demand, the question arises as to how player i makes the choice over λ_i, where $\lambda_i \in (0, 1)$.

Let $(x_1(t), x_2(t))$ be the trajectory given by the solution of the system A for an initial demand (x_1^o, x_2^o) and $\frac{x_2^o}{x_1^o} = r$ and $x_2^o + x_1^o > M$.

$\frac{d}{dt}(\frac{x_2(t)}{x_1(t)}) = \frac{x_1(t)\dot{x}_2(t) - x_2(t)\dot{x}_1(t)}{x_1^2(t)}$

$= \frac{x_1(t)\lambda_2[M - x_1(t) - x_2(t)] - x_2(t)\lambda_1[M - x_1(t) - x_2(t)]}{x_1^2(t)}$

$= \frac{[M - x_1(t) - x_2(t)][x_1(t)\lambda_2 - x_2(t)\lambda_1]}{x_1^2(t)}$

$= \frac{[M - x_1(t) - x_2(t)][\frac{\lambda_2}{\lambda_1} - \frac{x_2(t)}{x_1(t)}]x_1(t)\lambda_1}{x_1^2(t)}$

For $\frac{d}{dt}(\frac{x_2(t)}{x_1(t)}) > 0$, implies $[M - x_1(t) - x_2(t)][\frac{\lambda_2}{\lambda_1} - \frac{x_2(t)}{x_1(t)}] > 0$.

Since $x_1^o + x_2^o > M$, so $(M - x_1(t) - x_2(t)) < 0$ for $x_1(t), x_2(t)$ not equilibrium points.

Thus we get:

$[\frac{\lambda_2}{\lambda_1} - \frac{x_2(t)}{x_1(t)}] < 0.$

$\frac{\lambda_2}{\lambda_1} < \frac{x_2(t)}{x_1(t)}.$

$\Rightarrow \frac{\lambda_2}{\lambda_1} < \frac{x_2^o}{x_1^o}$ from the solution and case 2.

$\Rightarrow \frac{\lambda_2}{\lambda_1} < r$, given $\bar{\lambda}_1$.

Thus, player 2 must choose λ_2 for given $\bar{\lambda}_1$ such that $\lambda_2 < r\bar{\lambda}_1$.

From the foregoing analysis, we have obtained an upper bound for the λ_2 for given $\bar{\lambda}_1$, that is, $\lambda_2 \in (0, \bar{\lambda}_1 r)$, for $x_1^o + x_2^o > M$. Now we need to see how the share of the player 2 changes with the variation of λ_2 within the range concerned.

$$\frac{\partial}{\partial \lambda_2}(\frac{d}{dt}(\frac{x_2(t)}{x_1(t)})) = \frac{\partial}{\partial \lambda_2}(\frac{[M - x_1(t) - x_2(t)][\frac{\lambda_2}{\lambda_1} - \frac{x_2(t)}{x_1(t)}]\lambda_1}{x_1(t)})$$

$$= \frac{[M - x_1(t) - x_2(t)]\lambda}{x_1(t)} < 0, \quad \text{for} \quad x_1^o + x_2^o > M \quad \text{and} \quad x_1 + x_2 >$$

M, ... condition I.

Thus, if λ_2 decreases, then the relative demand of the player 2 increases over time. Thus, it is optimal for player 2 to choose the smallest λ_2 given $\bar{\lambda}_1$.

Similarly, player 1 will also try to maximize his share of the cake. Given $\bar{\lambda}_2$ and an initial demand (x_1^o, x_2^o), $\frac{x_2^o}{x_1^o} = r$ and $x_1^o + x_2^o > M$, the choice of λ_1 should be such that $\frac{d}{dt}(\frac{x_2(t)}{x_1(t)}) < 0$.

$$\frac{d}{dt}(\frac{x_2(t)}{x_1(t)}) = \frac{x_1(t)\dot{x}_2(t) - x_2(t)\dot{x}_1(t)}{x_1^2(t)}$$

$$= \frac{[M - x_1(t) - x_2(t)][\frac{\lambda_2}{\lambda_1} - \frac{x_2(t)}{x_1(t)}]x_1(t)\lambda_1}{x_1^2(t)}$$

For $\frac{d}{dt}(\frac{x_2(t)}{x_1(t)}) < 0$, requires $\frac{[M - x_1(t) - x_2(t)][\frac{\lambda_2}{\lambda_1} - \frac{x_2(t)}{x_1(t)}]x_1(t)\lambda_1}{x_1^2(t)}$

$< 0.$

Since $(M - x_1(t) - x_2(t)) < 0$ for $x_1^o + x_2^o > M$

$\Rightarrow (\frac{\lambda_2}{\lambda_1} - \frac{x_2(t)}{x_1(t)}) > 0$

$\Rightarrow \frac{\lambda_2}{\lambda_1} > \frac{x_2(t)}{x_1(t)}$

$\Rightarrow \frac{\lambda_2}{\lambda_1} > \frac{x_2^o}{x_1^o}$

$\Rightarrow \frac{\lambda_2}{\lambda_1} > r$, given $\bar{\lambda}_2$

$\Rightarrow \frac{\bar{\lambda}_2}{r} > \lambda_1$. Thus, we have obtained an upper bound of the value of λ_1 for a given $\bar{\lambda}_2$ for optimizing player 1.

Thus, we get that player 1 will choose λ_1 such that $\lambda_1 \in (0, \frac{\bar{\lambda}_2}{r})$. We need to check how the demand of the player 2 changes with the changes in λ_1.

$$\frac{\partial}{\partial \lambda_1}(\frac{d}{dt}\frac{x_2(t)}{x_1(t)})) = \frac{\partial}{\partial \lambda_1}(\frac{[M - x_1(t) - x_2(t)][\lambda_2 x_1(t) - \lambda_1 x_2(t)]}{x_1^2(t)})$$

$$= -\frac{(M - x_1(t) - x_2(t))x_2(t)}{x_1^2(t)}$$

$$= \frac{\partial}{\partial \lambda_1}(\frac{d}{dt}(\frac{x_2(t)}{x_1(t)})) > 0, \text{ for } x_1^o + x_2^o > M \text{ and } x_1 + x_2 > M... \text{ condition}$$
II.

If λ_1 decreases, then $(\frac{\partial}{\partial \lambda_1}(\frac{d}{dt}(\frac{x_2(t)}{x_1(t)})))$ decreases, or if λ_1 increases, then $(\frac{\partial}{\partial \lambda_1}(\frac{d}{dt}(\frac{x_2(t)}{x_1(t)})))$ increases. Thus, λ_1 must be the smallest value given $\bar{\lambda}_2$, if the player 1 wants to maximize his share.

In the model we have considered $\lambda_i \in (0, 1)$. Thus, it is an open set so we do not have any greatest lower bound which belongs to the set. We assume that $\lambda_i \in [\varepsilon_i, \delta_i]$, where i = 1, 2 and $0 < \varepsilon_i < \delta_i < 1$. The justification of this assumption is that both the players are going to make some adjustments when their demands are not feasible since it is better to make adjustments and reach an agreement rather than no adjustment and no agreement. So we can make the range of λ_i closed within some positive real values.[4]

From condition I, it is clear that, given any $\bar{\lambda}_1 \in [\varepsilon_1, \delta_1]$, and (x_1^o, x_2^o), player 2 will choose λ_2 such that $\lambda_2 = \varepsilon_2$ when $x_1^o + x_2^o > M$.

Again from condition II, it is clear that given any $\bar{\lambda}_2 \in [\varepsilon_2, \delta_2]$ and (x_1^o, x_2^o), player 1 will choose λ_1 such that $\lambda_1 = \varepsilon_1$, when $x_1^o + x_2^o > M$.

Thus, the optimal choice of player 1 and player 2 of λ_i, $i = 1, 2$ is ε_i when $x_1^o + x_2^o > M$.

Putting the values of $\lambda_i = \varepsilon_i$, $i = 1, 2$, in the solution of system A, we get $\frac{x_2}{\varepsilon_2} = \frac{x_1}{\varepsilon_1} + \bar{c}$.

Given that the players are going to choose the greatest lower bound of the range over which the rate of adjustment ($\lambda_i \in [\varepsilon_i, \delta_i]$, $i = 1, 2$) lies, the question arises as to what their initial demand, should be when each one of the player tries to maximize his own share.

---

[4] An explanation of the bounds on the rate of adjustment is given at the end of this section.

We know from our earlier discussion that the trajectories converge to an equilibrium point. The equilibrium point depends on the rate of adjustment and the initial point. When $(M - x_1^o - x_2^o) < 0$, we know that each player is going to choose the greatest lower bound of the range from which each of them can choose the rate of adjustment. Putting these values in the solution of the dynamic system, we can calculate the pay-off of each player in equilibrium, given an initial demand.

Suppose (x_1^*, x_2^*) is an equilibrium point.

$\Rightarrow \frac{x_2^*}{x_1^*} = \frac{\varepsilon_2}{\varepsilon_1} + \frac{\varepsilon_2 \bar{c}}{x_1^*}$ and $x_1^* + x_2^* = M$

$\Rightarrow x_1^* = \frac{\varepsilon_1 M - \varepsilon_1 \varepsilon_2 \bar{c}}{\varepsilon_1 + \varepsilon_2}$ and $x_2^* = \frac{\varepsilon_2 M + \varepsilon_1 \varepsilon_2 \bar{c}}{\varepsilon_1 + \varepsilon_2}$

From the solution and our discussion in this section, we get:

$\bar{c} = (\frac{x_2^o}{x_1^o} - \frac{\varepsilon_2}{\varepsilon_1}) \frac{x_1^o}{\varepsilon_2}$, where (x_1^o, x_2^o) is an initial point.

$$\Rightarrow x_1^* = \frac{\varepsilon_1 M - \varepsilon_1 \varepsilon_2 (\frac{x_2^o}{x_1^o} - \frac{\varepsilon_2}{\varepsilon_1}) \frac{x_1^o}{\varepsilon_2}}{\varepsilon_1 + \varepsilon_2} = \frac{\varepsilon_1 M - \varepsilon_1 x_2^o + \varepsilon_2 x_1^o}{\varepsilon_1 + \varepsilon_2}.$$

Proceeding similarly, we get $x_2^* = \dfrac{\varepsilon_2 M - \varepsilon_2 x_1^o + \varepsilon_1 x_2^o}{\varepsilon_1 + \varepsilon_2}$.

It is clear from the pay-off that if x_1^o is higher, then the pay-off of player 1 is higher. If x_2^o is higher, then the pay-off of player 2 is higher. So each player should demand the maximum possible demand so that the pay-off of each player attains the maximum possible value, given other things are constant. The size of the cake is M. So each player will make an initial demand of M when each of them is trying to maximize his share, given that the adjustment is done through the system A. The initial point is (M, M) when each of the players is trying to maximize his share.

If $\lambda_1 \in [\varepsilon_1, \delta_1]$, $\lambda_2 \in [\varepsilon_2, \delta_2]$ and $0 < \varepsilon_1 < \varepsilon_2$, player 1 chooses ε_1, player 2 chooses ε_2 and the initial demand is (M, M) then the pay-off of player 1 in equilibrium is $x_1^* = \frac{\varepsilon_2 M}{\varepsilon_1 + \varepsilon_2}$ and the pay-off of player 2 in equilibrium is $x_2^* = \frac{\varepsilon_1 M}{\varepsilon_1 + \varepsilon_2}$. The share of player 1 is greater than the share of player 2 in the limit since $\frac{x_2^*}{x_1^*} = \frac{\varepsilon_1}{\varepsilon_2} < 1 < \frac{\varepsilon_2}{\varepsilon_1}$. It satisfies the condition we had derived earlier for the limit point in case 3.

If $\lambda_1 \in [\varepsilon_1, \delta_1]$, $\lambda_2 \in [\varepsilon_2, \delta_2]$, and $0 < \varepsilon_2 < \varepsilon_1 < 1$, player 1 chooses ε_1, player 2 chooses ε_2 and the initial demand is (M, M) then the pay-off of player 1 in equilibrium is $x_1^* = \frac{\varepsilon_2 M}{\varepsilon_1 + \varepsilon_2}$ and the pay-off of player 2 in equilibrium is $x_2^* = \frac{\varepsilon_1 M}{\varepsilon_1 + \varepsilon_2}$. The share of player 1 is less than the share of player 2 in the limit since $\frac{x_2^*}{x_1^*} = \frac{\varepsilon_1}{\varepsilon_2} > 1 > \frac{\varepsilon_2}{\varepsilon_1}$. The condition we derived earlier for the limit point in case 2 is satisfied.

If $\lambda_1 \in [\varepsilon_1, \delta_1]$, $\lambda_2 \in [\varepsilon_2, \delta_2]$ and $0 < \varepsilon_1 = \varepsilon_2 < 1$, player 1 chooses ε_1, player 2 chooses ε_2 and the initial point is (M, M), given that each of the players wants to maximize his share, then the pay-off of player 1 in equilibrium is $x_1^* = \frac{\varepsilon_2 M}{\varepsilon_1 + \varepsilon_2}$ and the pay-off of player 2 in equilibrium is $x_2^* = \frac{\varepsilon_1 M}{\varepsilon_1 + \varepsilon_2}$. The share of player 1 is equal to the share of player 2 in the limit since $\frac{x_2^*}{x_1^*} = 1 = \frac{\varepsilon_2}{\varepsilon_1}$. It satisfies the condition we derived earlier for case 1.

This rate of adjustment can be interpreted as an index of the level of patience or capacity to wait of each player. The level of patience or capacity to wait can be understood as how quickly the players are willing to give in or end the bargaining to reach an agreement. Thus, the range of rate of adjustment can signify the range over which the bargaining power of a player lies. The lower bound of this range gives the maximum extent of the capacity to wait or the level of patience of each player and upper bound gives the minimum extent of the capacity to wait or the level of patience of each player. If player 1 is eager to or quickly wants to reach an agreement compared to player 2 and at the same time wants to maximize his share, it means the that lower bound of the range of rate of adjustment of player 1 is greater than the lower bound of the rate of adjustment of player 2. It implies that the bargaining power of player 1 is lower than the bargaining power of player 2.

Conclusion

In the bargaining between two players to divide a cake, if the bargaining takes place through an adjustment process (dynamic system A), the outcome is dependent on the initial point and the rate of adjustment. When we assume that both the players are trying to maximize their own shares and the range over which each player can choose his rate of adjustment is the same, the outcome is equal share $(\frac{M}{2}, \frac{M}{2})$. The outcome is not an equal share of the cake even if each player wants to maximize his own share when the capacity to wait or the level of patience is not similar. The player with the higher level of patience or capacity to wait gets the higher share.

References

Binmore, K. 1992. *Fun and Games: A Text on Game Theory.* New Delhi: AITBS.

Binmore, K., A. Rubinstein and A. Wolinsky. 1986. 'The Nash Bargaining Solution in Economic Modelling', *RAND Journal of Economics*, 17(2):176–88.

Crawford, V. P. 1982. 'A Theory of Disagreement in Bargaining', *Econometrica*, 50(3):607–37.

Cross, J. G. 1965. 'A Theory of the Bargaining Process', *The American Economic Review*, 55(1/2):67–94.

Harsanyi, J. C. 1956. 'Approaches to the Bargaining Problem Before and After the Theory of Games: A Critical Discussion of Zeuthen's, Hicks', and Nash's Theories', *Econometrica*, 24(2): 144–57.

———. 1963. 'A Simplified Bargaining Model for the n-Person Cooperative Game', *International Economic Review*, 4(2): 194–220.

———. 1977. *Rational Behaviour and Bargaining Equilibrium in Games and Social Situations*. Cambridge, New York, Melbourne: Cambridge University Press.

Kalai, E. and M. Smorodinsky. 1975. 'Other Solutions to Nash's Bargaining Problem', *Econometrica*, 43(3):513–18.

Lensberg, T. and W. Thomson. 1988. 'Characterizing the Nash Bargaining Solution without Pareto-Optimality', *Social Choice and Welfare*, 5(2):247–59.

Luce, R. D. and H. Raiffa. 1957. *Games and Decisions: Introduction and Critical Survey*. New York: John Wiley and Sons, Inc.

Nash, J. F., Jr. 1950. 'The Bargaining Problem', *Econometrica*, 18(2): 155–62.

Rubinstein, A. 1982. 'Perfect Equilibrium in a Bargaining Model', *Econometrica*, 50(1):97–109.

Rubinstein, A., Z. Safra, and W. Thomson. 1992. 'On the Interpretation of the Nash Bargaining Solution and Its Extension to Non-expected Utility Preferences', *Econometrica*, 60(5): 1171–86.

Schelling, T. C. 1956. 'An Essay on Bargaining', *The American Economic Review*, 46(3):281–306.

Shaked, A. and J. Sutton. 1984. 'Involuntary Unemployment as a Perfect Equilibrium in a Bargaining Model', *Econometrica*, 52(6):1351–64.

Sutton, J. 1986. 'Non-cooperative Bargaining Theory: An Introduction', *The Review of Economic Studies*, 53(5):709–24.

CHAPTER 5

Increasing Returns, Non-traded Goods and Wage Inequality

Brati Sankar Chakraborty and Abhirup Sarkar

This essay is yet another attempt to theoretically explain the rising wage gap between skilled and unskilled labour, a phenomenon that is being observed in different parts of the world for different lengths of time. The increase in wage dispersion has been most pronounced in the United States where the skill premium has been consistently increasing since the late 1970s. In the US, after an increase in the 1980s, wage inequality between high-school graduates and non-high-school graduates somewhat stabilized from the 1990s. However, the wages of college graduates and postgraduates, relative to that of non-graduates, have been sharply increasing for the last three decades.[1] For other Organisation for Economic Co-operation and Development (OECD) countries, there has either been a fall in the relative wage of the unskilled or an increase in their rate of unemployment or both, though the degree has varied from country to country (Katz and Autor 1999). The evidence on rising wage inequality has been somewhat mixed for developing countries. Zhu and Trefler (2005) reported that only about half of 20 developing and newly industrialized countries experienced rising inequality in the 1990s. Moreover, the skill premium increased in those countries where exports became more skill intensive. A number of studies have concentrated on the experience of Mexico after the country joined the North American Free Trade Agreement (NAFTA). While Esquivel and Rodriguez-Lopez (2003), Feenstra and Hanson (1997), Hanson and Harrison (1995), Wood

---

[1] See Autor et al. (2008), Katz and Autor (1999) and Lemieux (2008).

(1995) and others have reported rising wage inequality in Mexico in the 1980s and the 1990s, Robertson (2007) has found evidence of a narrowing wage gap in the country in the post-NAFTA period.

Roughly speaking, two broad streams of thought can be identified which explain the rising wage premium. First, a large part of the literature ascribes the rise in the wage premium to skill-biased technological change and a consequent increase in the relative demand for skilled labour (Acemoglu 2002; Autor et al. 1998, 2008; Bound and Johnson 1992; Krusell et al. 2000). Second, globalization or increasing integration with the international market has also been proposed to be a significant factor causing a rise in the wage premium (Borjas et al. 1991; Feenstra and Hanson 1996, 1999). There is yet a third stream of thought which looks at the interaction of the two factors to explain the increasing wage premium (Acemoglu 2002; Zeira 2007).

The present essay attempts to contribute to the second stream of thought. More specifically, it gives a theoretical explanation of the rising wage premium in terms of trade liberalization. Symmetric movements in the wage gap is not consistent with the 2 × 2 Heckscher–Ohlin–Samuelson (HOS) model, which would predict relative skill wages to go up in the skill-abundant country and come down in the skill-scarce one following trade. Therefore, some authors like Esquivel and Rodriguez-Lopez (2003) argue that for less developed countries like Mexico, skill-biased technological change and integration with the international market have produced opposite effects on the wage premium—the former has increased it, while the latter has reduced it. On the net, however, the effect of skill-biased technical change has dominated the effect of international integration, and, therefore, we find an overall increase in the wage premium. A number of authors have, thus, come out of the rigidity of the traditional HOS framework to explain rising wage inequality through trade.

Jones (1999) has proposed a variant of the HOS model with two countries (North and South), three goods and two factors (skilled and unskilled labour). The goods are uniquely ranked in terms of intensities. The good with middle ranked intensity is produced in both the countries, and the one with the highest and lowest skill intensities are produced exclusively in the developed North and the less developed South respectively, with the South exporting the good with the middle intensity. Trade liberalization by the North lead to an improvement in the terms of trade and a rise in demand for skilled labour in the South. In the North, lower import tariff reduces the domestic price of the middle good, which is the unskilled labour-intensive good for the North, and along with it the unskilled wage. The result, however, crucially depends on the pattern of trade. If, for example, the South were to import the good with the middle intensity, trade liberalization would reduce wage inequality in both countries.

Marjit and Acharyya (2003) suggest yet another route, namely, the intermediate goods trade, through which trade might symmetrically increase the skill premium. Feenstra and Hanson (1996), in an oft-cited paper, redesign the Dornbusch et al. (1980) model by adding a third factor—capital. In their model, a single manufacturing output is assembled from a continuum of intermediate inputs. Such inputs are produced by skilled labour, unskilled labour and capital. In equilibrium, the South produces and exports a range of inputs and the North does the rest. A rise in the stock of capital in the South shifts the intermediate intensity goods from the developed North to the underdeveloped South, raising the relative demand for skilled labour in both countries and, thus, symmetrically increasing the wage gap. Trefler and Zhu (2001) closely build up on the Feenstra and Hanson (1996) insight. In their model, similar product shifting from the North to the South is initiated by a technological catch-up in the South. Zhu and Trefler (2005) have brought in international outsourcing to explain a uniform rise in skill premium.

All these explanations use models of perfect competition and rely on differences in factor proportions as a basis for trade. Therefore, remaining within a framework of perfect competition, they focus on trade between dissimilar countries. On the other hand, empirical studies suggest that most of the contemporary world trade takes place in similar products and between countries with similar factor proportions (Baldwin and Martin 1999; Helpman 1999). Therefore, it seems natural that an explanation of rising wage inequality should use a framework of intra-industry trade and increasing returns as proposed by Krugman (1981) and Ethier (1982).

The present essay does precisely that. A number of recent papers have used the imperfect competition and intra-industry trade framework to explain the rising wage inequality. Of these, Unel (2010) and Monte (2011) build up models of firm heterogeneity, based on the work of Melitz (2003), to show that a fall in trading costs increases the demand for skilled labour and, hence, raises the skill premium. Epifany and Gancia (2008) consider inter-industry as well as intra-industry trade in a two-sector economy with imperfect competition and increasing returns. They come up with the result that removal of trade barriers increases the relative wage of skilled labour provided elasticity of substitution in consumption between the goods is greater than unity and provided scale economies are higher in the skill-intensive sector. Dinopoulos et al. (2011) use quasi-homothetic consumer preferences and non-homothetic production technology to demonstrate that depending on parameter values, a move from autarky to free trade may reduce or raise the relative wage of skilled labour.

The contribution of the present essay lies in its simplicity. The purpose is to drive home the simple but fundamental point that in a world of increasing returns, productivity of skilled labour can be enhanced through trade by expanding the size of the market in all countries participating in world trade. We consider a model where there is one traded and one non-traded sector. The traded sector uses skilled labour and the non-traded sector uses unskilled labour, an assumption which is vindicated by Matsuyama (2007) who demonstrated that in contrast to domestic trade, international trade makes more intensive use of skilled labour. The traded sector exhibits increasing returns and imperfect competition. Therefore, as trade opens up, through an expansion in the variety of produced inputs, productivity of labour in the traded sector increases in each country, which in turn leads to a rise in the skill premium across board. Quasi-linear preferences underlie the analysis, and, in this respect, our model is close to Helpman and Itskhoki (2010) and Helpman et al. (2010).

Two variants of the basic model are also developed in the essay. In one variation, a distinction is made between skilled and unskilled labour by postulating the asymmetry that the skilled have the ability to perform the task of both skilled and unskilled, while the unskilled cannot do the job of the skilled. If demand conditions are such that skilled labour cannot be fully employed in the skill-using increasing returns to scale (IRS) sector, then part of the skilled labour force goes to join the unskilled job and, hence, skilled labour, in general, can merely earn the unskilled wage. Trade via intermediate goods can generate sufficient external economies such that supply prices in the IRS sector fall significantly and are then accommodated by the demand to operate at a level that fully utilizes skill labour in the skill-using sector. Thus, skill and unskilled wage rates diverge. Trade, thus, allows to fully utilize hitherto underutilized skilled labour. This we identify to be closely in the spirit of the thesis proposed by Myint (1958) several decades back. Myint in a somewhat different context identified trade as a vent for surplus, the idea being that trade opened a vent or an outlet for a resource that had been previously underutilized. This was an apt description of the trajectory of development driven by agricultural exports in the second half of the nineteenth century that transformed the economies of Canada and the United States. Our context is surely different. We show that when the size of the market limits the scale of operation of a skill-intensive sector, trade, through external economies, can sufficiently reduce average costs so that a scale of production that fully utilizes the available skilled labour, can be accommodated by the demand. Hence, trade opens up the opportunity of fully utilizing skilled resources that had till then remained underutilized.

The second variant considers endogenous skill formation. Using our framework we demonstrate that international trade, by raising the skill premium, tends to increase the incentive to acquire skills and, hence, raises skill formation in all countries. The sharpness of our results partly hinges on the fact that we have deliberately assumed the unskilled labour using sector to be non-traded. We have done so to focus solely on the channel of trade-related market expansion leading to higher productivity in a world of increasing returns. If instead, we had allowed both sectors to be traded, the standard Stolper–Samuelson type effects would give rise to multiple possibilities. These possibilities are explored in our companion papers Chakraborty and Sarkar (2008, 2010). In what follows, the basic model is developed in the second section. The third and fourth sections contain variations of the basic model. The fifth section concludes the essay.

The Basic Model

The economy is populated with two distinct types of agents. We choose to call them skilled and unskilled labour. Each type of labour is endowed with one unit of labour time, which they supply inelastically. The total amount of skilled and unskilled labour endowment in the economy is given by $\bar{H}$ and $\bar{L}$ respectively.

Production

The economy produces two goods, 1 and 2, where X_1 and X_2 are the outputs respectively. Good 1 is produced using unskilled labour under constant returns to scale technology and sold in a competitive market. We assume that one unit of unskilled labour is required to produce one unit of good 1. Thus, the price of good 1, denoted p_1, equals the unskilled wage rate w_u. Good 2, on the other hand, is produced using differentiated intermediate inputs. The production technology for X_2

follows the Dixit–Stiglitz (1977) specification and is given by

$$X_2 = [\sum_{i=1}^{n} y_i^{\rho}]^{1/\rho} \qquad 0 < \rho < 1, \tag{5.1}$$

where y_i is the input of intermediate good i. Intermediate goods are imperfect substitutes and ρ measures the degree of differentiation of intermediate inputs. Given the number of intermediate inputs, the production function (5.1) exhibits constant returns to scale, but there is increasing returns to higher degree of specialization as measured by the number of intermediate varieties n. These economies are external to the firm but internal to the industry, that is, producers take n as given. As in Ethier (1982), we assume that all intermediate goods have identical cost functions. The cost of producing quantity x of a given variety of intermediate input is $C_x = (a + bx)w_s$, where a and b are the fixed and marginal requirements of skilled labour respectively, and w_s is the wage rate of skilled labour. The presence of fixed cost gives rise to internal economies of scale at the firm level. An individual producer of X_2 maximizes profits subject to the production function considering n to be parametrically given. This gives rise to the inverse input demand function for each intermediate input[2]

$$y_i = \frac{(q_i)^{-\sigma} \sum_{i=1}^{n} q_i y_i}{\sum_{i=1}^{n} q_i^{1-\sigma}}, \tag{5.2}$$

thus, each producer of intermediate inputs equate marginal revenue to marginal cost

$$q_i(1 - \frac{1}{\sigma}) = bw_s.$$

Taking note of the fact that $\sigma = \frac{1}{1-\rho}$

$$\Rightarrow q_i = \frac{bw_s}{\rho}. \tag{5.3}$$

Thus, prices of intermediate goods are a constant mark-up over the marginal cost. With identical technology, all firms charge the same price for intermediate goods ($q_i = q \ \forall i$). Free entry in the production of intermediate inputs drives down profits to zero (the Chamberlinian large group case). Thus, the operating surplus must be just enough to

---

[2] See Helpman and Krugman (1985).

cover the fixed cost

$$\frac{q}{\sigma}x_i = aw_s. \tag{5.4}$$

Dividing equation (5.4) by (5.3) we get

$$x_i = \frac{b\rho}{a(1-\rho)}. \tag{5.5}$$

This also implies that output x_i is the same for all producers ($x_i = x \ \forall i$). The symmetry in output choice across firms, that is, ($x_i = x$) and demand supply equilibrium in intermediate goods market, that is, ($y_i = x$), taken together, would allow us to express equation (5.1) as

$$X_2 = n^\alpha x, \tag{5.6}$$

where $\alpha \equiv \frac{1}{\rho}$. Further, note that (5.5) implies output per firm (x) is a constant. Thus, equation (5.6) implies that any expansion of X_2 would be in terms of increased n, and this, as has already been noted, implies increasing returns to scale at the industry level in X_2 production. If in equilibrium n is the effective number of produced varieties, then the total amount of skilled labour used in the production of intermediate goods is given by

$$H = n(a + bx). \tag{5.7}$$

Note that x is a constant which, in turn, implies that all changes in n and, thereby, in the output of X_2 are brought about singularly by changes in H.

Preferences

All agents share the same quasi-linear utility function given by

$$U = C_1^\beta + C_2; 0 < \beta < 1. \tag{5.8}$$

The quasi-linear form notionally captures the idea that agents might even go without good 2. And in this sense, this good is not a basic one. As we will see, one might have an equilibrium where sector 2 production does not come into being. First-order conditions for utility maximization imply

$$\beta C_1^{\beta-1} = \lambda p_1 \text{ and} \tag{5.9}$$

$$1 = \lambda p_2, \tag{5.10}$$

where p_1 and p_2 are the prices of good 1 and 2 respectively, and λ is the associated Lagrange multiplier. Equations (5.8) and (5.9) imply

$$p \equiv \frac{p_2}{p_1} = \frac{1}{\beta} c_1^{1-\beta}, \tag{5.11}$$

where p is the relative price of good 2.

The Autarkic General Equilibrium Supply and Demand Relation and the Skilled–Unskilled Wage Ratio

We now make a distinction between the relative supply price p^s and the relative demand price p^d of good 2. An expression of the former is obtained in this sub-section, while that for the latter is derived in the next. Noting that zero profit condition prevails in the production of final output X_2, we have

$$p_2 X_2 = nqx, \tag{5.12}$$

where the left-hand side is the total revenue and the right-hand side is the total cost. Substituting for X_2 from equation (5.6), equation (5.12) boils down to

$$p_2 = n^{1-\alpha} q. \tag{5.13}$$

Using equations (5.3) and (5.7), equation (5.13) can be rewritten as

$$p_2 = Z H^{1-\alpha} w_s, \tag{5.14}$$

where

$$Z \equiv \left[\frac{1-\rho}{a} \right]^{1-\alpha} \frac{b}{\rho}.$$

Equation (5.14) is nothing but the price and average cost equality. This is our fundamental supply-side equation and it essentially follows Ethier (1982). But we subsequently intend to tailor this equation somewhat differently for the purpose of our model. Using equation (5.14) and noting that $p_1 = w_u$,

$$p^s = \frac{p_2}{p_1} = Z H^{1-\alpha} \left(\frac{w_s}{w_u} \right) = Z \bar{H}^{1-\alpha} \left(\frac{w_s}{w_u} \right), \tag{5.15}$$

where the second part of the equality follows from the full employment of skilled labour. We chose to call this price the supply price p^s and that is naturally so because the equation has been derived exclusively from supply side relations.

On the demand-side, equation (5.11) can be integrated with the factor market equilibrium to arrive at an expression for the general equilibrium demand. First note that both skilled and unskilled labour must consume the same amount of good 1. This follows from noting equation (5.11). Consumption of good 1 is a function of p alone. All consumers facing the same price will consume the same amount of good 1. For each agent, $C_1 = (\frac{\bar{L}}{\bar{L}+\bar{H}})$, where the numerator is the total production of good 1, and the denominator gives the total number of people consuming good 1. Inserting this expression of C_1 in equation (5.11) we arrive at the relative demand price

$$p^d = \frac{p_2}{p_1} = \frac{1}{\beta} \left(\frac{\bar{L}}{\bar{L}+\bar{H}} \right)^{1-\beta} . \qquad (5.16)$$

The skilled to unskilled wage ratio in the autarkic equilibrium is solved for by equating p^s and p^d obtained from equations (5.15) and (5.16) respectively.

$$Z\bar{H}^{1-\alpha} \left(\frac{w_s}{w_u} \right) = \frac{1}{\beta} \left(\frac{\bar{L}}{\bar{L}+\bar{H}} \right)^{1-\beta} \qquad (5.17)$$

Trade

Let two countries having the aforemetioned structure be allowed to engage in trade of intermediate inputs and final good 2. Good 1 is assumed to remain non-traded. We call the countries home and foreign (whenever needed, we denote them by b and f respectively). Countries are similar preference and technology wise but can possibly differ in their quantities of factor endowments.

Now let us focus on the market clearing conditions for intermediate goods. Demand supply equality for intermediate goods require

$$x^b = y_b^b + y_f^b \qquad (5.18)$$

and

$$x^f = y_b^f + y_f^f \qquad (5.19)$$

where x^b and x^f are the supplies of representative brand of intermediate input of home and foreign country respectively, and y_j^i denotes the amount of intermediate input produced in the ith country and used by the jth country producers of good 2. Thus, the left-hand side of equations (5.18) and (5.19) denote the total world supply, and the right-hand side denotes the total world demand of intermediate inputs of home and foreign respectively.

Now noting the form of the demand function, it follows

$$\frac{y_b^b}{y_b^f} = \frac{y_f^b}{y_f^f} = \left(\frac{q^b}{q^f}\right)^{-\sigma} = \frac{x^b}{x^f}, \tag{5.20}$$

where q^i now denotes the price of a representative brand of intermediate input produced in the ith country. But now recall that output per firm in both home and foreign are equal, that is, $x^b = x^f$ under the assumption of identical technology and is given by equation (5.5). Thus, from equation (5.20), it follows that the prices of intermediate inputs in both the countries should be equalized, that is, $q^b = q^f$. Now noting that intermediate good prices are set as a constant mark-up over skilled wages (equation (5.3)), skilled wages are also equalized across countries. Therefore, the following proposition is immediate.

Proposition 1.   *Free trade in skills using final and intermediate goods equalizes skilled wages in both the countries.*

With price of intermediate goods produced in both the countries now equal (that is, $q^b = q^f = q$ say), it must be true that a country will be using the same amount of each brand of intermediate input whether produced at home or foreign in the production of final good 2, which implies $y_b^b = y_b^f$ and $y_f^b = y_f^f$. Now with zero profit condition prevailing in the final good 2 production,

$$p_2 X_2^j = n^b q^b y_j^b + n^f q^f y_j^f, \quad j = b, f \tag{5.21}$$

where X_2^j is the output of good 2 produced in country j, and n^b and n^f are the number of varieties produced in home and foreign respectively. Recalling that $q^b = q^f$ and $y_j^b = y_j^f$, and using the production function given in equation (5.1), equation (5.21) reduces to

$$p_2 = (n^b + n^f)^{1-\alpha} q. \tag{5.22}$$

This is evidently the trade counterpart of equation (5.13). As in equation (5.14), equation (5.22) reduces to

$$p_2 = Z(H^b + H^f)^{1-\alpha} w_s, \tag{5.23}$$

where w_s is the common skilled wage rate prevailing in both the countries; H^b and H^f are the amounts of skilled labour employed in intermediate goods production in the home and in the foreign country respectively.

Good 1 being non-traded, p_1 and thereby w_u can differ across countries. Thus, even with p_2 being equal, the relative price of good 2 can differ across countries. Thereby, it is necessary to identify the relative supply price of good 2 distinctly for the two countries. Using equation (5.23) and observing that $p_1^j = w_u^j$ (where p_1^j and w_u^j are the price of good 1 and the unskilled wage rate respectively, prevailing in country j),

$$p^{sj} = \frac{p_2}{p_1^j} = Z(H^b + H^f)^{1-\alpha}\left(\frac{w_s^j}{w_u^j}\right) = Z(\bar{H}^b + \bar{H}^f)^{1-\alpha}\left(\frac{w_s^j}{w_u^j}\right), \quad (5.24)$$

where p^{sj} and w_s^j is the relative supply price of good 2 and skilled wage respectively, prevailing in country $j = b, f$ (of course $w_s^b = w_s^f$). This is just the trade counterpart of equation (5.15).

Good 1 being non-traded, the demand-side equation (5.16) remain unaltered (just take note of how equation (5.16) was derived) under this trade regime. Thus, for any country j, the skilled to unskilled wage ratio is given by equating equation (5.24) and equation (5.16), yielding

$$Z(\bar{H}^b + \bar{H}^f)^{1-\alpha}\left(\frac{w_s^j}{w_u^j}\right) = \frac{1}{\beta}\left(\frac{\bar{L}^j}{\bar{L}^j + \bar{H}^j}\right)^{1-\beta}, \quad (5.25)$$

where $\bar{L}^j$ is the unskilled labour endowment in country j. Comparing equation (5.25) and (5.17), the next proposition evidently follows.

Proposition 2. *With unskilled labour being used in the good remaining non-traded, free trade in skill using final and intermediate goods raises skilled to unskilled wage ratio in both the countries.*

The First Variant of the Basic Model

In this variant of the basic model worked out in the previous section, we assume that skilled labour can perform both unskilled and skilled jobs, and they choose the one which holds higher reward. Unskilled labour, on the other hand, is tied down to the unskilled job and is not suited for skilled work. This assumption, we believe, captures in a very stylized manner a real-life situation and that this is real life does not require much persuasion. This otherwise innocent-looking assumption, as we will see, has serious implications for our model. If the skilled wage rate falls below the unskilled wage rate, all skilled workers join the unskilled labour force; so it must be true that $w_s \geq w_u$. Everything else remains the same as in the previous section.

The Autarkic General Equilibrium Supply and Demand Relations and the Skilled–Unskilled Wage Ratio

Let us now focus on the factor market. Note that until the moment the whole of skilled labour has been absorbed in intermediate goods sector (that is, $H < \bar{H}$), skilled labour can be employed in this sector at the wage rate of unskilled labour (that is, $w_s = w_u$). This is simply because the residual skilled labour remains employed in sector 1 and earns the unskilled wage rate unity. This, therefore, implies that in this relevant regime, equation (5.15) of the previous section holds with $w_s = w_u$.

$$p^s = \frac{p_2}{p_1} = ZH^{1-\alpha} \quad \text{for} \quad H < \bar{H} \qquad (5.26)$$

The moment skilled labour has been completely employed in the intermediate goods sector (that is, $H = \bar{H}$), equation (5.15) reduces to

$$p^s = \frac{p_2}{p_1} = Z\bar{H}^{1-\alpha} \left(\frac{w_s}{w_u} \right) \quad \text{for} \quad H = \bar{H}, \qquad (5.27)$$

where H is the total amount of skilled labour employed in the production of intermediate goods and $\bar{H}$ is the total amount of skilled labour available in the economy. In equation (5.26), w_s remains frozen at w_u. There being increasing returns to scale, increase in the output of good 2 depresses the average cost and, therefore, the relative price of good 2. In equation (5.27), H remains frozen at $\bar{H}$ and output of good 2 does not change, and any increase in relative price of good 2 translates into an increase in relative skilled wages. The two regimes corresponding to equations (5.26 and 5.27) are depicted as the curve SUM in Figure 5.1. The downward sloping section SU of this curve depicts equation (5.26). Here, $\frac{w_s}{w_u}$ remains fixed at unity and any increase in H depresses p^s. It can readily be checked that this section of the curve is asymptotic to the axis and is also convex. To see this, note that in equation (5.26) as $H \to 0, p^s \to \infty$. Furthermore, from equation (5.26),

$$\frac{dp^s}{dH} = (1 - \alpha)ZH^{-\alpha} < 0 \qquad (5.28)$$

and

$$\frac{d^2p^s}{dH^2} = -\alpha(1 - \alpha)ZH^{-(\alpha+1)} > 0. \qquad (5.29)$$

Note that point U corresponds to a relative price $p^s = Z\bar{H}^{1-\alpha}$. This is the minimum relative price at which good 2 can be sold. At U, skilled labour is employed at the wage rate of unskilled labour, and the total amount of skilled labour $\bar{H}$ has been absorbed in intermediate goods production, so the output of good 2 is at its maximum. Noting that there is increasing returns to scale, this implies that the average cost of production and, hence, the relative price of good 2 is at its minimum. On the other hand, to the left of U on the segment SU, though the skilled wage is frozen at the level of the unskilled wage, skilled labour employed (H) in sector 2 is less than $\bar{H}$ and, therefore, output of good 2 is less than that at U. Hence, relative average cost and, thereby, relative price of good 2 on this segment is higher than that at U. On the segment UM, which corresponds to equation (5.27), skilled labour has been completely absorbed in intermediate production so output of good 2 is at its maximum and there cannot be any further expansion of the same. Any rise in p^s is, therefore, translated into a rise in $\frac{w_s}{w_u}$ to bring relative average cost in line with p^s, as can be seen from equation (5.27). Thus, on the segment UM, $\frac{w_s}{w_u} \geq 1$ with $\frac{w_s}{w_u} = 1$ at U and $\frac{w_s}{w_u} > 1$ at all other points.

On the demand side, equation (5.11) from the previous section can be integrated with the factor market equilibrium to arrive at an expression for the general equilibrium demand. First note that from equation (5.11), it follows that all agents skilled and unskilled should consume the same amount of good 1 at any given p. Thus, $C_1 = (\frac{\bar{L}+(\bar{H}-H)}{\bar{L}+\bar{H}})$, where the numerator is the total production of good 1, and the denominator gives the total number of people consuming good 1. To see that the numerator is the total amount of good 1 produced in the economy, note that, with H being the amount of skilled labour employed in the intermediate goods sector, $(\bar{H} - H)$ amount of skilled labour is left to work in sector 1 over and above $\bar{L}$ unskilled labour who can only work in sector 1. Recalling that production of one unit of good 1 requires one unit of labour, $(\bar{L} + (\bar{H} - H))$ is the total amount of good 1 produced in the economy. Inserting this expression of C_1 in equation (5.11) we arrive at

$$p^d = \frac{p_2}{p_1} = \frac{1}{\beta}\left(\frac{\bar{L}+(\bar{H}-H)}{\bar{L}+\bar{H}}\right)^{1-\beta}. \tag{5.30}$$

Equation (5.30) is the modified version of equation (5.16) of our basic model. This demand expression can, thus, be depicted on the p, H plane as shown by the curve DC in Figure 5.1. It can readily be

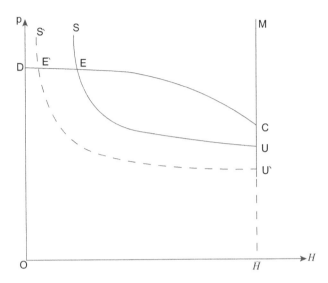

FIGURE 5.1A Full Utilization of Skill

checked that $\frac{dp^d}{dH}$ and $\frac{d^2p^s}{dH^2}$ are both negative.

$$\frac{dp^d}{dH} = -\frac{(1-\beta)}{\beta(\bar{L}+\bar{H})}\left(\frac{\bar{L}+(\bar{H}-H)}{\bar{L}+\bar{H}}\right)^{-\beta} < 0 \qquad (5.31)$$

$$\frac{d^2p^d}{dH^2} = -\frac{(1-\beta)}{(\bar{L}+\bar{H})^2}\left(\frac{\bar{L}+(\bar{H}-H)}{\bar{L}+\bar{H}}\right)^{-(1+\beta)} < 0 \qquad (5.32)$$

Hence, the curve DC in Figure 5.1 is concave and downward sloping.

We now have all the resources to determine the autarkic equilibrium. The supply-side curve SUM and the demand-side curve DC determines the equilibrium of the economy. Three alternative possibilities can arise as shown in Figures 5.1A, 5.1B and 5.1C.

In Figures 5.1A and 5.1B, the economy exhibits multiple equilibria at points D, E and C and at D, E, V respectively. Under reasonable presumptions of Marshallian adjustment (as is customary to assume in the increasing returns to scale literature),[3] one can see that point E is an unstable equilibrium in both these cases, with the demand curve intersecting the supply curve from below. So in Figure 5.1A, D and C and in

---

[3] See Ethier (1982).

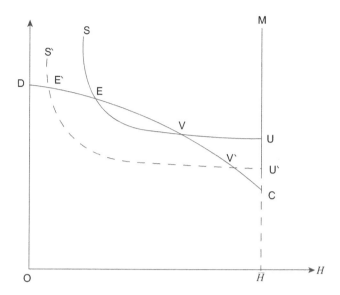

FIGURE 5.1B Under-utilization Equilibrium

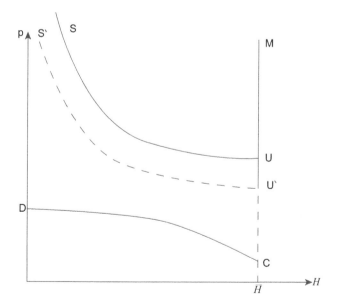

FIGURE 5.1C Skill Using Sector Never Takes Off

Figure 5.1B, D and V are the two stable equilibria. At D in both figures, sector 2 production never takes off, and in the vicinity of point D supply price exceeds demand price. Thus, under Marshallian adjustment, small attempts at increasing production of good 2 (which is the same as increasing H) would not work. With supply price exceeding the demand price, the economy comes back to point D. At C in Figure 5.1A and at V in Figure 5.1B, sector 2 is operative. But, as is evident, there is a crucial point of difference in the two cases shown in Figures 5.1A and 5.1B. At the stable equilibrium C in Figure 5.1A, skilled labour has been completely employed in the skill using intermediate goods sector and noting that the segment UM of the supply curve corresponds to $\frac{w_s}{w_u} > 1$, skilled wage is greater than the unskilled wage. On the other hand, at V in Figure 5.1B, though the skill using sector 2 is operative, skilled labour has not been completely absorbed in intermediate goods production and noting that the segment SU corresponds to $\frac{w_s}{w_u} = 1$, both skilled and unskilled wages are equal. And no wonder this happens. With skilled labour not being completely absorbed in the intermediate goods sector, some of the skilled workers remain working in the unskilled job in sector 1 earning a wage of w_u. Consequently, the economy-wide skilled wages are tied down to the level of unskilled wages. We choose to call an equilibrium of this kind, as shown by point V in Figure 5.1B, an *underutilization equilibrium*. This, we believe, has a semblance to the argument put forward by Myint, where he was making a case in favour of international trade as a vent for surplus. As we will show later, international trade can deliver a country from such an underutilization equilibrium to full utilization of its skilled labour. It is straightforward to see that the difference in the two cases, shown in Figures 5.1A and 5.1B, lies in the fact that in Figure 5.1 the demand curve intersect the vertical portion of the supply curve stretch UM at $H = \bar{H}$, and in Figure 5.1B the demand curve lies below the UM stretch at $H = \bar{H}$. Alternatively, in Figure 5.1A (Figure 5.1B) the relative demand price at $H = \bar{H}$ (which from equation (5.30) is given by $p^d = \frac{1}{\beta}(\frac{\bar{L}}{\bar{L}+\bar{H}})^{1-\beta}$) is greater (less) than the minimum relative supply price of good 2 at $H = \bar{H}$ (which corresponds to the point U, and from equation (5.26) is given by $Z\bar{H}^{1-\alpha}$). Thus, strong-scale economies or a high α favours the case shown in Figure 5.1A. In Figure 5.1B; which corresponds to a case of low α, the supply price, even at the largest possible scale of operation of sector 2 ($H = \bar{H}$), is not sufficiently low as to be matched by a corresponding demand price (see that point U lies above C). Consequently the economy cannot fully absorb the skilled work force in the skill using sector. Figure 5.1C corresponds to a case where the supply price is

uniformly higher than the demand price. Hence, the unique equilibrium is given by point D. This would be the case if the strength-scale
economies or which is the same as α, is sufficiently low. In such a
case, sector 1 is the only operative sector. And all wages, skilled and
unskilled, would be equal.

The observations made are summarized in the following manner:
The economy exhibit multiple equilibria. The following three situations
exhaust all the possibilities:

1. The economy has two stable equilibria (D and C, as shown in
   Figure 5.1A): one in which sector 2 is non-operative and skilled
   wage is equal to unskilled wage and another with an operative
   sector 2 with skilled labour completely absorbed in that sector
   and with skilled wage higher than the unskilled wage. It is evident
   that a necessary and sufficient condition for such a situation to
   arise is given by

$$\frac{1}{\beta}\left(\frac{\bar{L}}{\bar{L}+\bar{H}}\right)^{1-\beta} > Z\bar{H}^{1-\alpha}.$$

2. The economy has two stable equilibria (D and V, as shown in
   Figure 5.1B): one in which sector 2 is non-operative and skilled
   wage is equal to unskilled wage and another with an operative sector 2 with skilled labour partially absorbed in that sector and with
   skilled wage remaining equal to the unskilled wage. A necessary
   and sufficient condition for such a situation to arise is given by

$$\frac{1}{\beta}\left(\frac{\bar{L}}{\bar{L}+\bar{H}}\right)^{1-\beta} < Z\bar{H}^{1-\alpha}$$

and

$$\exists H \in (0,\bar{H}) \text{ such that } \frac{1}{\beta}\left(\frac{\bar{L}+(\bar{H}-H)}{\bar{L}+\bar{H}}\right)^{1-\beta} > Z\bar{H}^{1-\alpha}.$$

3. The economy has a unique equilibrium in which sector 2 production never takes off (point D, as shown in Figure 5.1C). All skilled
   and unskilled workers are employed in sector 1 and they earn
   the same wage. A necessary and sufficient condition for such a
   situation to arise is given by

$$\frac{1}{\beta}\left(\frac{\bar{L}+(\bar{H}-H)}{\bar{L}+\bar{H}}\right)^{1-\beta} < ZH^{1-\alpha} \quad \forall H \in (0,\bar{H}). \qquad (5.33)$$

From these findings we arrive at the following three propositions.

Proposition 3. *Under autarky three types of equilibria are possible: (a) where sector 2 production never takes off, (b) where sector 2 production takes off but is unable to absorb the entire skilled labour force, and (c) where sector 2 employs the entire skilled labour force. In situations (a) and (b), there is no inequality of income between skilled and unskilled labour ($w_s = w_u$), while (c) represents an equilibrium exhibiting wage inequality ($w_s > w_u$).*[4]

Proposition 4. *A necessary condition for wage inequality to exist in autarky equilibrium is given by*

$$\frac{1}{\beta}\left(\frac{\bar{L}}{\bar{L}+\bar{H}}\right)^{1-\beta} > Z\bar{H}^{1-\alpha}.$$

Proposition 5. *A sufficient condition for no inequality to hold in autarky equilibrium is given by*

$$\frac{1}{\beta}\left(\frac{\bar{L}}{\bar{L}+\bar{H}}\right)^{1-\beta} < Z\bar{H}^{1-\alpha}.$$

The inequality in proposition 4 needs to be interpreted. First, an increase in the proportion of unskilled labour in the economy increases the left-hand side and, hence, makes wage inequality more likely. This effect works through the demand side. More unskilled labour relative to skilled labour expands the relative production of sector 1, creating more income in that sector. This, in turn, increases demand for the product produced by sector 2 leading to its expansion. Second, an increase in the absolute endowment of skilled labour reduces the right-hand side (recall that $\alpha > 1$) making wage inequality more likely. This is a pure supply-side effect working through increasing returns. An increase in skilled labour endowment reduces the minimum relative price at which the entire skilled labour force is employed in sector 2 and, hence, increases the chance of full utilization of skilled labour. Finally, note that the case where sector 2 fails to take off exhibits a coordination failure or a lack of demand. Here, at zero level of production of sector 2, the relative price at which the first unit can be supplied is arbitrarily high, while the price at which the first unit is demanded remains finite.

---

[4] There is a pathological case where the demand curve intersects the supply curve at the supply curve's lowest point where it is kinked. In this case, the entire skilled labour force is just employed in sector 2 but $w_s = w_u$. We are ignoring this case.

Hence, production never takes off. If production could be started, both the demand price and the supply price would fall, and some other equilibrium with positive production in sector 2 could have been reached. There is, of course, the other possibility that the demand price lies below the supply price for all levels of H, so the only possible equilibrium is the no take-off equilibrium. An important point needs clarification here. In an equilibrium with underutilization of skilled labour, both skilled and unskilled labour fetches the same reward. It might then be, not unreasonably, claimed that if skill accumulation were to be costly, labourers would not acquire skill at all. We should make here clear the purpose of our model-building exercise. We are beginning with a stock of skilled labour that might be considered to be historically given or thought of as a distribution of innate abilities. Given that stock, we explore the conditions under which that gets fully utilized or otherwise. This helps us to capture meaningfully Myint's notion of underutilization of resources and show, as we do in the subsequent section, how trade can possibly help to come out of such a situation, though of course with adverse distributional consequences. In a later section, we will explore the consequences of having purposive accumulation of skill in a similar model, where we do not any more have an equilibrium with underutilization of skilled labour, but the story of trade-driven wage inequality survives, along with other interesting possibilities.

Trade

Let two countries having the aforementioned structure engage in commodity trade. The structure of trade is exactly the same as discussed in the second section; final good 2 and the intermediate goods are traded, and good 1 remains non-traded. Absolutely similar arguments as provided preceding proposition 1, guarantee that

Proposition 6.   *Free trade in skill using final and intermediate goods equalizes skilled wages in both the countries.*

Similar routine manipulations, as provided in equations (5.21–5.24) and noting of the arguments preceding equation (5.26), allow us to write the relative supply price for any country $i, j \in \{h, f\}$ and $j \neq i$ as

$$p^{sj} = \frac{p_2}{p_1} = Z(H^j + H^i)^{1-\alpha} \quad \text{for} \quad H^j < \bar{H}^j. \tag{5.34}$$

The moment skilled labour has been completely employed in the intermediate goods sector (that is, $H^j = \bar{H}^j$), equation (5.34) reduces to

$$p^{sj} = \frac{p_2}{p_1} = Z(\bar{H}^j + H^i)^{1-\alpha} \left(\frac{w_s^j}{w_u^j} \right) \quad \text{for} \quad H^j = \bar{H}^j. \tag{5.35}$$

On the other hand, good 1 being non-traded, the demand-side equation (5.30) for any country j remains unaltered (just take note of the way equation (5.30) was derived) under this trade regime.

$$p^{dj} = \frac{p_2}{p_1} = \frac{1}{\beta} \left(\frac{\bar{L}^j + (\bar{H}^j - H^j)}{\bar{L}^j + \bar{H}^j} \right)^{1-\beta} \tag{5.36}$$

Thus, in the panel of Figures 5.1A, 5.1B and 5.1C pertaining to autarky, for any country j, the SUM curve shifts down under the trade regime. The new SUM curve is given by equation (5.34, 5.35). Thus, for each levels of H^j, the supply price given by equation (5.34) is lower than the supply price given by equation (5.26) due to the presence of the extra term H^i in equation (5.34). The DC curve stays put under this trade regime as equation (5.36) and equation (5.30) are the same equations. Thus, for any country j, it follows that if the country in autarky is at an underutilization equilibrium (that is, $H^j < \bar{H}^j$), then trade surely leads to higher H^j. Of course, if the country in autarky is already at full utilization equilibrium with whole of the skilled labour force absorbed in the skill using sector 2, then there is no scope of further expansion of H^j. The same is true for country i. This, as one may see, is not the complete characterization of the equilibrium. An increase in H^j will have a feedback and, in turn, increase H^i, which, in turn, will increase H^j, and so on, until iteratively the process comes to a halt. What we have just noticed is that $i, j \in \{h, f\}$ and $i \neq j$, where H^j is a non-decreasing function of H^i and H^j is bounded above by $\bar{H}^j$.

Having noticed this relationship, we can now determine the complete equilibrium. We plot H^h as a non-decreasing function H^f, where the domain of H^f is $[0, \bar{H}^f]$ and H^h takes its autarkic value at $H^f = 0$ and is bounded above by $\bar{H}^h$. This we call the h graph in Figures 5.2A–5.2F. Similarly, we plot H^f as a non-decreasing function H^h, where the domain of H^h is $[0, \bar{H}^h]$, and H^f takes its autarkic value at $H^h = 0$ and is bounded above by $\bar{H}^f$. This we call the f graph in Figures 5.2A–5.2F. The complete equilibrium is determined by the intersection of the h and f graph. Myriad kinds of equilibria are possible as shown in Figures 5.2A–5.2F.

Figure 5.2A: Curve AB shows the h graph and curve MN shows the f graph. Both the home and the foreign were at an underutilization

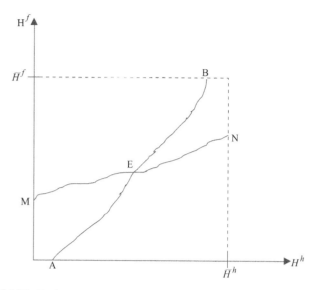

FIGURE 5.2A Under-utilization of Skill in Both Home and Foreign in Autarky and in Trade

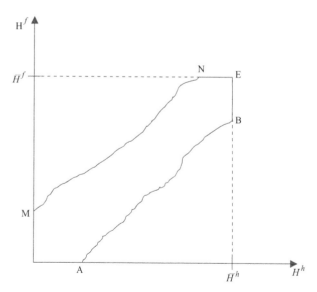

FIGURE 5.2B Under-utilization of Skill in Both Home and Foreign in Autarky and Full Utilization of Skill in Both, Under Trade

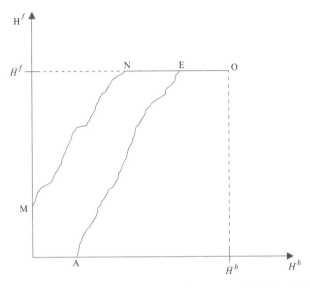

FIGURE 5.2C Under-utilization of Skill in Both Home and Foreign in Autarky and ull tilization in Foreign and Under-utilization in Home under Trade

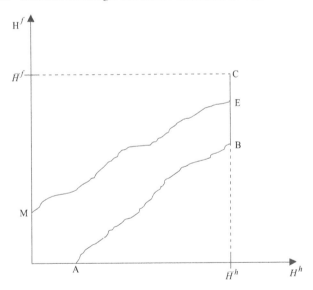

FIGURE 5.2D Under-utilization of Skill in Both Home and Foreign in Autarky and Full Utilization in Foreign and Under-utilization in Home, under Trade

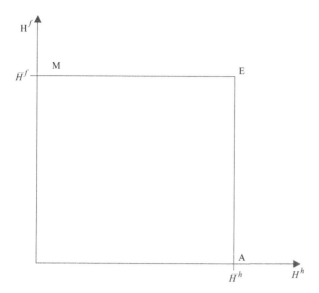

FIGURE 5.2E   Full Utilization of Skill in Both Home and Foreign in Autarky and in Trade

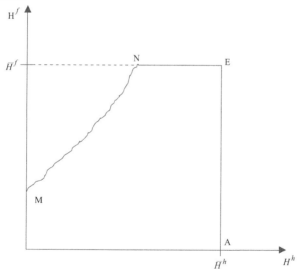

FIGURE 5.2F   Full Utilization Equilibrium in Home Both under Autarky and Trade and Foreign Moves from an Under-utilization Equilibrium under Autarky to Full Utilization under Trade

equilibrium in autarky. E is the trade equilibrium in which both home and foreign have increased the utilization of skill, but both are still at an underutilization equilibrium.

Figure 5.2B: Curve ABE shows the h graph and curve MNE shows the f graph. Both the home and the foreign were at an underutilization equilibrium in autarky. E is the trade equilibrium in which both home and foreign are at full utilization equilibrium.

Figure 5.2C: Curve AE shows the h graph and curve MNO shows the f graph. Both the home and the foreign were at an underutilization equilibrium in autarky. E is the trade equilibrium in which foreign is at full utilization equilibrium, and home, though it has increased skill utilization, is still at an underutilization equilibrium.

Figure 5.2D: Curve ABC shows the h graph and curve ME shows the f graph. Both the home and the foreign were at an underutilization equilibrium in autarky. E is the trade equilibrium in which both home and foreign have increased the utilization of skill, home is at full utilization equilibrium and foreign remains at an underutilization equilibrium.

Figure 5.2E: Curve AE shows the h graph and curve ME shows the f graph. E is the trade equilibrium. Home and the foreign are at full utilization equilibrium both under autarky and trade.

Figure 5.2F: Curve AE shows the h graph and curve MNE shows the f graph. Foreign was at an underutilization equilibrium and home at full utilization in autarky. E is the trade equilibrium in which home remains and foreign arrives at full utilization equilibrium.

Trade: Vent for Surplus and Wage Inequality

Let us start with the most straightforward case, in which trade leads to an increase in skill premium in both the countries. And, in this, we will also try to argue that trade plays the a role of a vent for surplus, in the spirit of the thesis proposed by Hla Myint. Let us assume that the parameters of the model are such that both the economies, home and foreign, begin from a situation where the autarkic equilibrium is of the kind depicted by point V in Figure 5.1B. That is to say, both the countries have an operative sector 2, but skilled labour remains underutilized. And, thereby, in both the countries, skilled and unskilled wages are equal.

Now with the opening up of trade, it can always be possible that the trading equilibrium is of the kind, depicted by point E in Figure 5.2B, where both the countries have finally reached a state where skilled labour is fully employed in sector 2. Clearly such an equilibrium ensures a higher wage for skilled workers than unskilled workers in both the countries. In terms of Figures 5.1A, 5.1B and 5.1C the final equilibrium, after the iteration has come to a halt, has been attained somewhere on the vertical segment U'M of the S'U'M curve for both the countries.

Proposition 7. *If both the countries, beginning from an underutilization equilibrium, attain full employment of skilled labour in sector 2, then the skilled to unskilled wage ratio rises unambiguously in both the countries.*

Thus, we have a very plausible theory of trade-led rise in skill premium in both the trading countries. The mechanism is intuitively pretty clear. Trade in intermediate goods generate externalities which reduce the relative average cost of producing good 2 in both the countries. If to begin with the autarky, the minimum relative average cost (which corresponds to the full utilization of skilled labour in the intermediate goods sector and skilled wage equal to unskilled wage) of producing good 2 is higher than the relative demand price evaluated at full absorption of skilled labour in the skill-using intermediate goods sector, skilled labour cannot be fully absorbed in the skill-using sector. Part of the skilled work force, therefore, remains engaged in sector 1. Skilled wage, thus, remains tied down to the level of unskilled wage. Trade, by bringing down the minimum average cost to a level that can be accommodated by the demand price, helps absorb skilled labour in the skill-using sector fully. Thereby, skilled and unskilled wages diverge. What is crucial in the mechanism involved, is that trade helps utilize fully hitherto underutilized skilled labour.

Yet another case could be both countries having an equilibrium of the kind depicted as point C in Figure 5.1A in autarky, and the trade equilibrium is of the kind depicted as point E in Figure 5.2E. Thus, both under autarky and trade, these countries are fully utilizing the skilled labour in the skill-using sector. Even under such a situation, inequality could rise in both the countries following trade. To see this, note that for any county j, the relative skilled wage under autarky in this situation can be solved by equating the relative supply and demand prices from equation (5.27) and equation (5.30) evaluated at $H^j = \bar{H}^j$, yielding

$$\left(\frac{w_s^j}{w_u^j}\right)^a = \frac{\frac{1}{\beta}\left(\frac{\bar{L}}{\bar{L}+\bar{H}^j}\right)^{1-\beta}}{Z(\bar{H}^j)^{1-\alpha}}, \tag{5.37}$$

where $\left(\frac{w_s^j}{w_u^j}\right)^a$ denotes the autarkic skilled to unskilled wage ratio in the jth country. Similarly, the solution for skilled to unskilled wage ratio under trade for an equilibrium like point E in Figure 5.2E would be given by solving equations (5.35) and (5.36) evaluated at $H^j = \bar{H}^j$ and $H^i = \bar{H}^i$, thus, obtaining

$$\left(\frac{w_s^j}{w_u^j}\right)^t = \frac{\frac{1}{\beta}\left(\frac{\bar{L}^j}{L^j + H^j}\right)^{1-\beta}}{Z(\bar{H}^j + \bar{H}^i)^{1-\alpha}}, \tag{5.38}$$

where $\left(\frac{w_s^j}{w_u^j}\right)^t$ denotes the skilled to unskilled wage ratio in the jth country under trade. Comparing equations (5.37) and (5.38), it is evident $\left(\frac{w_s^j}{w_u^j}\right)^t > \left(\frac{w_s^j}{w_u^j}\right)^a$.

Proposition 8.   *If both the countries fully employ skilled labour in sector 2, both under autarky and under trade, even then the skilled to unskilled wage ratio demonstrably has risen with trade.*

The Second Variant of the Basic Model

In the previous section which we call 'the first variant of the basic model', we assume that skilled labour can perform both unskilled and skilled jobs, and they choose the one which holds higher reward. Unskilled labour, on the other hand, is tied down to the unskilled job and is not suited for skilled work. This basic assumption led us to talk meaningfully about an equilibrium in which skilled labour is less than fully absorbed in the skill-using sector 2. This we called the underutilization equilibrium. But a feature of the underutilization equilibrium is that both skilled and unskilled labour fetch the same reward. It might then be, not unreasonably, claimed that if skill accumulation were to be costly, labourers would not acquire skill at all. As we have already noted, that the purpose of our model-building exercise is to conceive of an economy beginning with a given stock of skilled labour, which might be considered to be historically given or as a distribution of innate abilities. Given that stock, we explore the conditions under which that gets fully utilized or otherwise. This helps us to capture meaningfully Myint's notion of underutilization of resources. In this section, we will explore the consequences of having purposive accumulation of skill in a similar model, where we do not any more have an equilibrium with underutilization of skilled labour in the earlier sense, but the story of trade-driven wage inequality survives, along with other interesting possibilities.

The Labour Market and Skill Accumulation

The economy is populated with a continuum of agents differing in their abilities to acquire skill. The agents are distributed over the unit interval [0, 1] according to some distribution function $F(k)$, with density function $f(k) \in [0, 1]$. Each type of agent is initially endowed with one unit of unskilled labour. $\bar{H}$ is the total amount of unskilled labour available to the economy. An agent of type k has to expend $e(k)$ of this unskilled labour to become skilled. So if this agent decides to acquire skill, after doing so, she is left with $(1 - e(k))$ amount of skilled labour. Alternatively, we may assume that a k-type agent has to buy and use up $e(k)$ amount of skilled labour to transform her one unit of unskilled labour into one unit of skilled labour. It is assumed that $e'(k) < 0$, that is, as we go up along the interval [0, 1], the basic ability level of a worker increases. As we shall see later, the two alternative specifications of skill formation are equivalent in terms of the working of our model. For now, however, it suffices to note that the total amount of skilled and unskilled labour in this model is endogenous because depending upon one's type and the relative market wage of skilled and unskilled labour, an agent may or may not decide to acquire skill.

Except for this reformulation, everything else is assumed to be the same as in the previous section(s).

The Autarkic General Equilibrium Supply and Demand Relation and the Skilled–Unskilled Wage Ratio

On the demand side, equation (5.11) can be integrated with the factor market equilibrium to arrive at an expression for the general equilibrium demand. First note that both skilled and unskilled labour must consume the same amount of good 1. This follows from noting equation (5.11). Consumption of good 1 is a function of p alone. All consumers facing the same price will consume the same amount of good 1. Denoting the total amount of unskilled labour available for production by U, we can write the consumption of good 1 by each agent as $C_1 = \frac{U}{\bar{H}}$, where the numerator is the total production of good 1, and the denominator gives the total number of people consuming good 1. Inserting this expression in equation (5.11), we arrive at

$$p^d = \frac{p_2}{p_1} = \frac{1}{\beta} \left(\frac{U}{\bar{H}} \right)^{1-\beta}. \tag{5.39}$$

A worker of type k will acquire skill if and only if

$$w_s(1 - e(k)) \geq w_u \tag{5.40}$$

since a type-k worker has to spend $e(k)$ of her own raw labour (or alternatively, has to use $e(k)$ units of skilled labour) to become skilled. Hence, her net income after becoming skilled is given by the left-hand side of (5.40). If the worker decides to acquire skill, her net income has to be greater than or equal to the income she can earn by remaining unskilled. We assume that $e'(k) < 0$, $e(0) = 1$ and $e(1) = 0$. Thus, the worker at the lowest end of the spectrum, the one with the least ability, has no incentive to acquire skills, while the one with the highest ability will always acquire skills. Let k^* be the type of worker who is indifferent between remaining unskilled and acquiring skill. Then we have

$$\frac{w_s}{w_u} = \frac{1}{(1 - e(k^*))}. \tag{5.41}$$

Since $e(k)$ is decreasing in k, all workers with $k > k^*$ must acquire skill and all workers with $k < k^*$ must choose to remain unskilled. Therefore, the supply of skilled labour is given by

$$H = \bar{H} \int_{k^*}^{1} (1 - e(k)) f(k) dk \tag{5.42}$$

and the supply of unskilled labour is given by

$$U = \bar{H} \int_{0}^{k^*} f(k) dk. \tag{5.43}$$

Plugging the expressions for skilled and unskilled labour in demand and supply equations (5.39) and (5.15), and using (5.41) to substitute for $\frac{w_s}{w_u}$ in equation (5.15), we obtain supply and demand prices solely as functions of the single variable k^*:

$$p^s(k^*) = \frac{Z \left[\bar{H} \int_{k^*}^{1} (1 - e(k)) f(k) dk \right]^{1-\alpha}}{(1 - e(k^*))} \tag{5.44}$$

$$p^d(k^*) = \frac{1}{\beta} \left(\int_{0}^{k^*} f(k) dk \right)^{1-\beta} \tag{5.45}$$

The shape of the p^d function is unambiguous. An increase in k^* increases the demand price. Also the graph of $p^d(k^*)$ starts at zero with $k^* = 0$ and goes up to a finite number at $k^* = 1$, as shown in Figures

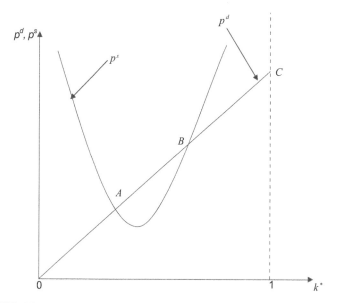

FIGURE 5.3A B Is an Unstable Equilibriuml Flanked by Two Stable Equilibria;
A and C

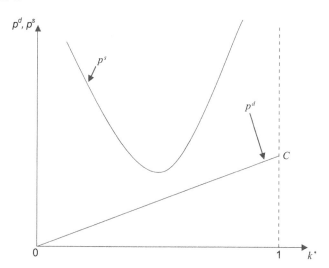

FIGURE 5.3B   C Is the Unique Stable Equilibrium in Which the Economy
Remains Primitive

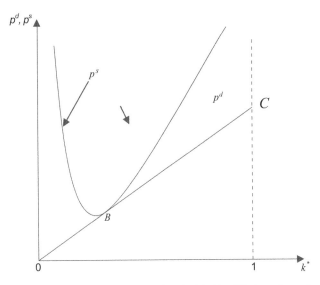

FIGURE 5.3C   A Pathological case: B is a Stable Equilibrium from the Left
and Unstable from the Right

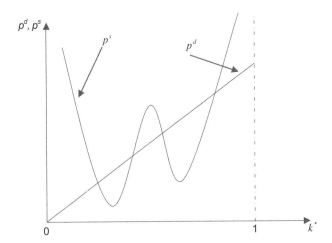

FIGURE 5.3D   Possibility of Innumerable Equilibria Wherein Each Unstable
Ones are Flanked by Two Stable Equilibria

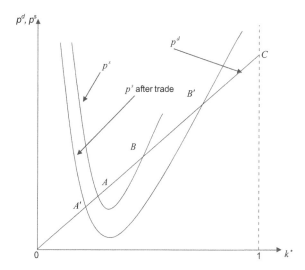

FIGURE 5.3E Primary Impact of Trade

5.3A–5.3E. On the other hand, it is clear from (5.44) that an increase in k^* has, in general, an ambiguous effect on the supply price p^s. Recalling that the exponent $(1 - \alpha) < 0$, we find that both the numerator and the denominator go up with an increase in k^*, making the overall change in the supply price ambiguous. However, from our assumed boundary conditions $e(0) = 1$ and $e(1) = 0$, we can easily verify that $p^s \to \infty$ as $k^* \to 0$ or 1. This suggests a possible U-shape of the supply function (as in Figures 5.3A–5.3C). This is a mere suggestion though. Indeed, without knowing the exact form of the distribution function and the $e(k)$ function, we cannot specify the exact nature of the supply function and, in particular, how many ups and downs the graph of $p^s(k^*)$ exhibits (like in Figure 5.3D). For working convenience, we shall stick to a U-shaped graph for the moment. In fact, the readers will readily recognize that the analysis done with a U-shaped curve immediately extends to the case with a curve which might have many ups and downs (on this point, we have a discussion in footnote 4).

Uniform Distribution, Linear Ability Function

Suppose the distribution function is uniform, that is, $f(k) = 1$ and the ability function is linear and of the form $e(k) = 1 - k$. Then the supply price is given by

$$p^s(k^*) = \frac{Z\left[\bar{H}\left(\frac{1}{2} - \frac{k^{*2}}{2}\right)\right]^{1-\alpha}}{k^*}. \tag{5.46}$$

Straightforward calculations show that the function reaches a unique minimum at $k^* = \frac{1}{\sqrt{2\alpha-1}}$. Since $\alpha > 1$, we may conclude that the graph of the supply price function is U-shaped in the interval $0 < k^* < 1$.

Equilibrium

We proceed with the assumption that the supply price function is U-shaped. The demand price function, as we have already seen, is upward rising. Putting the two together we find that three types of equilibria are possible. In Figure 5.3A, there are three equilibria occurring at points A, B and C. Equilibrium points A and C are Marshallian stable, while in the same sense B is unstable. If we start with a k^* between A and B, demand price exceeds supply price and, hence, there is an expansion of output of good 2. This expansion can only come through an expansion of skilled labour employment in sector 2, which, in turn, entails a rise in skill formation and a consequent fall in k^* so that we move towards the equilibrium point A. Similarly, when we start to the left of A, supply price exceeds demand price and there is a contraction of output of good 2, leading to an increase in k^*. Again, C is an equilibrium because even though at C supply price exceeds demand price, k^* has no further possibility of increasing. It can also be seen that it is stable. C is an equilibrium point where there is no skill formation in the economy and no production of good 2. Finally, equilibrium at point B is unstable—the economy will either settle at A or C following a small perturbation from B. In Figure 5.3B, the only equilibrium is at C where the economy remains primitive and unskilled. In Figure 5.3C, apart from the primitive equilibrium at C, there is an equilibrium at B which is stable from the left-hand side but unstable from the right. In what follows, we are going to ignore the unstable equilibria and focus only on the stable ones. From equation (5.44), it follows that an increase in the size of the economy, that is, an increase in $\bar{H}$ shifts the supply price function downwards. This implies that smaller economies are likely to have equilibrium represented by Figure 5.3B. In other words, small isolated economies are likely to remain primitive. This is due to economies of scale, the advantage of which can not be appropriated by a small isolated economy. For a large economy, the possibility of remaining primitive is still there, as shown by point C in Figure 5.3A. However, for these economies the bad equilibrium can materialize only as a result of coordination failure. A consorted effort by the economic agents can bring the economy to the good equilibrium at A. Our findings so far can be summarized in the following proposition:

Proposition 9.   *In our economy, two types of equilibria are possible: a bad equilibrium where no skill is acquired by the workers and a good equilibrium where there is skill formation. For small isolated economies, the bad equilibrium is the only possible outcome. For large economies, equilibrium can be either good or bad, and the bad equilibrium can occur only due to coordination failure.*

Under a general ability function and a general distribution function, the p^s curve might have many ups and downs but with $p^s \to \infty$ as $k^* \to 0$ or 1, as shown in Figure 5.3D. This adds no additional insight and the analysis remains the same as in an U-shaped curve. Only that in this case, there are many more stable and unstable equilibria (see footnote 5).

Trade

We now introduce international trade. Let two countries having the structure described earlier engage in commodity trade. We call them home and foreign (whenever needed, we denote them by superscripts h and f respectively). Countries are similar in terms of preference and technology but can possibly differ in their quantities of labour endowments H^h and H^f. The cost of acquiring skill is also the same in the two countries. We assume final good 2 and also the intermediate goods to be freely tradable; good 1 remains non-tradable as earlier. Now let us focus on the market clearing conditions for intermediate goods. Similar arguments, as provided preceding proposition 1, deliver the following proposition.

Proposition 10.   *Free trade in skill using final and intermediate goods equalizes skilled wages in both the countries.*

Similar routine manipulations as provided in equations (5.21–5.24) allow us to write the relative supply price for any country $i, j \in \{h, f\}$ and $j \neq i$ as

$$p^{sj} = \frac{p_2}{p_1} = Z(H^j + H^i)^{1-\alpha} \left(\frac{w_s^j}{w_u^j} \right), \qquad (5.47)$$

where H^j is the amount of skilled labour employed in intermediate goods production in the country j. This yields the following supply price function for any country j

$$p^{sj}(k^{*j}) = \frac{Z \left[\left(\bar{H}^j \int_{k^{*j}}^1 (1-e(k))f(k)dk \right) + \left(\bar{H}^i \int_{k^{*i}}^1 (1-e(k))f(k)dk \right) \right]^{1-\alpha}}{(1 - e(k^{*j}))},$$

(5.48)

where under this trade regime, k^{*j}, $j \in \{b,f\}$ satisfies

$$\frac{w_s^j}{w_u^j} = \frac{1}{(1 - e(k^{*j}))}.$$

(5.49)

Comparing equations (5.48) and (5.44) for any country j, it is clear that the relative supply price of good 2 is lower, for any given k^{*j}, in the integrated world economy than in the isolated domestic economies (due to the presence of the additional term, $(\bar{H}^i \int_{k^{*i}}^1 (1 - e(k))f(k)dk)$ in the right-hand side of equation (5.48)). This is clearly due to an increase in the scale of operation. On the other hand, good 1 being non-traded, the demand price equation (5.45) remains the same, even after trade opens up (this, one can readily check going through the arguments preceding equation (5.39)).

Wage Inequality and Skill Accumulation

It is clear from the preceding analysis that for any country j, international trade shifts the graph of the supply price function downwards, keeping that of the demand price function unchanged. This is shown in Figure 5.3E. If the economy was at an interior stable equilibrium (which we have assumed to be the case), like at A (in Figure 5.3E), the new equilibrium shifts to A', thus, lowering k^{*j} and increasing skill accumulation, and, thereby, employment ($H^j = \bar{H}^j \int_{k^{*j}}^1 (1 - e(k))f(k)dk$) in sector 2 of country j. Once again, this is not a one-shot process. This increase in H^j feeds into ith country's corresponding equation for p^{si} (equation 5.48) and shifts down the supply price function for the ith country, thereby lowering k^{*i} and increasing $H^i (= \bar{H}^i \int_{k^{*i}}^1 (1 - e(k))f(k)dk)$, which, in turn, will increase H^j by feeding into p^{sj} in equation (5.48). This process continues until H^j and H^i converge to their equilibrium values. That the process converges to the equilibrium values can be readily seen. Observe that we have shown that H^b is an increasing function of H^f and that H^b will always be less than $\bar{H}^b \int_0^1 (1 - e(k))f(k)dk$ (as the supply price graph in Figure 5.3E is asymptotic to the p^s axis, k^{*b}

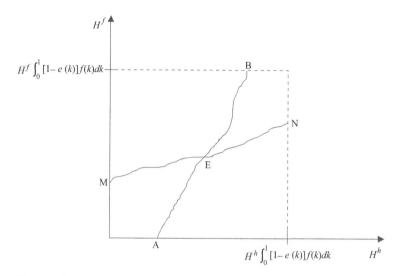

FIGURE 5.4 Determination of the Trade Equilibrium

is always greater than zero). H^j and H^i converge to their equilibrium values. That the process converges to the equilibrium values can be readily seen. Observe that H^b is an increasing function of H^f, and that H^b will always be less than $\bar{H}^b \int_0^1 (1 - e(k)) f(k) dk$ (as the supply price graph in Figure 5.3E is asymptotic to the p^s axis, k^{*b} is always greater than zero).

Having noticed this relationship, we can now determine the complete equilibrium. We plot H^b as an increasing function of H^f, where the domain of H^f is $[0, \bar{H}^f \int_0^1 (1 - e(k)) f(k) dk]$ and H^b takes its autarkic value at $H^f = 0$ and is always less than $\bar{H}^b \int_0^1 (1 - e(k)) f(k) dk$. This we denote as the b graph in Figure 5.4A. Similarly, we plot H^f as an increasing function H^b, where the domain of H^b is $[0, \bar{H}^b \int_0^1 (1 - e(k)) f(k) dk]$ and H^f takes its autarkic value at $H^b = 0$ and is always less than $\bar{H}^f \int_0^1 (1 - e(k)) f(k) dk$. This we denote as the f graph in Figure 5.4. The complete equilibrium is determined by the intersection of the b and f graph. Thus, the trade equilibrium has higher H^b and H^f compared to autarky and, thereby, lower k^{*b} and k^{*f} (that is to say, higher skill formation and higher employment in the skill using sector

2). Observing equation (5.49), lower k^{*j}, $j \in \{h,f\}$ implies higher $\frac{w_s^j}{w_u^j}$. [5]

Proposition 11.   *Free international trade increases skill formation and also the skilled–unskilled wage ratio in both the countries participating in trade.*

Conclusion

This work focuses on the role of non-traded goods in generating symmetric movements in the skilled to unskilled wage ratio in a model of trade. Consumers have quasi-linear utilities, and the traded good is produced under increasing returns to scale in a monopolistically competitive market structure. Alternative scenarios are considered: First, where the supply of skilled and unskilled labour is inelastically given. This case, starkly brings out the fact that trade can, through a very natural route, raise wage inequality in both the trading countries. Second, we consider the case where unskilled labour is tied down to unskilled job but skilled labour can potentially be employed in both the skilled and unskilled job. This case, besides holding the possibility of generating symmetric increase in skill premium in both the trading countries, demonstrates that trade can help increase utilization of underutilized skilled labour—a result very much in the spirit of Myint's 'vent for surplus'. Third, we introduce the possibility of accumulating skill by incurring a cost. Herein, we show that the skilled to unskilled wage ratio can increase in both the trading countries; alongside, trade leads to higher skill acquisition.

---

[5] According to Samuelson's correspondence principle (1947), unstable production equilibria are almost never to be observed in the real world. Even if the initial equilibrium were to be unstable, Samuelson (1971) argues that perverse comparative statics results would never obtain. This is the global correspondence principle. Taking the clue from the global correspondence principle, we can show that even if the initial equilibrium is at B (in Figure 5.3E), which is unstable, opening up to trade will lead to higher skill formation, and the new equilibrium will be arrived at A'. To see this, note that as the p^s curve shifts down, the demand price p^d exceeds the supply price p^s at initial k^* (at B). This then, according to the proposed Marshallian adjustment rule, should increase the output of X_2, which implies a higher skill formation and, thereby, lower k^*. Argument on a similar line has been used in Ide and Takayama (1991). Also see Wong (1995: 224).

References

Acemoglu, D. 2002. 'Directed Technical Change', *Review of Economic Studies*, 69(4):781–809.

Autor, D. H. and L. Katz. 2008. 'Trends in US Wage Inequality: Revising the Revisionists, Review of Economics and Statistics', 90(2):300–23.

Autor, D. H., L. Katz and A. Krueger. 1998. 'Computing Inequality: Have Computers Changed the Labour Market', *Quartarly Journal of Economics*, 113(4):1169–214.

Baldwin, R. and P. Martin. 1999. 'Two Waves of Globalization: Superficial Similarities, Fundamental Differences', in H. Siebert (ed.), *Globalization and Labour*. Tubingen: J.C.B. Mohr for Kiel Institute of World Economics, pp. 3–59.

Borjas, G., R. Freeman and L. Katz. 1991. 'On the Labour Market Effects of Immigration and Trade', The National Bureau of Economic Research (NBER) Working Paper No. 3761.

Bound, J. and G. Johnson. 1992. 'Changes in the Structure of Wages in the 1980s: An Evaluation of Alternative Explanations', *American Economic Review*, 82(3):371–92.

Chakraborty, B. S. and A. Sarkar. 2008. 'Trade, Wage Inequality and the Vent for Surplus', in Sugata Marjit and Eden S. H. Yu (eds), *Contemporary and Emerging Issues in Trade Theory and Policy*. UK: Emerald Group Publishing Limited, pp. 251–73.

————. 2010. 'Trade and Wage Inequality with Endogenous Skill Formation', in B. Basu, B. Chakrabarti, S. R. Chakravarty and Gangopadhyay (eds), *Econophysics and Economics of Games, Social Choices and Quantitative Techniques*. Milan: Springer Verlag Italia, pp. 306–19.

Dinopoulos, E., C. Syropoulos, B. Xu and Y. V. Yotov. 2011. 'Interindustry Trade and the Skill Premium: Theory and Evidence', *Journal of International Economics*, 84(1):15–25.

Dixit, A. and J. E. Stiglitz. 1977. 'Monopolistic Competition and Optimum Product Diversity', *American Economic Review*, 67:297–308.

Dornbusch, R., S. Fischer and P. A. Samuelson. 1980. 'Heckscher-Ohlin Trade Theory with a Continuum of Goods', *Quarterly Journal of Economics*, 95(2):203–24.

Epifany, P. and G. A. Gancia. 2008. 'The Skill Bias of World Trade', *Economic Journal*, 118(530):927–60.

Esquivel, G. and J. A. Rodriguez-Lopez. 2003. 'Technology Trade and Wage Inequality in Mexico before and after NAFTA', *Journal of Development Economics*, 72(2):543–65.

Ethier, W. J. 1982. 'National and International Returns to Scale in the Modern Theory of International Trade', *American Economic Review*, 72(3):389–405.

Feenstra, R. and G. Hanson. 1996. 'Foreign Investment, Outsourcing and Relative Wages', in R. Feenstra, G. Grossman and D. Irwin (eds), *Political Economy of Trade Policy: Papers in Honour of Jagadish Bhagawati*. Cambridge, Mass.: MIT Press, pp. 89–127.

———. 1997. 'Foreign Direct Investment and Relative Wages: Evidence from Mexico's Maquiladoras', *Journal of International Economics*, 42(3–4):371–93.

———. 1999. 'The Impact of Outsourcing and High Technology Capital on Wages: Estimates for the United States 1979–1990', *Quarterly Journal of Economics*, 114(3): 907–40.

Hanson, G. and A. Harrison. 1995. 'Trade, Technology and Wage Inequality', NBER Working Paper No. 5110.

Helpman, E. 1999. 'The Structure of Foreign Trade', *Journal of Economic Perspectives*, 13(2):121–44.

Helpman, E. and O. Itskhoki. 2010. 'Labour Market Rigidities, Trade and Unemployment', *Review of Economic Studies*, 77(3):1100–37.

Helpman, E., O. Itskhoki and S. Redding. 2010. 'Inequality and Unemployment in a Global Economy', *Econometrica*, 78(4):1239–83.

Helpman, E. and P. Krugman. 1985. *Market Structure and International Trade*. Cambridge: MIT Press.

Ide, T. and A. Takayama. 1991. 'Variable Returns to Scale, Paradoxes and Global Correspondence in the Theory of International Trade', in A. Takayama, M. Ohyama and H. Ohta (eds), *Trade, Policy and International Adjustments*. San Diego: Academic Press, pp. 108–54.

Jones, R. W. 1999. 'Heckscher-Ohlin Trade Models for the New Century', Mimeo, University of Rochester.

Katz, L. and D. Autor. 1999. 'Changes in the Wage Structure and Earnings Inequality', in Orley Ashenfelter and David Card (eds), *Handbook of Labour Economics*, Vol. 3, Part 1. Amsterdam: North Holland, pp. 1463–555.

Krugman, P. 1981. 'Intra-industry Specialization and the Gains from Trade', *Journal of Political Economy*, 89:959–73.

Krusell, P., L. E. Ohanian, J. V. Rios-Rull and G. L. Violante. 2000. 'Capital-Skill Complimentarity and Inequality: A Macroeconomic Analysis', *Econometrica*, 68(5):1029–53.

Lemieux, T. 2008. 'What Do We Really Know about Changes in Wage Inequality', Working Paper, University of British Columbia.

Marjit, S. and R. Acharyya. 2003. *International Trade, Wage Inequality and the Developing Economy: A General Equilibrium Approach*. Heidelberg: Physica-Verlag.

Matsuyama, K. 2007. 'Beyond Icebergs: Towards a Theory of Biased Globalization', *Review of Economic Studies*, 74(1): 237–53.

Melitz, M. J. 2003. 'The Impact of Trade on Intra-industry Reallocations and Aggregate Industry Productivity', *Econometrica*, 71(6): 1695–725.

Monte, F. 2011. 'Skill Bias, Trade and Wage Dispersion', *Journal of International Economics*, 83(2):202–18.

Myint, Hla. 1958. 'The "Classical Theory" of International Trade and the Underdeveloped Countries', *Economic Journal*, 68(270): 317–37.

Robertson, R. 2007. 'Trade and Wages: Two Puzzles from Mexico', *The World Economy*, 30(9):1378–98.

Samuelson, P. A. 1947. *Foundations of Economic Analysis*. Cambridge, MA: Harvard University Press.

———. 1971. 'On the Trail of Conventional beliefs about the Transfer Problem', in J. N. Bhagwati, R.W. Jones, R. A. Mundell and J. Vanek (eds), *Trade, Balance of Payments and Growth: Papers in International Economics in Honor of Charles P. Kindelberger*. Amsterdam: North Holland, pp. 327–51.

Trefler, D. and S. C. Zhu. 2001. 'Ginis in General Equilibrium: Trade, Technology and Southern Inequality., NBER Working Paper No. 8446.

Unel, B. 2010. 'Firm Heterogeneity, Trade and Wage Inequality', *Economic Dynamics and Control*, 34(6):1369–79.

Wong, Kar-yiu. 1995. *International Trade in Goods and Factor Mobility*. Cambridge, Mass.: MIT Press.

Wood, A. 1995. 'How Trade Hurt Unskilled Workers', *Journal of Economic Perspectives*, 9(3):57–80.

Zeira, J. 2007. 'Wage Inequality, Technology, and Trade', *Journal of Economic Theory*, 137(1):79–103.

Zhu, S. C. and D. Trefler. 2005. 'Trade and Inequality in Developing Countries: A General Equilibrium Analysis', *Journal of International Economics*, 65(1):21–48.

CHAPTER 6

Equality, Priority and Distributional Judgements

S. Subramanian*

This essay is specifically concerned with the value that goes by the name of egalitarianism. The notes which follow are, more than anything else, an account of certain confusions experienced by the present author from a reading of Derek Parfit's (1997) essay on priority and equality. As such, they may reflect nothing more than a faulty reading of the text. On the other hand, and in the event that the reservations expressed here are not, after all, a product of misinterpretation, there may be some value in the questions raised. A preliminary part of this essay is based heavily on an earlier work of mine (Subramanian 2011), and is also related to the perspective advanced in Thomas Christiano and Will Braynan (2008). Additionally, my appreciation of some of the issues involved has been considerably aided by the work of John Broome (2003) and Marc Fleurbaey (2001), and it will be seen that I draw on both writers—sometimes in agreement and sometimes not—in presenting my views. In terms of the final outcome, my sympathies are largely with Fleurbaey's conclusions in the matter. I should add that the entire problem of distributional judgements in an environment of uncertainty, which has been dealt with by both Broome and Fleurbaey, is neglected in the present discussion.

---

* I would like to thank, without implicating, John Broome, Thomas Christiano, Sanjay Reddy and Henry Richardson for comments on earlier versions of this essay.

The following is a very brief summary of Parfit's (1997) position on equality and priority, as I understand it. Parfit's difficulty with egalitarianism seems to reside in his perception that there is, ultimately, no purely egalitarian justification available, in certain situations, for the reasonable judgement we may make that a particular equal distribution of a smaller sum of well-being is preferable to a particular unequal distribution of a larger sum. In Parfit's view, the case in favour of egalitarianism must rest in one of two views: (*a*) that an equal distribution of well-being is intrinsically good; and (*b*) that it is right to pursue equality in the cause of justice or fairness (or some other value). The first view is a *Telic* Egalitarian view, while the second is a *Deontic* Egalitarian view. Telic Egalitarianism, in Parfit's judgement, falls foul of what he calls the Levelling Down Objection: this is the objection that one cannot hold that it is in *any* respect good to move towards equality by just pulling down the better-off person's well-being level to that of the worse-off person. What, then, of the alternative avenue of justification, Deontic Egalitarianism? Parfit, in this context, conceives of a scenario called the Divided World situation, in which the inequality of a distribution neither has any unfavourable effects nor is attributable to injustice or unfairness or some similar casualty of a desired value: in the Divided World, one cannot have a Deontic Egalitarian argument for favouring an equal distribution of a smaller sum of well-being over an unequal distribution of a larger sum. If egalitarianism—of either the Telic or Deontic variety— is of no help in rationalizing such a preference, one must resort to some other view for achieving a satisfactory rationalization; the view which Parfit advances is the Priority View, which requires that 'benefiting people matters more the worse off these people are' (Parfit 1997: 213). The Priority View is distinguished from the Egalitarian view on grounds that the former is concerned only with people's absolute levels of well-being, while the latter is concerned with the relativities arising from inter-personal comparisons of well-being. Briefly, the grounds for equality are more pertinently located in Priority than in Equality itself.

In what follows, we have, first, a description of what is claimed to be a plausible view of Pluralist Telic Egalitarianism which is not vulnerable to the Levelling Down Objection, and which can, in fact, satisfactorily address the Divided World situation. Second, the validity of linking the status of belief in equality with the 'relative *versus* absolute' basis of the distinction between Egalitarianism and Prioritarianism is reviewed, and found wanting. Third, it is suggested that there is a specific 'distribution-invariance'/'distribution-sensitivity' dichotomy for which a specific 'absolute'/'relative' dichotomy *is* relevant: the resulting distinction, it is claimed, is useful for differentiating two types of Egalitarian rather than for differentiating Prioritarians from Egalitarians. It is concluded that the distinction between Prioritarianism and Egalitarianism claimed by Parfit is not one of profound conceptual significance as far as a critique of Egalitarianism is concerned.

On the Robustness of Egalitarianism to Parfit's Objections

Parfit (1997) draws a distinction between two kinds of Telic Egalitarianism, which he calls, respectively, Pure Telic Egalitarianism and Pluralist Telic Egalitarianism, both of which are united in endorsing the *Principle of Equality*, which upholds the view that 'it is in itself bad if some people are worse off than others' (Parfit 1997: 204). The distinction between the two kinds of Telic Egalitarianism is identified in the following terms by Parfit (1997: 205):

> If we cared only about equality, we would be *Pure* Egalitarians. If we cared only about utility, we would be Utilitarians. Most of us accept a pluralist view: one that appeals to more than one principle or value. According to *Pluralist Egalitarians*, it would be better both if there was more equality, and if there was more utility. In deciding which of two outcomes would be better, we give weight to both these values.

I have claimed elsewhere (Subramanian 2011: 10) that the following descriptions of the categories of Pure and Pluralist Telic Egalitarianism are both inherently plausible and compatible with Parfit's differentiation (as set out in the quote) of the two notions:

> *Pure Telic Egalitarianism* requires that, given any two equi-dimensional distributions of well-being, the more equal distribution be judged to be the better one.

> *Pluralist Telic Egalitarianism* requires that, given any two equi-dimensional distributions of well-being with the same sum-total of well-being, the more equal distribution be judged to be the better one; and given any two equal equi-dimensional distributions of well-being, the distribution with the larger sum-total of well-being be judged to be the better one.

It is noted in Subramanian (2011) that while Pure Telic Egalitarianism, as defined earlier, is certainly vulnerable to the Levelling Down

Objection, this is not true of Pluralist Telic Egalitarianism, which—as defined earlier—is simply not committed to comparing distributions of different sums of well-being. By holding the sum total of well-being constant, one avoids commitment to a needlessly strong version of Pluralist Telic Egalitarianism, a version which requires that if any one distribution is more equal than another, then the former must be judged to be better than the latter in at least the one respect of equality. Such a formulation of Pluralist Telic Egalitarianism makes the notion easy game for the Levelling Down Objection. Parfit achieves his ends precisely by saddling Pluralist Telic Egalitarianism with this strong baggage: why must all egalitarians accept this interpretation of their ethic? The point is not to assert that Pluralist Telic Egalitarianism will survive the Levelling Down Objection under Parfit's 'unrestricted' characterization (which of course it will not, and which Pure Telic Egalitarianism does not), but rather to point out, precisely, that such a characterization is neither the only nor the most reasonable one available.

Putting it differently, one's moral intuition, it seems, can be very clear about favouring equal over unequal distributions of a *given* sum total of well-being: why must one, as a person that cares for equality at all, necessarily be seized of a similar certitude regarding the superiority, even if only in one respect, of (for example) an equal distribution of a small sum of well-being over a (Pareto-dominating) unequal distribution of a larger sum of well-being? In particular, it does not appear to be fair (or logical) to criticize an egalitarian because she confines her egalitarian impulses to a restricted domain of application and, at the same time, trip her up with the Levelling Down objection when she expands the domain of application! More significantly, the 'value' of equality can be focused upon precisely under a *ceteris paribus* clause (one in which, specifically, the aggregate level of well-being is kept constant).

The matter is amenable to elaboration with the help of an example. Suppose one were inclined to judge sculptures favourably by, inter alia, assigning some intrinsic value to the *size* of the sculptures. This should surely not *require* one to say that in the respect of size, at least, a misshapen but large sculpture has something to commend it vis-à-vis a delicate but small sculpture! One would imagine that an eminently acceptable way of attaching intrinsic value to size is to say that sculpture A is a better one than sculpture B if A is a blown-up version of B (that is, A is identical to B except for a scale factor greater than one). Why is the 'intrinsic' nature of this value in any way compromised by restricting A to be a scaled-up version of B? (Indeed, and symmetrically, one can imagine many persons holding exactly the contrary intrinsic value of 'small is beautiful' by requiring that A is better than B whenever A is a scaled-*down* version of B.) Analogously, people of inegalitarian persuasion will typically have no systematically intrinsic preference for equal over unequal distributions of a given sum of well-being.

It is worth noting here that Parfit's Levelling Down Objection has been dealt with, in the foregoing, by defining Pluralist Telic Egalitarianism in such a way that it avoids any entailment of Levelling Down as an acceptable principle. The two-person distribution of well-being (50,50) does not, in a concession to Levelling Down, have to be declared superior to the distribution (50,100) in at least the one respect of equality, because the Pluralist Telic Egalitarian principle, as it has been defined here, is not obliged to pronounce judgement on comparisons of distributions which have different aggregate levels of well-being. This defence of Egalitarianism is in contrast to the argument resorted to by Larry Temkin (2000), who questions the view that the Levelling Down Objection is indeed objectionable: in his view, the Levelling Down Objection has acquired a certain quality of unexceptionableness entirely because of a near-universal (and, presumably, inadequately examined) subscription to what he calls the Slogan, more commonly known to economists as the Pareto Principle, and which Broome has called 'the Principle of Personal Good'. Here is how Temkin states the Slogan (Temkin 2000: 126):

The Slogan. One situation *cannot* be worse (or better) than another if there is *no one* for whom it *is* worse (or better).

Temkin contests the prevailing view of the unassailable moral appeal of the Slogan, and so calls into question the position that there is something necessarily repugnant about Levelling Down. The argument in the present essay simply sidesteps the question of whether the Levelling Down Objection deserves the status of a Sacred Cow: it avoids what is arguably an avoidable controversy. While the definition of Pluralist Telic Egalitarianism employed in this essay does not entail the Levelling Down Objection, it also does not entail the Slogan—though it is not inimical to the Slogan. A simple restatement of the Pluralist Telic Egalitarian principle for a two-person society, as enunciated in this essay, should clarify the issue. First, suppose $\succ$ to be a binary relation of strict betterness. The version of Pluralist Telic Egalitarianism (PTE) which has been advanced in this essay can be shown to subscribe, without contradiction, to the following three principles, which I call α, β and γ respectively. Principles α and β, between them, characterize PTE, while Principle γ is, essentially, the Slogan.

Principle α. For all well-being levels $x, a, b > 0$, if $a \neq b$ and $a + b = 2x$, then $(x, x) \succ (a, b)$. (That is, for any two-person society, given any aggregate level of well-being, an equal distribution of the aggregate is better than an unequal distribution.)

Principle β. For all well-being levels $x, y > 0$, if $x > y$, then $(x, x) \succ (y, y)$. (That is, for any two-person society, an equal distribution of well-being levels is greater than another equal distribution of well-being levels, if aggregate well-being is greater in the first case than in the second.)

Principle γ (The Slogan). For all well-being levels $x, c, d > 0$, if $c > d$, then $(x, c) \succ (x, d)$. (That is, for any two-person society, if one person's well-being level is raised while keeping the other person's level constant, then this is an improvement.)

Given three two-person distributions of well-being $(10, 100)$, $(10, 10)$ and $(55, 55)$, by Principle α, $(55, 55) \succ (10, 100)$, and by Principle γ, $(10, 100) \succ (10, 10)$. Principles α and γ in conjunction with transitivity of $\succ$ imply also that $(55, 55) \succ (10, 10)$, which, precisely, is what Principle β demands. Briefly, the egalitarian argument in this essay gets around the Levelling Down Objection by showing that there is an eminently reasonable way of describing Pluralist Telic Egalitarianism so that it does not either entail the Objection or call into question the appeal of the Slogan. (The reader is invited to see also, in this context, the work of Christiano and Braynen 2008.)

If Parfit finds Telic Egalitarianism unsatisfactory as a basis for upholding the intrinsic value of equality, he also finds Deontic Egalitarianism unsatisfactory as a basis for upholding the instrumental value of equality. His Divided World example (Parfit 1997) is designed to demonstrate that there are certain situations in which Deontic Egalitarianism is of no avail in upholding equality as a virtue promoting other valued principles such as justice or fairness. Parfit invites us to consider two worlds, World 1 and World 2, each containing the same number of persons and completely cut off from one another, so that neither World is aware of the other's existence. Consider two alternative distributions of well-being, in the first of which each person in World 1 experiences a well-being level of 100 and each person in World 2 a well-being level of 200, while in the second distribution, each person in each World experiences a well-being level of 145 (all in appropriately chosen units). The two distributions can be represented by the ordered vectors $(100, 200)$ and $(145, 145)$ respectively. Many of us would be tempted to pronounce that $(145, 145) \succ (100, 200)$ from the consideration that even though the aggregate level of well-being in the distribution $(145, 145)$ is a little lower than in the distribution (100,200), this fact is more than compensated for by the feature that the first distribution is an equal one and the second distribution a very unequal one. Yet, since the two Worlds are Divided and neither World has any knowledge of the existence of the other, one cannot appeal to the requirements of justice or fairness or any allied instrumental cause for pronouncing the more equal distribution to be better than the less equal one; nor—given the complete insulation of each World from the other—can one appeal to any adverse effects which inequality might have as a rationalization of the preference for (145,145) over (100,200). In Parfit's view, Telic Egalitarianism falls foul of the Levelling Down Objection, while Deontic Egalitarianism falls foul of the Divided World example—whence the inability of Egalitarianism to support the moral intuition which favours an equal distribution of a smaller sum of well-being over an unequal distribution of a larger sum of well-being, as in the case of the distributions (145,145) and (100,200) just considered. Hence also Parfit's contention that, in view of this failure of Egalitarianism, one needs some other principle to justify one's preference for equality—and the principle he proposes is the Priority View.

It can be argued, however, that the Divided World example does not constitute any sort of conclusive case against egalitarianism. In Subramanian (2011), we are invited to consider a third hypothetical distribution (150,150), such that each person in each of the two Worlds experiences a well-being level of 150 units. Recalling the constitutive elements of Pluralist Telic Egalitarianism as we have defined it, in terms of the Principles α and β, it may be noted that $(150,150) \succ (100,200)$ by Principle α, and $(150,150) \succ (145,145)$ by Principle β. Call the distributions (150,150), (100,200) and (145,145) **a**, **b** and **c** respectively. For any pair of distributions **x** and **y**, let $P(\mathbf{x},\mathbf{y})$ stand for the 'extent to which' **x** is preferred to **y**. Let Q be an exact asymmetric ordering such that for all distributions **x**, **y**, **w**, **z**, $P(\mathbf{x},\mathbf{y})QP(\mathbf{w},\mathbf{z})$ will be taken to mean that the extent to which **x** is preferred to **y** is greater than the extent to which **w** is preferred to **z**. What we are speaking of is a form of ordinal comparison of intensities of preference. Returning to the distributions **a** = (150,150), **b** = (100,200) and **c** = (145,145) defined earlier, it is entirely conceivable that $P(\mathbf{a},\mathbf{b})QP(\mathbf{a},\mathbf{c})$ from the consideration that, at the same level of aggregate well-being, there is considerably more inequality in **b** than in **a**, while at the same level of equality, there is only a relatively smaller level of aggregate well-being in **c** than in **a**. To suggest that $P(\mathbf{a},\mathbf{b})QP(\mathbf{a},\mathbf{c})$ is also to suggest that **c** lies above **b** in one's preference ranking. Pluralist Telic Egalitarianism, as it has been defined in this essay, is not vulnerable to the Levelling Down Objection; further, it is compatible, even in a Divided World, with the judgement that an equal distribution of a smaller sum of well-being (such as **c**) is preferable to an unequal distribution of a larger sum of well-being (such as **b**). Briefly, the Levelling Down Objection and the Divided World example do not, after all, between them dispose of the case for Egalitarianism.

On the Practical Relevance of the Equality–Priority Distinction

As we have seen in the previous section, the Levelling Down Objection and the Divided World example, between them, serve as grounds for Parfit to advance the notion that, in some cases, our preference for equal over unequal distributions must be located in a non-Egalitarian view of the world. While the force of this claim has been questioned in the preceding discussion, this is not a sufficient reason for denying the possibility that a preference for equality could be grounded in some non-Egalitarian view. Parfit claims that the Priority View is such a non-Egalitarian view. It is the view that 'benefiting people matters more the worse off these people are' (Parfit 1997: 213). In what way is the Priority View distinct from Egalitarianism? Parfit says: 'Egalitarians are concerned with *relativities*: with how each person's level compares with the level of other people. On the Priority View, we are concerned only with people's absolute levels' (1997: 214). He also says: '[O]n the Priority View, benefits to the worse off matter more, but that is only because these people are at a lower *absolute* level. It is irrelevant that these people are worse off *than others*. Benefits to them would matter just as much even if there *were* no others who were better off' (1997: 214).

It is worth asking if these particular verbal distinctions translate into any operational distinctions of outcome when we are confronted with some specific practical problem of distribution, such as that of allocating a benefit of fixed size amongst a set of people constituting society. By way of example, let $\mathbf{x} = (10, 20)$ be an ordered two-person distribution of well-being levels or 'benefits'. Suppose we had a budget of 10 units of benefit to distribute. Fairly straightforwardly, both an egalitarian and a prioritarian would transfer the entire budget to the person with a well-being level of 10 in distribution **x**, to arrive at the distribution $\mathbf{x}' = (20, 20)$. Let us call a person who subscribes to the Priority View without believing in equality a '*Pure* Prioritarian'. A Pure Prioritarian might be expected to advance something like the following claim: 'in an exercise of optimal transfers, both an Egalitarian and I would recommend a movement from **x** to **x′**; but this is not a reason for you to confuse (Pure) Prioritarians and Egalitarians: the Egalitarian and I may make the same prescription, but he does it in order to achieve equality, whereas I do it in order to give priority to the worse off.' This, as far as it goes, is a valid claim of distinction but it is not at all clear how far the distinction actually goes. Setting aside the Pure Telic Egalitarian (who is altogether too much of a sitting duck), one would like to know if the difference in motivation between a Pure Prioritarian and an Egalitarian that Parfit claims ever causes any divergence in distributional judgements of what is better or what ought to be done, and if the divergence can be traced to the belief of the one and the non-belief of the other in equality. Without pre-judging the issue, it seems fair to suggest that from *Parfit's* own (1997) account, it is difficult to deduce any such divergence: one is, therefore, led to find Fleurbaey's position understandable when he says of the distinction between (Pure) Prioritarianism and Egalitarianism that '[It] mostly has to do with the reasons for, rather than the content of, judgments about distributions' (Fleurbaey 2001: 1). If this is so, one could be speaking of a distinction without a difference.

It may be objected here that inasmuch as utilitarianism could also support equality in a practical exercise of distribution, this fact should not serve as a basis for the pronouncement that utilitarian and egalitarian judgements differ only with respect to their reasons and not with respect to their content. In response to this objection, it is relevant to ask if utilitarianism invariably prescribes distributional equality. The assumption that all individuals are equipped with the *same* utility function is the force behind what Amartya Sen (1973) has called utilitarianism's 'ill-deserved reputation' for egalitarianism. Typically, a physically challenged person (PCP) may be deemed to be a less efficient pleasure machine than an able-bodied person (ABP) in transforming income into utility. Typically, utilitarianism will prescribe both an income and a total-utility distribution which allocates a larger share to ABP than to PCP. This being the case, there is no reason whatever for failing to see a distinction between egalitarianism (or prioritarianism), on the one hand, and utilitarianism, on the other, 'in practice'. This is the well-known problem of 'heterogeneity'. But the problem is not only with heterogeneity. Consider a case in which both individuals 1 and 2 in a two-person society have the *same* utility function U defined on income x: $U_i(x) = U(x) = \sqrt{x}$, $i = 1, 2$. (This is an increasing, strictly concave utility function, of the type favoured in canonical discussions of the nature of utility.) Suppose a total income of 50 is to be distributed between the two persons. The optimal utilitarian distribution will be

$\mathbf{x}^* = (25,25)$ and aggregate welfare, by the utilitarian calculus, will be 10 utils. Consider another distribution $\mathbf{y} = (0,100)$ of a total income of 100: aggregate welfare for this distribution, by the utilitarian calculus, is also 10 utils. A utilitarian is obliged to be indifferent between the distributions $\mathbf{x}^*$ and $\mathbf{y}$. There is little reason for the view that prioritarians and egalitarians are obliged to agree with the utilitarian. One should not have much difficulty in conceding that the distinction between egalitarianism and utilitarianism is also an overdrawn and functionally not very useful one if it were indeed the case that egalitarianism and utilitarianism invariably prescribed the same distributions in practice: only, they do not do so. Hence the view that when it comes to egalitarianism and prioritarianism—unlike in the case of egalitarianism (or prioritarianism) and utilitarianism—one could be speaking of a distinction without a difference.

As it happens, Parfit's 'absolute/relative' distinction can indeed, under a certain interpretation of that distinction, lead to a divergence in distributional judgements, although it is questionable if the divergence should be traced to the status of belief in equality (as will be discussed in the following section). Specifically, it does not, in any way, appear to be a necessity of logic that a Prioritarian—understood to mean someone who subscribes to the Priority View—should not believe in equality. Hence the earlier suggestion that if what is involved is only a matter of definition, then it would be convenient to call somebody who believes in the Priority View without believing in equality a *'Pure* Prioritarian'. It will be contended, in what follows, that any possible divergence in distributional judgements that may arise between 'relativists' and 'absolutists' does not necessarily imply a disagreement on the appeal of equality, such that 'absolutists' must necessarily be seen as adopting a stand in favour of a principle of Priority which is distinct from, and incompatible with, a principle of Equality.

Egalitarian Judgements and Additive Separability

While a Prioritarian is free to renounce any belief in equality, it is, I believe, perfectly open to an Egalitarian to find the Priority View ('benefiting people matters more the worse off these people are') appealing. Indeed, if Prioritarianism requires that 'benefits to the worse off should be given more weight' (Parfit 1997: 213), then it is difficult to imagine that any Egalitarian can quarrel with Prioritarianism on *this* ground. Certainly, and as already stated, a Prioritarian need not believe in equality: a person with such a view we have called a Pure Prioritarian. It appears to be safe to suggest, minimally, that the intersection between 'Non-pure' Prioritarians and Egalitarians is a non-empty set. Let us use the term 'P-Egalitarians' to describe Egalitarians belonging to this intersection. While all P-Egalitarians may be expected to agree that benefits to the worse off should be given more weight, there can be disagreement about precisely what sort of weighting structure should be employed in order to realize this objective. Parfit's 'absolute–relative' distinction could conceivably be related to this weighting structure question but the distinction would be relevant for differentiating between two sorts of P-Egalitarian rather than for differentiating Prioritarians and Egalitarians.

Specifically, it is useful, here, to invoke the economist's device of the social welfare function. Suppose income, for specificity, to be the space in which advantage or benefit is assessed. Let $\mathbf{a} = (a_1, ..., a_i, ..., a_n)$ be a non-decreasingly ordered n-vector of incomes, where a_i is the income of the ith poorest person and n is an element of the set $\mathcal{N}$ of positive integers. Let $\mathbf{X}_n$ be the set of non-decreasingly ordered n-vectors of income, and define $\mathbf{X}$ to be the set $\bigcup_{n \in \mathcal{N}} \mathbf{X}_n$. For every $\mathbf{a} \in \mathbf{X}$, $N(\mathbf{a})$ will stand for the set of individuals whose incomes are represented in $\mathbf{a}$, and $n(\mathbf{a})$ for the dimensionality of $\mathbf{a}$. *Social welfare* is a function $W : \mathbf{X} \to \mathcal{R}$ (where $\mathcal{R}$ is the set of real numbers), such that for every $\mathbf{a} \in \mathbf{X}$, $W(\mathbf{a})$ specifies a real number which is supposed to represent the amount of social welfare associated with the income vector $\mathbf{a}$. Typically, W is taken to be an increasing function of each person's income. For all $\mathbf{a} \in \mathbf{X}$ and $i \in N(\mathbf{a})$, we shall let $v(a_i; \mathbf{a})$ stand for the *valuation function* which assigns a real number to the ith poorest person's income, with the number signifying the social valuation placed on her income. The valuation function v is said to be *menu-independent* if, for all $\mathbf{a}, \mathbf{b} \in \mathbf{X}, j \in N(\mathbf{a})$ and $k \in N(\mathbf{b})$, $a_j = b_k$ implies $v(a_j; \mathbf{a}) = v(\mathbf{b}_k; \mathbf{a})$. The valuation function v is said to be *menu-dependent* if $\exists$ [$\mathbf{a}, b \in \mathbf{X}, j \in N(\mathbf{a}) \& k \in N(\mathbf{b})$] such that $a_j = b_k$ and $v(a_j; \mathbf{a}) \neq v(b_k; \mathbf{b})$. One way of writing a social welfare function is in terms of an additive average of the valuations of all individuals' incomes, that is, for all $\mathbf{a} \in \mathbf{X}$:

$$W(\mathbf{a}) = [1/n(\mathbf{a})]\Sigma_{i \in N(\mathbf{a})}v(a_i; \mathbf{a}). \tag{6.1}$$

For all $\mathbf{a} \in \mathbf{X}$, $W(\mathbf{a})$ will be said to an *additively separable social welfare function* if and only if

$$W(\mathbf{a}) = [1/n(\mathbf{a})]\Sigma_{i \in N(\mathbf{a})}v(a_i; \mathbf{a}) \text{ and } v \text{ is } \textit{menu-independent}. \tag{6.2}$$

Let $r_i(\mathbf{a}) \equiv (n(\mathbf{a}) + 1 - i)$ be the rank-order of the ith poorest person's income in $\mathbf{a}$. Consider a particular income-valuation function, given by $v^B(a_i; \mathbf{a}) = r_i(\mathbf{a})a_i$ for all $i \in N(\mathbf{a})$. Employing this valuation function in (6.1), we obtain what we call the Borda (Rank-Order Weighted) Social Welfare Function W^B:

$$W^B(\mathbf{a}) = [1/n(\mathbf{a})][n(\mathbf{a})a_1 + ... + (n(\mathbf{a}) + 1 - i)a_i + ... + a_n] \quad (6.3)$$

Consider a slight variation of the valuation function v^B, given by $v^{DW}(a_i; \mathbf{a}) = r_i^2(\mathbf{a})a_i$ for all $i \in N(\mathbf{a})$. If we employed this valuation function in (6.1), then we would obtain a social welfare function W^{DW}, attributable to Donaldson and Weymark (1980), and given by:

$$W^{DW}(\mathbf{a}) = [1/n(\mathbf{a})][n^2(\mathbf{a})a_1 + ... + (n(\mathbf{a}) + 1 - i)^2 a_i + ... + a_n]. \quad (6.4)$$

Suppose we took the income-valuation function—call it v^A—to be an identically increasing and strictly concave transform of a_i for all i, such that $v^A(a_i; \mathbf{a}) = (1/\lambda)a_i^\lambda$ for all $i \in N(\mathbf{a})$, where λ is any number greater than zero and less than one. Then, the social welfare function in (6.1) can be written (after the Atkinson 1970 fashion) as:

$$W^A(a) = (1/n(\mathbf{a})\lambda)(a_1^\lambda + ... + a_i^\lambda + ... + a_n^\lambda). \quad (6.5)$$

W^A is an example of an *additively separable function*, because $v^A(a_i; \mathbf{a})$ is menu-independent, while W^B and W^{DW} are examples of functions which, while they are additive, are *not* separable, because $v^B(a_i; \mathbf{a})$ and $v^{DW}(a_i; \mathbf{a})$ are menu-dependent. It is a property of an additively separable social welfare function that given any two (ordered) income vectors $\mathbf{a}$ and $\mathbf{b}$, the valuation placed on the jth poorest person's income in the vector $\mathbf{a}$ will be exactly the same as the valuation placed on the kth poorest person's income in the vector $\mathbf{b}$ if the two individuals should happen to share the same income. Thus, if W^A, for example, is the welfare function employed, and if the jth poorest person in some n-dimensional distribution $\mathbf{a}$ receives the same income a as the kth poorest person in some other m-dimensional distribution $\mathbf{b}$, then the valuation $v^A(a_j; \mathbf{a})$ placed on the jth poorest person's income in $\mathbf{a}$ is identical to the valuation $v^A(b_k; \mathbf{b})$ placed on the kth poorest person's income in $\mathbf{b}$: $v^A(a_j; \mathbf{a}) = v^A(b_k; \mathbf{b}) = (1/\lambda)a^\lambda$. The Borda Social Welfare Function is *not*, however, additively separable; and if W^B is the welfare function employed, then it is easy to check that $v^B(a_j; \mathbf{a}) = (n(\mathbf{a}) + 1 - j)a$, $v^B(b_k; \mathbf{b}) = (n(\mathbf{b}) + 1 - k)a$ and (unless $n(\mathbf{a}) - j = m(\mathbf{b}) - k$), $v^B(a_j; \mathbf{a}) \neq v^B(b_k; \mathbf{b})$. The same is also obviously true of the welfare function W^{DW}.

Notice that when the social welfare function is of the additively separable type, the valuation placed on a person's income depends only on the *absolute* level of that income, whereas when the social welfare function is of the Borda or Donaldson–Weymark type, the valuation placed on a person's income is also influenced by the *relative* place occupied by that income level in the distribution. Valuation, in an additively separable welfare function, is thus 'distribution-invariant' in a manner in which valuation, in a Borda-type welfare function, is not. It is *this* sort of 'absolute-relative' distinction which Parfit conceivably has in mind when he seeks to differentiate Prioritarianism from Egalitarianism; indeed, Broome (2003) insists that the distinction between Prioritarianism and Egalitarianism is to be found in an identification of Prioritarians with additively separable welfare functions and of Egalitarians with welfare functions that are not additively separable.

However, in my view, a distinction of this nature is applicable not in the context of Prioritarians and Egalitarians but in the context of the class of Egalitarians earlier referred to as 'P-Egalitarians'. Differences in distributional judgement can certainly arise between 'absolute valuationists' and 'relative valuationists', but these, in my view, are differences between two types of Egalitarian rather than between Prioritarians and Egalitarians. Thus, I am inclined to agree with Fleurbaey, when he says: 'insofar as [the distinction between Prioritarianism and Egalitarianism] bears on the content of distributional judgments, it merely draws a line within egalitarianism' (Fleurbaey 2001: 1).

In particular, it seems reasonable to suggest that P-Egalitarians can be categorized into two types: P_1-Egalitarians, who insist that the welfare function be additively separable, and P_2-Egalitarians, who insist that the welfare function should not be additively separable (of which two examples are the W^B and the W^{DW} functions). These two varieties of Egalitarian have a simple disagreement on the structural form in which benefits to the worse off should be given more weight. That the distinction between P_1- and P_2-Egalitarians could be a non-trivial one is reflected in the following considerations. While a welfare function can be seen as a kind of 'gain function', an inequality measure can be seen as a kind of 'loss function', and the latter can, through suitable manipulation, be derived as a sort of obverse of the former. Typically, inequality measures derived from additively separable welfare functions would be 'subgroup consistent', whereas inequality measures derived from welfare functions that are not additively separable would violate subgroup consistency, which is the requirement that, when a population is partitioned into mutually exclusive and collectively exhaustive subgroups, an increase in inequality in any one subgroup should increase overall inequality. Theil's inequality measure is an example of a subgroup consistent measure, while the Gini coefficient is an example of a measure which is not subgroup consistent. The properties of subgroup consistency and a stronger version of it, called decomposability, have for long been known to economists working on the measurement of inequality.[1] Whether or not subgroup consistency is a compulsively desirable property in an inequality index is also a fairly long-standing controversy amongst economists (Sen and Foster [1997] has an instructive review of the issues involved). In a particular comparison of two distributions **x** and **y**, it is possible that the Theil index pronounces **x** to display more inequality than **y**, and the Gini index reverses this ranking. This could be a cause for a potential conflict in the inequality judgements of P_1- and P_2-Egalitarians. Of course, this could also be a cause for a conflict between Pure Prioritarians and P_2-Egalitarians but, relevantly, not for a conflict between Pure Prioritarians and P_1-Egalitarians. It, therefore, appears to be misplaced to suggest that Prioritarians should be distinguished from Egalitarians by identifying the latter with a belief in equality and the former with a lack of such belief. In fact, divergences in welfare (and, therefore, inequality) judgements of distributions can also arise amongst those committed exclusively to welfare functions that are not additively separable, as the following reveals.

Imagine two 4-vectors of income **b** $= (24, 26, 40, 50)$ and **c** $= (20, 30, 44, 46)$ which share the same mean income of 35. It is easily verified that $W^B(\mathbf{b}) = W^B(\mathbf{c}) = 76$, while $W^{DW}(\mathbf{b})(= 207) > W^{DW}(\mathbf{c})(= 203)$. This sort of rank reversal seems to be inadequate reason to suggest that as between adherents of the Borda-type welfare functions and adherents of the Donaldson–Weymark-type welfare functions, one lot ought to be identified with Egalitarianism and the other with some distinct, non-Egalitarian principle. (Indeed, economists will be quick to recognize that the distinction between the two sets of evaluators resides, rather simply, in the differing appeal which Kolm's [1976] 'principle of diminishing transfers' has for them.) Briefly, divergences in the inequality ranking of distributions do not necessarily deserve to be invested with any more significance than as manifestations of differing varieties and degrees of 'equity-consciousness'. It seems to be neither warranted nor profitable to

---

[1] See, in particular, Shorrocks (1980, 1988).

counterpose Prioritarianism as a principle which is distinct and separate from Egalitarianism.

Conclusion

In this essay, an attempt has been made to argue that a reasonable interpretation of Egalitarianism enables it to survive the charge of its being vulnerable to the Levelling Down Objection and the Divided World example. This is not in any way to suggest that a Prioritarian can be coerced into believing in Equality—of course, this is not the case. That said, it is not clear that subscription to the Priority View without belief in Equality constitutes grounds for viewing the distinction between Prioritarianism and Egalitarianism as being either practically relevant for distributional judgements or conceptually significant for foundational analysis. It is hard to determine if there exists any Prioritarian argument which establishes a convincing case against an egalitarian endorsement of an Atkinson-type social welfare function. Broome invites us to consider such an interpretation in an effort, I believe, to confer some precise meaning on Parfit's 'relative–absolute' distinction. One can, however, hold, in response to this interpretation, that there is nothing inherently 'egalitarian' about rejecting subgroup consistency, as one might need to argue in order to insist that egalitarians may not subscribe to additively separable welfare functions. Putting it differently, while some Egalitarians may abjure additive separability, not all Egalitarians should be *required* to do so. In particular, it would be reasonable to expect from those that advance the Priority View as a distinct and substantively important concept vis-à-vis the Egalitarian View to provide evidence of this claim; the present essay questions precisely the Prioritarian success of this enterprise. Additionally, and very markedly differently from Prioritarian efforts, this essay does bring out the practical consequences of alternative weighting schemata, in terms of success or failure in satisfying subgroup consistency, decomposability and transfer-sensitivity—all of which are issues in respect of which Egalitarians can have differences of opinion among themselves, without having to see these differences as entailing the elicitation of deference to some distinct and counterposed ethic such as 'prioritarianism'. On balance, Fleurbaey's view of the matter is compelling, when he says: '[The Prioritarian-Egalitarian] distinction mostly has to do with the reasons for, rather than the content of, judgments about distributions; [and] ... insofar as it bears on the content of distributional judgments, it merely draws a line within egalitarianism' (Fleurbaey 2001: 1).

References

Atkinson, A. B. 1970. 'On the Measurement of Inequality', *Journal of Economic Theory*, 2(3):244–63.

Broome, J. 2003. 'Equality versus Priority: A Useful Distinction', forthcoming in C. Murray and D. Winkler (eds), *'Goodness' and 'Fairness': Ethical Issues in Health Resource Allocation*. World Health Organization. Available at http://users.ox.ac.uk/~sfop0060/

Christiano, T. and W. Braynen. 2008. 'Inequality, Injustice and Leveling Down', *Ratio*, 21(4):392–420.

Donaldson, D. and J. A. Weymark. 1980. 'A Single-Parameter Generalization of the Gini Indices of Inequality', *Journal of Economic Theory*, 22(1):67–86.

Fleurbaey, M. 2001. 'Equality versus Priority: How Relevant is the Distinction?', forthcoming in C. Murray and D. Winkler (eds), *'Goodness' and 'Fairness': Ethical Issues in Health Resource Allocation*. World Health Organization. Available at http://cerses.shs.univ-paris5.fr/marc-fleurbaey_eng.htm

Kolm, S.-Ch. 1976. 'Unequal Inequalities I', *Journal of Economic Theory*, 12(3):416–42; and 'Unequal Inequalities II', *Journal of Economic Theory*, 13(1):82–111.

Parfit, D. 1997. 'Equality and Priority', *Ratio* (new series), 10(3):202–21.

Sen, A. 1973. *On Economic Inequality*. Oxford: Clarendon Press.

Sen, A. and J. E. Foster. 1997. *On Economic Inequality: Expanded Edition with a Substantial Annexe*. Oxford: Clarendon Press.

Shorrocks, A. F. 1980. 'The Class of Additively Decomposable Inequality Measures', *Econometrica*, 48(3):613–25.

———. 1988. 'Aggregation Issues in Inequality Measurement', in W. Eichhorn (ed.), *Measurement in Economics: Theory and Applications in Economic Indices*. Heidelberg: Physica Verlag, pp. 429–51.

Subramanian, S. 2011. 'Are Egalitarians Really Vulnerable to the Levelling Down Objection and the Divided World Example?', *The Journal of Philosophical Economics*, IV(2):5–14.

Temkin, L. 2002. 'Equality, Priority, and the Levelling Down Objection', in A. Clayton and M. Williams (eds), *The Ideal of Equality*. Basingstoke and New York: Palgrave Macmillan, pp. 126–61.

CHAPTER 7

Contest under Interdependent Valuations

Rittwik Chatterjee*

In this essay, we will briefly study the theory of contest under interdependent valuations. Valuations are interdependent if the valuation of any contestant not only depends on her own type but also on the types of all the other contestants. Interdependent valuations can be of two types—affiliated valuation and common valuation. Under affiliated valuations, the valuations of the bidders are positively correlated with each other. Under affiliation, the Revenue Equivalence Theorem of independent private values (IPV) model no longer holds because the second-price sealed bid auction generates weakly higher expected revenue than the first-price sealed bid auction. In case of common value, all the bidders assign a common value to the object but do not know the exact value of the object. One of the important phenomenon that can occur in common value auction is 'winner's curse'. In this case, the winner (the highest bidder of the auction) will overpay. 'Winner's curse' occurs when the bidders estimate their respective valuation using only their own signals.

Contest is a widely known phenomenon. There are numerous essays those have studied different aspects of contests. Depending on the objective of the contest designer, several essays have studied how to design optimal contests (Glazer and Hassin 1988; Moldovanu and Sela 2001). There are different types of contests. The rent-seeking contest

---

* I want to thank Prof. Krishnendu Ghosh Dastidar for his valuable comments.

was first studied by Tullock (1980). Tournaments, which are another form of contests, have also been widely studied (Abrevaya 2002; Groh et al. 2003; Lazear and Rosen 1981; Taylor 1995).

In this paper, we will assume a special type of interdependent valution, namely, pure common value. Here, all the contestants assign the same value to all the prizes. By the type of a contestant, we mean the ability of that contestant. We will first describe our model by a set of assumptions. Throughout this essay we are going to assume that performance of any contestant is exactly equal to the effort she puts in the contest. Then we will study a contest with interdependent valuations under the assumption of a linear cost function. We first derive the equilibrium bidding strategy of a contestant, then we study whether it is optimal for the contest designer to offer a single 'winner take all' first prize or multiple prizes under the assumption that the contest designer can only offer either a single prize or two prizes. Then we analyse a contest with interdependent valuations under non-linear cost functions. Here, we derive the equilibrium bidding strategy of a contest. Finally, we analyse the case where the contest designer can offer more than two prizes (note that even in this case, the contest designer can offer at most k prizes, where k is the number of contestants). We derive the equilibrium bidding strategy of a contestant and comment that the results we have derived for the case where the contest designer can offer a single prize or two prizes still holds for the case where the contest designer can offer more than two prizes.

Contests with Interdependent Valuation

Generally, in the literature, we find that contests are studied in a particular way, that is, in most of the cases (if not all) the prizes are nothing but some amount of money. Here, we are interested in studying contests, where prizes are different commodities (or services) but not money. The crucial difference between the existing literature and our model is that if we consider money as prizes, then each of the prizes holds the same value for all the contestants (since the amount of each prize is the same for all the contestants) and common knowledge to all the contestants. In our case (where we are considering prizes to be in the form of some commodities or services), however, it may be different and private information (since different people are likely to have different valuations for the same commodity/service depending on their individual preference patterns). Also, in our case, the valuation of one contestant may depend on the valuations of all the other contestants—

we are interested in studying exactly this aspect of valuations in a contest.

So, first, in our model, the prizes are not money but commodities (or services) and, second, the valuations of the contestants are interdependent. Several real life examples can be thought of. First, there are several contests giving both money and other services as prizes. For example, in India singing contests are very popular. If someone wins a singing contest, then she not only gets some amount of money as the prize but also many contracts from different recording companies as well for singing in different places. The amount of prize money and the contracts are obviously dependent on that particular contest. Note that because there are several singing contests going on simultaneously and the contestant can participate in only one of them at a time, she must choose which contest to participate in. This decision may depend on what other contestants think about that contest. In that way, we have a situation of interdependent valuation. Currently, most of the popular contests not only offer money as prizes but also, directly or indirectly, many other facilities. So, our model is a good depiction of the way the contests are designed nowadays.

In our model, we are also interested in comparing two situations: first, a contest where only one prize is offered by the contest designer and, second, a contest where several prizes are offered. In the case where prizes are nothing but money, we have seen that it is always optimal for the contest designer[1] to offer a single prize when cost functions of the contestants are linear and concave, and if the cost functions are suffciently convex, then offering multiple prizes are optimal (Moldovanu and Sela 2001). We will show that this is not generally true for our model.

In our model, we assume that there are several contestants contesting for one or many commodities (or services). They have certain abilities, which are private information to them, and their valuations on the prizes are interdependent. Each one of them must choose an effort level which will guide their performances in the contest. But efforts are costly. The costs are dependent on the abilities. So, a lower ability contestant has to incur a higher cost as compared to a contestant who has a higher ability for the same level of performance. Efforts must be chosen simultaneously. Finally, we are assuming pure common value for our

---

[1] Whose objective is to maximize the sum of expected performances.

analysis. We have studied our model under different cost structures and compare our results to the results of Moldovanu and Sela (2001).

We will now formally study contests with interdependent valuations.

The Model and Its Assumptions

- Consider a contest where $p > 0$ prizes are awarded.
- There are k contestants. The set of contestants is $K = \{1, ..., k\}$.
- Each contestant has some private information concerning the value of each prize. Contestant i's private information is summarized as the realization of the random variable $A_i \in [m, 1]$, called the i's signal, where $1 > m > 0$. The realization of A_i is nothing but the ability of the contestant i.
- We assume that contestants' signals are independent and identically distributed with the distribution function $F(.)$. We also assume that $F(.)$ has a corresponding density $f(.)$ and has full support.
- The value of the jth prize ($V^{[j]}$) to contestant i can be expressed as a function of all the contestants' signals, that is, $V^{[j]} = \widehat{V}^{[j]}(A_1, A_2, ..., A_k)$. Immediately, one can see that we are assuming *pure common value* in which all the contestants assign the same values to all the prizes—the valuations of the contestants are identical. We assume that the valuation function is a common knowledge to all the contestants.
- For all $j \in [1, p]$, $\widehat{V}^{[j]}(0, 0, ..., 0) = 0$ and $E\left[\widehat{V}^{[j]}\right] < \infty$.
- We assume that for all $j \in [1, p]$, $\widehat{V}^{[j]}$ is symmetric in the last $k - 1$ components. This means that from the perspective of a particular contestant, the signals of the other contestants can be interchanged without affecting the value.
- For all $j \in [1, p - 1]$, $\widehat{V}^{[j]}(.) \geqslant \widehat{V}^{[j+1]}(.)$, that is, for all the contestants, the valuation of the first prize is greater than or equal to the valuation of the second prize, and so on.
- In the contest, each player i makes an effort x_i. Efforts are undertaken simultaneously.
- We assume that the cost function (a function of effort and ability) is increasing in effort and decreasing in ability. An effort x_i causes a disutility (or cost) denoted by $\frac{1}{a_i}C(x_i)$.[2] We assume that cost is a strictly increasing function of effort (that is, $C^{-1}(.)$ exists

---

[2] The treatment of the case where i's cost function is given by $\delta(1/a_i)x_i$, with δ strictly monotone increasing, is completely analogous.

and is a strictly increasing function) and $C(0) = 0$. We will analyse contests with linear, strictly concave and strictly convex cost
functions.

- The contestant with the highest performance wins the first prize
  $V^{[1]}$ while the contestant with second highest performance wins
  the second prize $V^{[2]}$, and so on, until all the prizes are allocated.[3]
  Therefore, the pay-off of contestant i who has ability a_i and makes
  an effort x_i is either $V^{[j]} - \frac{1}{a_i}C(x_i)$ if i wins prize j or $-\frac{1}{a_i}C(x_i)$ if i
  does not win a prize. We assume that $C'(.) > 0$.
- Performance (ϕ_i) of player i is equal to $P(x_i)$. We assume that
  $P'(.) > 0$.
- We show that at equilibrium, the contestant whose ability is m puts
  in zero effort, that is, at equilibrium, the following equation must be
  satisfied $x_i(m, .) = 0 \ \forall i = 1, ..., k$. Note that the equilibrium effort
  of any contestant is a function of the abilities of all the contestants, that is, for all $i \in [1, k]$, $x_i = b(a_1, a_2, ..., a_k)$. Therefore, at
  equilibrium, we have $\phi_i = b(a_1, a_2, ..., a_k)$. We are interested in an
  increasing symmetric equilibrium only, so that at equilibrium b is
  a strictly increasing function of ability of the contestant i, that is,
  $b_i > 0$ throughout the domain of the function b. Moreover, as we
  have assumed, at equilibrium, an agent with the lowest ability always puts in zero effort, that is, $b_i(a_1, ..., a_{i-1}, m, a_{i+1}, ..., a_k) = 0$.
  Therefore, the performance of the contestant whose ability is m is
  zero at equilibrium.[4]
- Each contestant i chooses her effort in order to maximize her expected utility (given the other competitors' efforts and given the
  value functions of the different prizes). (Alternatively each contestant i chooses her performance to maximize expected utility as a_i
  is known to i).
- The contest designer determines the number of prizes having positive value and the distribution of the total prize sum among the
  different prizes in order to maximize the expected value of the sum
  of the performances, $\sum_{i=1}^{k} \phi_i$ (given the contestants' equilibrium
  performance function).

---

[3] Let $b > 1$ contestants tie for prize j. If $b \leqslant p - j + 1$, we assume that prizes
$j, ..., j + b - 1$ are randomly allocated among the tied players. If $b > p - j +$
1, then prizes $j, ..., p$ and a total of $b - (p - j + 1)$ zero prizes are randomly
allocated among the tied players.
[4] We are implicitly assuming that the performance and effort cannot be negative.

- Let us define the function

$$v^{[j]}(a_i, y_j) = \begin{cases} E\left[V^{[1]} \,\middle|\, A = a_i, Y_1 = y_1\right] & \text{if } j = 1 \\ E\left[V^{[j]} \,\middle|\, A = a_i, Y_j = y_j, Y_{j-1} = y_{j-1}, a_i < y_{j-1}\right] & \text{otherwise} \end{cases}$$

to be the expectation of the value of the contestant i for the prize j, when the signal she receives is a_i and the jth highest signal among the other contestants, Y_j, is y_j. These functions are the same for all the contestants because of symmetry. For all $j \in [1, p]$, let us assume $v^{[j]}$ are non-decreasing functions in a_i and y. Let us also assume that for all $j \in [1, p]$, $v^{[j]}$ are strictly increasing in a_i. Moreover, since for all $j \in [1, p]$, $\widehat{V}^{[j]}(m, m, ..., m) = 0$, $v^{[j]}(m, m) = 0$, and assume that for all $j \in [1, p-1]$, $v^{[j]}(.) \geqslant v^{[j+1]}(.)$. Finally, we assume, for all $j \in [1, p]$, $v^{[j]}(z, .) > 0 \; \forall z > m$.

Let us assume $p = 2$ and $k \geq 3$. We now derive the equilibrium bidding strategy of a contestant. Let us define $\bar{v}^{[2]}(a_i, y_1) = E\left[V^{[2]} \mid A = a_i, Y_1 = y_1\right]$ to be the expectation of the value of the contestant i for the second prize, when the signal he or she receives is a_i and the highest signal among the other contestants, Y_1, is y_1. Let us suppose that all the contestants except the contestant i follow the increasing and differentiable strategy $b(.)$. Clearly it is not optimal for any contestant to put in an effort more than $b(1)$. Let us define $G^{[j]}(.) = \frac{(k-1)!}{(i-1)!(k-i)!} \times (1 - F(a))^{i-1}(F(a))^{k-i}$ as the probability of winning the jth prize and let $g^{[j]}(.)$ be the first derivative of $G^{[j]}(.)$ with respect to a.

Linear Cost and Performance Functions

First let us assume a linear cost function (that is, the cost function is given by $C(x_i) = \frac{x_i}{a_i}$) and a linear performance function (that is, the performance function is given by $P(x_i) = x_i$). Consider a case where the contest designer is offering two prizes. The expected pay-off of the contestant i when her signal is a_i and she puts in an effort equal to $b^{[2]}(z)$ is

$$\Pi(z, a_i) = \int_m^z v^{[1]}(a_i, y_1)g^{[1]}(y_1)dy_1 + \int_m^z v^{[2]}(a_i, y_2)g^{[2]}(y_2)dy_2 - \frac{b^{[2]}(z)}{a_i}.$$

The first-order condition for the expected profit maximization is

$$v^{[1]}(a_i, z)g^{[1]}(z) + v^{[2]}(a_i, z)g^{[2]}(z) - \frac{b^{[2]\prime}(z)}{a_i} = 0$$

$$\Leftrightarrow v^{[1]}(a_i, z)g^{[1]}(z) + v^{[2]}(a_i, z)g^{[2]}(z) = \frac{b^{[2]\prime}(z)}{a_i}$$

$$\Leftrightarrow v^{[1]}(a_i, z)a_i g^{[1]}(z) + v^{[2]}(a_i, z)a_i g^{[2]}(z) = b^{[2]\prime}(z).$$

At a symmetric equilibrium, it is optimal to bid according to $z = a_i$; so setting $z = a_i$ in the first-order condition, we obtain the differential equation

$$v^{[1]}(a_i, a_i)a_i g^{[1]}(a_i) + v^{[2]}(a_i, a_i)a_i g^{[2]}(a_i) = b^{[2]\prime}(a_i). \qquad (7.1)$$

Since, by assumption, $v(m, m) = 0$, it is the case that $b(m) = 0$. Thus, associated with equation (7.1), we have the boundary condition $b(m) = 0$. The solution to the differential equation (7.1) together with the boundary condition $b(m) = 0$, as stated in proposition 7.1, constitutes a symmetric equilibrium.

Proposition 1. *Symmetric equilibrium strategies in the contest are given by*

$$b^{[2]}(a_i) = \int_m^{a_i} v^{[1]}(z, z)z g^{[1]}(z)dz + \int_m^{a_i} v^{[2]}(z, z)z g^{[2]}(z)dz.$$

Proof. See Appendix 7A.1

Later in this essay we will show that our argument here can be easily generalized for the case $p > 2$.

Consider another case where only the highest performer gets a prize and that prize consists of both the prizes as discussed earlier. We will now compare these two cases.

Proposition 2. *Symmetric equilibrium strategies in the contest are given by*

$$b^{[1]}(a_i) = \int_m^{a_i} v^{[1]}(z, z)z g^{[1]}(z)dz + \int_m^{a_i} \bar{v}^{[2]}(z, z)z g^{[1]}(z)dz.$$

Proof. See Appendix 7A.2.

Let us define $A(a_i) = \int_m^{a_i} v^{[2]}(z, z)z g^{[1]}(z)dz$ and $B(a_i) = \int_m^{a_i} v^{[2]}(z, z)z g^{[2]}(z)dz$. Next we compare the two different sums of expected performances and get the following proposition.

Proposition 3. *It is optimal to offer a single winner-take-all first prize if the following condition holds*

$$\int_m^1 \left[\int_m^{a_i} v^{[2]}(z, z)z g^{[2]}(z)dz \right] f(a_i)da_i$$

$$- \int_m^1 \left[\int_m^{a_i} \bar{v}^{[2]}(z, z)z g^{[1]}(z)dz \right] f(a_i)da_i < 0.$$

Proof. See Appendix 7A.3.

First let us assume that for all $a_i > m$, $\bar{v}^{[2]}(a_i, .) \geqslant v^{[2]}(a_i, .)$, that is, the expected value of the second prize, given the next highest ability, when there are two prizes and the contestant gets the second prize due to the fact that she finishes the contest with the second position is less than or equal to the expected value of the second prize, given the next highest ability, when the contestant gets the second prize along with the first prize due to the fact that there is a single prize that equals the sum of the first and the second prizes and she wins the contest. Therefore, we have

$$\Phi_1 = k \int_m^1 \left[\int_m^{a_i} v^{[1]}(z, z)zg^{[1]}(z)dz \right] f(a_i)da_i$$

$$+ k \int_m^1 \left[\int_m^{a_i} \bar{v}^{[2]}(z, z)zg^{[1]}(z)dz \right] f(a_i)da_i$$

$$\geqslant k \int_m^1 \left[\int_m^{a_i} v^{[1]}(z, z)zg^{[1]}(z)dz \right] f(a_i)da_i + k \int_m^1 A(a_i)f(a_i)da_i$$

and

$$\Phi_2 = k \int_m^1 \left[\int_m^{a_i} v^{[1]}(z, z)zg^{[1]}(z)dz \right] f(a_i)da_i + k \int_m^1 B(a_i)f(a_i)da_i.$$

We will now prove seven lemmas which will play an important role in proving our main results. These seven lemmas are very similar to the seven lemmas provided in Moldovanu and Sela (2001), and we will proceed exactly in the same way.

Lemma 1. *Under the assumptions stated earlier, the following seven conditions hold:*

1. $A(m) = B(m) = 0$
2. $\forall c \in (m, 1)$ $A(c) > 0$, $A'(c) > 0$
3. Let $c*$ be such that $F(c^*) = \frac{k-2}{k-1}$, then $B'(c^*) = 0$; $\forall c \in (m, c^*)$ $B'(c) > 0$ and $\forall c \in (c^*, 1)$ $B'(c) < 0$
4. $|B'(c)| > |A'(c)|$ for c in a neighbourhood of m
5. $A(1) > B(1)$
6. For any $k \geqslant 3$, there exists a unique point $c^{**} \neq m$ such that $A(c^{**}) = B(c^{**})$
7. $\int_m^1 (B(c) - A(c))F'(c)dc < 0$

Proof. See Appendix 7A.4.

We now prove our next main results.

Proposition 4. *Under the set-up discussed earlier, it is always optimal to offer a single first prize.*

Proof. See Appendix 7A.5.

Note that proposition 7.4 crucially depends on the assumption that for all $a_i > m$, $\bar{v}^{[2]}(a_i, .) \geqslant v^{[2]}(a_i, .)$. Now consider a case where we assume that for all $a_i > m$, $\bar{v}^{[2]}(a_i, .) < v^{[2]}(a_i, .)$, that is, the expected value of the second prize, given the next highest ability, is strictly lower if the contestant gets the second prize along with the first prize in the case where there is a single prize that equals the sum of the first and the second prizes and she wins the contest, compared to the case where there are two prizes and the contestant gets the second prize due to the fact that she finishes the contest with the second position.

The equilibrium bidding strategy of a contestant and Φ_2 do not change, but we have

$$\Phi_1 = k \int_m^1 b^{[1]}(a_i) f(a_i) da_i$$
$$\leqslant k \int_m^1 \left[\int_m^{a_i} v^{[1]}(z, z) z g^{[1]}(z) dz \right] f(a_i) da_i$$
$$+ k \int_m^1 \left[\int_m^{a_i} v^{[2]}(z, z) z g^{[1]}(z) dz \right] f(a_i) da_i.$$

And, therefore,

$$(\Phi_1 - \Phi_2)/k$$
$$\leqslant \int_m^1 \left[\int_m^{a_i} v^{[1]}(z, z) z g^{[1]}(z) dz \right] f(a_i) da_i + \int_m^1 A(a_i) f(a_i) da_i$$
$$- \int_m^1 \left[\int_m^{a_i} v^{[1]}(z, z) z g^{[1]}(z) dz \right] f(a_i) da_i + \int_m^1 B(a_i) f(a_i) da_i$$
$$= \int_m^1 \left[A(a_i) - B(a_i) \right] f(a_i) da_i > 0.$$

So, in this case, either $\Phi_1 > \Phi_2$ or $\Phi_1 < \Phi_2$ or they are equal. If $\Phi_1 > \Phi_2$ holds, then it is better to offer a single first prize; on the other hand, if $\Phi_1 < \Phi_2$, then it is better to offer multiple prizes. Therefore, we have shown that even if both the cost and the performance functions are linear, then also in case of interdependent valuations, offering multiple prizes may be a better choice for the contest designer.

Proposition 5. *If for all $a_i > m$, $\bar{v}^{[2]}(a_i, .) < v^{[2]}(a_i, .)$, then it may be better to offer multiple prizes.*

This result is quite different from the results in previous literature; for instance, one of the earlier essays in the literature shows that, '*When cost functions are linear or concave in effort, it is optimal to allocate the entire prize sum to a single "first" prize*, Moldovanu and Sela (2001). By introducing interdependent valuations, we have shown that even if the cost and the performance functions are linear in effort, it may be better to offer multiple prizes.

Remark: First, note that when prizes are money, we have for all $a_i > m$, $\bar{v}^{[2]}(a_i, .) = v^{[2]}(a_i, .)$. Second, proposition 7.5 shows that if the difference $\left(\bar{v}^{[2]}(a_i, .) - v^{[2]}(a_i, .)\right)$ is sufficiently high, then the winner of the first prize (when the contest is offering a single prize) values the second object much less than does the winner of the second prize (when the contest offers two prizes). Therefore in that case, if one splits the prizes, and offers multiple prizes, then the expected performances of all the contestants will rise. So, the sum of the expected performances will also rise. So, it will be better for the contest designer to offer multiple prizes under such circumstances.

Example 1. Assume that the abilities are distributed uniformly. Suppose $\bar{v}^{[2]}(a_i, .) = a_i^{10}$ and $v^{[2]}(a_i, .) = a_i$, and there are $k > 4$ contestants. So, $g^{[1]}(a) = (k-1)a^{k-2}$ and $g^{[2]}(a) = (k-1)[(k-2) - (k-1)a]a^{k-3}$.

Now, $\int_m^{a_i} v^{[2]}(z, z) z g^{[2]}(z)\, dz = (k-1)\left[\frac{k-2}{k}a_i^k - \frac{k-1}{k+1}a_i^{k+1}\right]$ and $\int_m^{a_i} \bar{v}^{[2]}(z, z) z g^{[1]}(z)\, dz = \frac{k-1}{k+10}a_i^{k+10}$. Therefore, $\int_m^1 [\int_m^{a_i} v^{[2]}(z, z) z g^{[2]}(z)\, dz] f(a_i)\, da_i = (k-1)\left[\frac{k-2}{k(k+1)} - \frac{k-1}{(k+1)(k+2)}\right]$, and we also have $\int_m^1 \left[\int_m^{a_i} \bar{v}^{[2]}(z, z) z g^{[1]}(z)\, dz\right] f(a_i)\, da_i = \frac{k-1}{(k+10)(k+11)}$. Finally, if $k > 4$, then it is optimal for the contest designer to offer multiple prizes because in that case we have $(k-1)\left[\frac{k-2}{k(k+1)} - \frac{k-1}{(k+1)(k+2)}\right] > \frac{k-1}{(k+10)(k+11)}$. Note that the cost function here is linear, and this shows the difference between our results and results derived by Moldovanu and Sela.

Non-linear Cost and Performance Functions

Now we are going to concentrate on non-linear cost and performance functions. In case of a non-linear cost function, C can take any shape, but we will only focus on concave and convex cost functions. Also, the same holds true for the performance function (P).

Proposition 6. *The symmetric equilibrium bidding strategy is given by*

$$b^{[2]}(a_i) = \Omega^{-1}\left[\int_m^{a_i} v^{[1]}(z, z) z g^{[1]}(z)\, dz + \int_m^{a_i} v^{[2]}(z, z) z g^{[2]}(z)\, dz\right],$$

where $\Omega = C\left(P^{-1}\right)$.

Proof. See Appendix 7A.6.

Now let us calculate the sum of expected performances in case of non-linear cost functions. The sum of expected performances for all the contestants in the case of two prizes is given by

$$\Phi_2 = k \int_m^1 b^{[2]}(a_i) f(a_i) da_i$$
$$= k \int_m^1 \Omega^{-1} \left[\int_m^{a_i} v^{[1]}(z, z) z g^{[1]}(z) dz + \int_m^{a_i} v^{[2]}(z, z) z g^{[2]}(z) dz \right] f(a_i) da_i \cdot$$

In this section, we will briefly show that the results we derived earlier can be extended to the case where $k > p > 2$ very easily. We will proceed exactly the same way as we did earlier, that is, we will first derive the equilibrium bidding strategy of a contestant in case of $k > p > 2$, and then we will show that proposition 4 and proposition 5 still hold.

Proposition 7. *Suppose $k > p > 2$, then the symmetric equilibrium strategies in the contest are given by*

$$b^{[p]}(a_i) = \Omega^{-1} \left[\sum_{j=1}^p \int_m^{a_i} v^{[j]}(z, z) z g^{[j]}(z) dz \right].$$

Proof. See Appendix 7A.8.

The sum of expected performances of all the contestants is given by

$$\Phi_p = k \int_m^1 b^{[p]}(a_i) f(a_i) da_i$$

$$= k \int_m^1 \Omega^{-1} \left[\sum_{j=1}^p \int_m^{a_i} v^{[j]}(z, z) z g^{[j]}(z) dz \right] f(a_i) da_i.$$

Let us assume again that Ω^{-1} is a linear function such that $\Phi_p = k \int_m^1 \left[\sum_{j=1}^p \int_m^{a_i} v^{[j]}(z, z) z g^{[j]}(z) dz \right] f(a_i) da_i$. Again if we also assume that $\bar{v}^{[j]}(a_i, .) \geqslant v^{[j]}(a_i, .) \; \forall j \in [2, p]$ where $\bar{v}^{[j]}(a_i, y_1) = E\left[V^{[j]} \mid A_i = a_i, Y_1 = y_1 \right]$, then it is routine to check that all the seven lemmas hold for each $j \in [2, p]$ and, therefore, it is optimal to offer a single prize. On the other hand, if it is the case that $\bar{v}^{[j]}(a_i, .) \leqslant v^{[j]}(a_i, .) \; \forall j \in [2, p]$, then even if we assume a linear cost function, it may be the case that offering multiple prizes is optimal for the contest designer. In case of private valuation, $\bar{v}^{[j]}(a_i, .) = v^{[j]}(a_i, .) \; \forall j \in [2, p]$ so that it is optimal to offer a single prize,[5] but interdependent valuation makes things

---

[5] See Moldovanu and Sela (2001).

much more complicated even in the case of linear cost and performance functions.

Conclusion

Contest under interdependent valuations is much more complicated than that under private values. We have analysed contest under interdependent valuations with multiple prizes; here, we have assumed that the valuations of all the contestants for all the prizes are functions of the abilities of all the contestants.

We have first derived equilibrium bidding strategy of a contestant where the contest designer can offer at most two prizes. Consider two cases. In both the cases, the cost and the performance functions are linear in effort. Now, in the first case, there are two prizes[6] P_1 and P_2, and the expected valuation of P_2 to the second prize winner of the contest is V_2. In the second case, there is a single prize P which is a bundle of goods consisting of P_1 and P_2, and the expected valuation of P_2 to the first prize winner of the contest is $\overline{V}_2$. We have shown that if $\overline{V}_2 \geqslant V_2$, then it is optimal to offer a single prize, otherwise it may be optimal to offer multiple prizes. In case of private value $\overline{V}_2 = V_2$, therefore, it is optimal to offer a single prize.[7] So the private value case is a special case of interdependent valuations.

Next we have derived the equilibrium bidding strategy of a contestant with general cost and performance functions. Finally, we have derived the equilibrium bidding strategy of a contestant where the contest designer can offer more than two prizes. We have argued that it may be the case that even with linear cost and performance functions offering multiple prizes is optimal. This stands in contrast to the private value case.

Appendix 7A.1

Note that because $v^{[1]}(a_i, a_i)a_i g^{[1]}(a_i) + v^{[2]}(a_i, a_i)a_i g^{[2]}(a_i) = b^{[2]/}(a_i)$ and because all $a_i > m$ imply for all $j \in [1, p]$, $v^{[j]}(a_i, .) > 0$, we have

$$v^{[1]}(a_i, a_i)a_i g^{[1]}(a_i) + v^{[2]}(a_i, a_i)a_i g^{[2]}(a_i)$$
$$\geqslant \left[g^{[1]}(a_i) + g^{[2]}(a_i)\right] a_i v^{[2]}(a_i, a_i)$$
$$= (k - 1)(k - 2)F(a_i)^{k-3}(1 - F(a_i))F'(a_i)a_i v^{[2]}(a_i, a_i) > 0.$$

---

[6] Both the prizes are indivisible in nature.

[7] Our study, therefore, generalize the study of Moldovanu and Sela (2001).

Now consider a contestant who bids $b^{[2]}(z)$ when her signal is a_i. The expected profit from such a bid can be written as

$$\Pi(z, a_i) = \int_m^z v^{[1]}(a_i, y_1)g^{[1]}(y_1)dy_1 + \int_m^z v^{[2]}(a_i, y_2)g^{[2]}(y_2)dy_2 - \frac{b^{[2]}(z)}{a_i}$$

since $b^{[2]}$ is increasing.

Differentiating with respect to z yields

$$\frac{\partial \Pi}{\partial z} = v^{[1]}(a_i, z)g^{[1]}(z) + v^{[2]}(a_i, z)g^{[2]}(z) - \frac{b^{[2]\prime}(z)}{a_i}.$$

If $z < a_i$, then since $v^{[1]}(a_i, z) > v^{[1]}(z, z)$ and $v^{[2]}(a_i, z) > v^{[2]}(z, z)$, we obtain that

$$\frac{\partial \Pi}{\partial z} > v^{[1]}(z, z)g^{[1]}(z) + v^{[2]}(z, z)g^{[2]}(z) - \frac{b^{[2]\prime}(z)}{a_i}$$
$$> v^{[1]}(z, z)g^{[1]}(z) + v^{[2]}(z, z)g^{[2]}(z) - \frac{b^{[2]\prime}(z)}{z} = 0.$$

Similarly, if $z > a_i$, then $\frac{\partial \Pi}{\partial z} < 0$. Thus, $\Pi(z, x)$ is maximized by choosing $z = x$.

Appendix 7A.2

Consider a contest in which the highest performer gets both the prizes as a winner-take-all single prize, that is, there is a single first prize (v) only such that $v(.) = v^{[1]}(.) + \bar{v}^{[2]}(.)$. Then the pay-off of contestant i when the equilibrium bidding strategy is $b^{[1]}$ is given by

$$\Pi(z, a_i) = \int_m^z v(a_i, y_1)g^{[1]}(y_1)dy_1 - \frac{b^{[1]}(z)}{a_i}$$
$$= \int_m^z \left[v^{[1]}(a_i, y_1) + \bar{v}^{[2]}(a_i, y_1) \right] g^{[1]}(y_1)dy_1 - \frac{b^{[1]}(z)}{a_i}.$$

It is routine to check that in this case the symmetric equilibrium bidding strategy of a contestant with ability a_i is given by

$$b^{[1]}(a_i) = \int_m^{a_i} \left[v^{[1]}(z, z) + \bar{v}^{[2]}(z, z) \right] zg^{[1]}(z)dz$$

by providing similar arguments as in Appendix 7A.1.

Appendix 7A.3

The expected sum of performances of all the contestants in the case of two prizes is

$$\Phi_2 = k \int_m^1 b^{[2]}(a_i) f(a_i) da_i$$
$$= k \int_m^1 \left[\int_m^{a_i} v^{[1]}(z, z) z g^{[1]}(z) dz + \int_m^{a_i} v^{[2]}(z, z) z g^{[2]}(z) dz \right] f(a_i) da_i$$
$$= k \int_m^1 \left[\int_m^{a_i} v^{[1]}(z, z) z g^{[1]}(z) dz \right] f(a_i) da_i$$
$$+ \int_m^1 \left[\int_m^{a_i} v^{[2]}(z, z) z g^{[2]}(z) dz \right] f(a_i) da_i.$$

Similarly, the expected sum of performances of all the contestants in the case of a single first prize is

$$\Phi_1 = k \int_m^1 b^{[1]}(a_i) f(a_i) da_i$$
$$= k \int_m^1 \left[\int_m^{a_i} \left[v^{[1]}(z, z) + \bar{v}^{[2]}(z, z) \right] z g^{[1]}(z) dz \right] f(a_i) da_i$$
$$= k \int_m^1 \left[\int_m^{a_i} v^{[1]}(z, z) z g^{[1]}(z) dz \right] f(a_i) da_i$$
$$+ k \int_m^1 \left[\int_m^{a_i} \bar{v}^{[2]}(z, z) z g^{[1]}(z) dz \right] f(a_i) da_i.$$

Finally, note that

$$(\Phi_2 - \Phi_1)/k = \int_m^1 \left[\int_m^{a_i} v^{[1]}(z, z) z g^{[1]}(z) dz \right] f(a_i) da_i$$
$$+ \int_m^1 \left[\int_m^{a_i} v^{[2]}(z, z) z g^{[2]}(z) dz \right] f(a_i) da_i$$
$$- \int_m^1 \left[\int_m^{a_i} v^{[1]}(z, z) z g^{[1]}(z) dz \right] f(a_i) da_i$$
$$+ \int_m^1 \left[\int_m^{a_i} \bar{v}^{[2]}(z, z) z g^{[1]}(z) dz \right] f(a_i) da_i$$
$$= \int_m^1 \left[\int_m^{a_i} v^{[2]}(z, z) z g^{[2]}(z) dz \right] f(a_i) da_i$$
$$- \int_m^1 \left[\int_m^{a_i} \bar{v}^{[2]}(z, z) z g^{[1]}(z) dz \right] f(a_i) da_i.$$

Appendix 7A.4

These lemmas are very similar to Moldovanu and Sela (2001); only the $A(c)$ and $B(c)$ functions are different.

Lemma 1, 2 and 3 are trivial from the definitions of $A(c)$, $B(c)$ and their respective derivatives.

Note that

$$A(c) = (k - 1) \int_m^c v^{[2]}(a, a) a F(a)^{k-2} F'(a) da$$
$$B(c) = (k - 1) \int_m^c v^{[2]}(a, a) a F(a)^{k-3} F'(a) [(k - 2) - (k - 1) F(a)] da$$
$$A'(c) = (k - 1) v^{[2]}(c, c) c F(c)^{k-2} F'(c)$$
$$B'(c) = (k - 1) v^{[2]}(c, c) c F(c)^{k-3} F'(c) [(k - 2) - (k - 1) F(c)].$$

4. If $c \in (m, c*)$, then

$$|B'(c)| - |A'(c)| = B'(c) - A'(c)$$
$$= (k-1)v^{[2]}(c, c)cF(c)^{k-3}F'(c)[(k-2) - kF(c)] > 0,$$

if c is close enough to m such that $F(c) < \frac{k-2}{k}$.

5. Let $\bar{c}$ be such that $F(\bar{c}) = \frac{k-2}{k}$ and because by assumption $v^{[2]}(z, z) > 0$ $\forall z > m$, and as we have already assumed, $v^{[j]}$ are nondecreasing functions in a_i and y, and for all $j \in [1, p]$, $v^{[j]}$ are strictly increasing in a_i, we have

$$A(1) - B(1)$$
$$= (k-1)\int_m^1 v^{[2]}(t, t)tF(t)^{k-3}F'(t)[kF(t) - (k-2)]dt$$
$$= (k-1)\int_m^{\bar{c}} v^{[2]}(t, t)tF(t)^{k-3}F'(t)[kF(t) - (k-2)]dt$$
$$\quad + (k-1)\int_{\bar{c}}^1 v^{[2]}(t, t)tF(t)^{k-3}F'(t)[kF(t) - (k-2)]dt$$
$$> (k-1)v^{[2]}(\bar{c}, \bar{c})\bar{c}\left[\int_m^{\bar{c}} F(t)^{k-3}F'(t)[kF(t) - (k-2)]dt\right.$$
$$\quad \left. + \int_{\bar{c}}^1 F(t)^{k-3}F'(t)[kF(t) - (k-2)]dt\right]$$
$$= (k-1)v^{[2]}(\bar{c}, \bar{c})\bar{c}\int_m^1 F(t)^{k-3}F'(t)[kF(t) - (k-2)]dt$$
$$= (k-1)v^{[2]}(\bar{c}, \bar{c})\bar{c}\int_0^1 z^{k-3}[kz - (k-2)]dz$$
$$= (k-1)v^{[2]}(\bar{c}, \bar{c})\bar{c}\left[\frac{k}{k-1}z^{k-1} - z^{k-2}\right]_0^1$$
$$= v^{[2]}(\bar{c}, \bar{c})\bar{c} > 0.$$

The fourth equality is obtained by assuming $z = F(t)$. Then it follows that

- $a = m$ implies $z = F(m) = 0$,
- $a = 1$ implies $z = F(1) = 1$ and
- $dz = F'(t)dt$.

6. The first result of the lemma shows that both $A(c)$ and $B(c)$ curves start from the origin. The second result of the lemma implies that the curve $A(c)$ always lies in the positive quadrant, and it is strictly increasing for all $c > m$. The third result illustrates that $B(c)$ is a concave function. That is to say initially $B(c)$ increases with the ability and reaches a maximum at ability equal to $c*$, and after that it decreases. The fourth result shows that the curve $B(c)$ in the neighbourhood of its starting point lies above $A(c)$. The fifth result shows that $B(c)$ again intersects $A(c)$ at ability $c*|*$, where $c*|* < 1$. And after that $B(c)$ is always less

than $A(c)$. Combining all these results, we have this result, which claims that except at $c = m$ the curves $A(c)$ and $B(c)$ will intersect at a point $c * |* > m$.

7. We know that $B(c) - A(c) > 0 \forall c \in (m, c * | *)$ and that $B(c) - A(c) < 0 \forall c \in (c **, 1)$. Again, because by assumption $v^{[2]}(z, z) > 0 \; \forall z > m$, and as we have already assumed, $v^{[j]}$ are non-decreasing functions in a_i and y and for all $j \in [1, p]$, $v^{[j]}$ are strictly increasing in a_i, we have

$$\int_m^1 (B(c) - A(c)) F'(c) dc$$
$$= \int_m^c ** (B(c) - A(c)) F'(c) dc + \int_c **^1 (B(c) - A(c)) F'(c) dc$$
$$= (k-1) \int_m^{c**} \left[\int_m^c v^{[2]}(a, a) a F(a)^{k-3} [(k-2) - kF(a)] F'(a) da \right] F'(c) dc$$
$$+ (k-1) \int_{c**}^1 \left[\int_m^c v^{[2]}(a, a) a F(a)^{k-3} [(k-2) - kF(a)] F'(a) da \right] F'(c) dc$$
$$< (k-1) v^{[2]}(c**, c**) c** \int_m^{c**} \left[\int_m^c F(a)^{k-3} [(k-2) - kF(a)] F'(a) da \right] F'(c) dc$$
$$+ (k-1) v^{[2]}(c**, c**) c** \int_{c**}^1 \left[\int_m^c F(a)^{k-3} [(k-2) - kF(a)] F'(a) da \right] F'(c) dc$$
$$= (k-1) v^{[2]}(c**, c**) c** \int_m^1 \left[\int_m^c F(a)^{k-3} [(k-2) - kF(a)] F'(a) da \right] F'(c) dc$$
$$= (k-1) v^{[2]}(c**, c**) c** \int_m^1 \left[\int_0^{F(c)} z^{k-3} [(k-2) - kz] dz \right] F'(c) dc$$
$$= (k-1) v^{[2]}(c**, c**) c** \int_m^1 \left[z^{k-2} - \tfrac{k}{k-1} z^{k-1} \right]_0^{F(c)} F'(c) dc$$
$$= (k-1) v^{[2]}(c**, c**) c** \int_m^1 \left[F(c)^{k-2} - \tfrac{k}{k-1} F(c)^{k-1} \right] F'(c) dc$$
$$= (k-1) v^{[2]}(c**, c**) c** \int_0^1 \left[v^{k-2} - \tfrac{k}{k-1} v^{k-1} \right] dv$$
$$= (k-1) v^{[2]}(c**, c**) c** \left[\tfrac{v^{k-1}}{k-1} - \tfrac{v^k}{k-1} \right]_0^1 = 0.$$

The fourth equality is obtained by assuming $z = F(a)$. Then it follows that

- $a = m$ implies $z = F(m) = 0$,
- $a = c$ implies $z = F(c)$, and
- $dz = F'(a) da$.

The seventh equality is obtained by assuming $v = F(c)$. Then it follows that

- $c = m$ implies $v = F(m) = 0$
- $c = 1$ implies $v = F(1) = 1$, and
- $dv = F'(c) dc$.

Appendix 7A.5

$(\Phi_1 - \Phi_2)/k$

$$\geqslant \int_m^1 \left[\int_m^{a_i} v^{[1]}(z,z)zg^{[1]}(z)dz \right] f(a_i)da_i + \int_m^1 A(a_i)f(a_i)da_i$$

$$\qquad - \int_m^1 \left[\int_m^{a_i} v^{[1]}(z,z)zg^{[1]}(z)dz \right] f(a_i)da_i + \int_m^1 B(a_i)f(a_i)da_i$$

$$= \int_m^1 A(a_i)f(a_i)da_i - \int_m^1 B(a_i)f(a_i)da_i$$

$$= \int_m^1 \left[A(a_i) - B(a_i) \right] f(a_i)da_i$$

We know from Lemma 7 that $\int_m^1 \left[A(a_i) - B(a_i) \right] f(a_i)da_i > 0$.

Appendix 7A.6

First note that Ω^{-1} exists because by assumption C and P are both strictly increasing functions of effort. Also, we know that Ω^{-1} is a strictly increasing function. The expected pay-off of the contestant i when her signal is a_i and she puts in effort $b^{[2]}(z)$ is

$$\Pi(z, a_i) = \int_m^z v^{[1]}(a_i, y_1)g^{[1]}(y_1)dy_1$$

$$\qquad + \int_m^z v^{[2]}(a_i, y_2)g^{[2]}(y_2)dy_2 - \frac{\Omega(b^{[2]}(z))}{a_i}.$$

The first-order condition is

$$v^{[1]}(a_i, z)g^{[1]}(z) + v^{[2]}(a_i, z)g^{[2]}(z) - \Omega'(b^{[2]}(z))\frac{b^{[2]\prime}(z)}{a_i} = 0$$

$$\Leftrightarrow v^{[1]}(a_i, z)g^{[1]}(z) + v^{[2]}(a_i, z)g^{[2]}(z) = \Omega'(b^{[2]}(z))\frac{b^{[2]\prime}(z)}{a_i}$$

$$\Leftrightarrow v^{[1]}(a_i, z)a_ig^{[1]}(z) + v^{[2]}(a_i, z)a_ig^{[2]}(z) = \Omega'(b^{[2]}(z))b^{[2]\prime}(z).$$

At a symmetric equilibrium, it is optimal to bid according to $z = a_i$; so setting $z = a_i$ in the first-order condition, we obtain the differential equation

$$v^{[1]}(a_i, a_i)a_ig^{[1]}(a_i) + v^{[2]}(a_i, a_i)a_ig^{[2]}(a_i) = \Omega'(b^{[2]}(a_i))b^{[2]\prime}(a_i). \quad (7.2)$$

Since, by assumption, $v(m, m) = 0$, it is the case that $b(m) = 0$. Thus associated, with equation (7.2), we have the boundary condition $b(m) = 0$. The solution to the differential equation (7.2) together with the boundary condition $b(m) = 0$ constitutes a symmetric equilibrium, which is given as

$$b^{[2]}(a_i) = \Omega^{-1} \left[\int_m^{a_i} v^{[1]}(z,z)zg^{[1]}(z)dz + \int_m^{a_i} v^{[2]}(z,z)zg^{[2]}(z)dz \right].$$

Note that the equilibrium bidding function is a strictly increasing function of ability because $\Omega^{-1}(.)$ is strictly increasing and we have already proved in the section on linear cost and performance functions that $\int_m^{a_i} v^{[1]}(z,z)zg^{[1]}(z)dz + \int_m^{a_i} v^{[2]}(z,z)zg^{[2]}(z)dz$ is a strictly increasing function of ability in the domain $(m, 1)$. Because cost and performance are strictly increasing functions of effort, one can check the second-order condition in the way shown in the Appendix 7A.1.

Appendix 7A.7

Note that in this case, the pay-off function of the contestant i when her signal is a_i and she puts in effort $b^{[p]}(z)$ is given by

$$\Pi(z, a_i) = \sum_{j=1}^p \int_m^z v^{[j]}(a_i, y_j)g^{[j]}(y_j)dy_j - \frac{\Omega(b^{[p]}(z))}{a_i}.$$

The rest of the proof is similar to $p = 2$ case as presented earlier.

References

Abrevaya, J. 2002. 'Ladder Tournaments and Underdogs: Lessons from Professional Bowling', *Journal of Economic Behavior and Organization*, 47(1):87–101.

Glazer, Amihai and Refael Hassin. 1988. 'Optimal Contests', *Economic Inquiry*, 26(1):133–43.

Groh, C., B. Moldovanu, A. Sela and U. Sunde. 2003. 'Optimal Seedings in Elimination Tournaments', *Economic Theory*, 49(1):59–80.

Lazear, E. P. and S. Rosen. 1981. 'Rank-Order Tournaments as Optimum Labor Contracts', *Journal of Political Economy*, 89(5):841–64.

Moldovanu, B. and R. Sela. 2001. 'The Optimal Allocation of Prizes in Contests', *The American Economic Review*, 91(3):542–58.

———. 'Contest Architecture', *Journal of Economic Theory*, 126(1):70–96.

Taylor, Curtis R. 1995. 'Digging for Golden Carrots: An Analysis of Research Tournaments', *American Economic Review*, 85(4):873–90.

Tullock, Gordon. 1980. 'Efficient Rent-Seeking', in James M. Buchanan, Robert D. Tollison and Gordon Tullock (eds), *Towards a Theory of the Rent-Seeking Society*. College Station, TX: Texas A&M University Press, pp. 97–112.

CHAPTER 8

Auctions with Synergy

Srobonti Chattopadhyay and Rittwik Chatterjee

The notions of superadditive and subadditive values are very important in the context of auctions with synergy. Superadditive or subadditive values characterize many types of objects. Superadditive values are said to be present when having more than one object together yields a value higher than the sum of the individual values of the objects. This is also termed as positive synergy. This means that supposing that there are two objects, A and B, and denoting the valuations of bidder i for them by $x^i(A)$ and $x^i(B)$ respectively, and the valuation for the package consisting of A and B by $x^i(A \cup B)$, we say there exists a positive synergy if $x^i(A \cup B) > x^i(A) + x^i(B)$.[1]

Similarly, when having more than one objects yields a value lower than the sum of the individual values of the objects, there is a situation with subadditive values. This is also known as negative synergy. This means that there exists negative synergy if $x^i(A \cup B) < x^i(A) + x^i(B)$.[2]

One ready example of an object with positive synergy is a radio-frequency spectrum, as discussed by Milgorm (2004). Other than that, Hendricks and Porter (1988) talk about the presence of positive synergy for drainage tracts (that is, oil tracts adjacent to tracts on which deposits have been discovered). Leufkens et al. (2010) refer to synergies (cost benefits) for bidders through winning multiple contracts for construction, military procurement, and so on.

---

[1] Superadditive value has been defined following Krishna (2010).
[2] Subadditive value has been defined following Krishna (2010).

Literature Review

Krishna and Rosenthal (1996) model a radio-frequency spectrum auction for which there had been significant economies of scale in the amount of the spectrum covering a particular geographic area and economic advantages of various types associated with owning licenses that collectively cover large and/or continuous geographic areas. They consider two types of bidders: local bidders, who are interested in just one unit and global bidders, interested in more than one units. They observe that the synergies are most significant for the bidders who are interested in establishing large personal communications service (PCS) networks. Their essay seeks to capture the interactions of the following three elements: the simultaneous sale of multiple items at auction; the presence of two kinds of bidders, local and global; and increasing returns for the global bidders. In case of simultaneous second price sealed-bid auctions, involving a single global bidder, two objects, and the same numbers of local bidders for each auction, the bidding strategies are calculated. Then they provide more general cases involving more than one global bidders and multiple objects. Finally they compare such simultaneous auction formats to sequential auctions.

Rosenthal and Wang (1996) analyse simultaneous auctions with synergies and common values. They consider m objects which are offered for sale in a simultaneous, first price sealed bid auction. They consider these objects to be arranged on a circle, so that each object has two neighbouring objects. For each object there are three groups of interested bidders. First, there is the local group, whose members are interested just in a single object. Therefore, for them no synergy factor exists. There are two types of 'global' groups. The members in these groups are interested in any object together with its neighbour on left and on right respectively. For both these groups, the positive synergy element is quite significant. The common values of the individual objects are perfectly correlated, so that either all the objects are high-valued, or all are all low-valued. Each bidder receives a private, binary-valued signal on which she can condition her bid. These signals are assumed to be conditionally independent given the true state. The synergy term is positive only in the high state. The essay constructs two qualitatively different equilibria in mixed strategies, valid only over a nonempty subset of the set of possible parameter-value combinations for the model. Winner's curse considerations suggest that the local bidders are at a severe disadvantage in this model, but the disadvantage is never large enough to prevent them from participating and a local indeed wins with positive probability in both equilibria. The results of the essay show that the increase in the size of the synergy term makes global bidders more aggressive and unambiguously improves both efficiency and seller's revenue. Also, efficiency increases in the number of global bidders and the presence of local bidders unambiguously reduces seller's expected revenue as compared to the case in which no locals are present.

Menezes and Monteiro (2004) elaborate on sequential auctions with synergies. They consider sequential auctions separately for the cases of positive and negative synergies. Their framework involves a more general form of synergies as compared to Krishna and Rosenthal (1996). When two units together yield a higher value than the sum of the individual units separately, whichever bidder wins the first object has a greater opportunity to realize the synergy. Therefore, the first period price includes a premium that reflects this opportunity. The results they derive show that expected prices decline in the presence of positive synergies and increase in the presence of negative synergies. Thus, they suggest that positive synergies can be one of the possible factors that contribute to price decline anomaly in sequential auctions. Their results suggest, that, first, the seller is indifferent between selling the objects simultaneously as a bundle or sequentially when synergies are positive; second, when synergies are negative, the sequential auction might yield higher expected revenue than the simultaneous auction. Third, in presence of positive synergy buying an object at the same price as the first object never happens in a symmetric equilibrium. Contrary to this, if there is an equilibrium where this option of buying an additional object at the same price as the first object is never exercised, then the equilibrium prices may either increase or decrease. Therefore, the net effect on the seller's revenue of the introduction of such an option is ambiguous.

Menezes and Monteiro (2005) also analyse muti-unit auctions with synergies for single unified formats. They discuss the bidding strategies under the sequential auctions, and different single-stage auctions like discriminatory auctions, uniform price auctions and optimal auctions separately for positive and negative synergies. Here also, they show that expected prices decline in subsequent stages.

Xu et al. (2010) analyse auctions with synergy and resale. They consider two bidders, two objects and a sequential auction. Here, the winner of the package obtains a synergy from the second object. If reselling occurs after the two auctions, it proceeds as either a monopoly or a monopsony take-it-or-leave-it offer. They find that post-auction resale has a significant impact on bidding strategies in the auctions: Under the monopoly offer, there does not exist any equilibrium (symmetric or asymmetric) where the bidders reveal their types truthfully with positive probability. Under the monopsony offer, however, symmetric, increasing bidding strategies for both the objects can be identified. While resale increases efficiency, its effect on expected revenue and probability of exposure are both ambiguous.

Most of the literature, however, deals with cases where the synergy parameters are the same for the agents who have either superadditive or subadditive values. As discussed earlier, Menezes and Monteiro (2004) have analysed the issue of asymmetric synergy parameters with sequential second-price auctions. Therefore, it seems interesting to explore the case of a single-stage unified auction where different agents have different synergy parameters. In this essay, we restrict ourselves to only sealed-bid formats of single-stage unified multiple unit auctions.

There are primarily three standard sealed-bid multiple unit auction formats: the discriminatory auction, the uniform price auction and the Vickrey auction. Here, we must note that in multiple unit auctions, every bidder submits a bid vector, each element of which indicates the bid for distinct individual units. All the bid vectors are taken together and then, supposing that there are k units offered for sale, the k highest bids are selected as the winning bids and the objects are accordingly awarded to the corresponding bidders. In the discriminatory auction, the winning bidders have to pay their own bids. In the uniform price auction, all the winning bidders have to pay the same price. Now, the standard results in auction literature suggest that this price, in a symmetric equilibrium, can be either the highest losing bid or the lowest winning bid or any price in between these two; however, the general convention is to set the highest losing bid as the uniform price to be paid by all the winning bidders (Krishna 2010: 177). In the Vickrey auction, the bidder who wins, say, k^i units out of k units is supposed to pay k^i highest losing bids of the other bidders, that is, k^i highest losing bids excluding her own. When there is a single unit demand for all bidders, the uniform price auction and the Vickrey auction become identical.

In this essay, to start with, we consider just two agents and a Vickrey auction. We first derive the general formula for both negative and positive synergies separately.

The Model

In this section, we first state the assumptions of the model and then elaborate on the cases of positive and negative synergies separately.

Structure of the Model

There are two units of a homogeneous commodity. There are two bidders each having a demand for both the units. Each bidder has a synergy in demand, but the synergy parameter is different for the two bidders. The valuation for the first unit (or a single unit) of the concerned commodity for each bidder is distributed over the same interval $[0, \omega]$ following the same distribution function $F(.)$ which has a continuous density $f(.)$. The valuations are private information and they are distributed independently. The distribution function (and, hence, the density) and the interval are common knowledge. The synergy parameters for bidders 1 and 2 are α and γ respectively so that their respective marginal valuation vectors are $(x, (\alpha - 1)x)$ and $(y, (\gamma - 1)y)$, where x and y are respectively the valuations for the first unit for bidders 1 and 2. The values of the synergy parameters α and γ are common knowledge. The seller has a zero valuation for each unit. We assume all the agents, that is, the bidders as well as the seller, to be risk neutral. The bidders submit their bids in order to maximize their expected pay-offs. Here, in each of the following cases, we derive the formula for expected payments for each bidder and, therefore, the expected revenue to the seller in a general framework. We must note here that our analysis holds true when the mechanism satisfies individual rationality, that is, the bidders are at least as well off from participating in the auction as from abstaining.[3]

Case of Positive Synergy

We look at a Vickrey auction involving these two bidders. The results from the existing literature suggest that both the bidders will bid their true demand function (Krishna 2010) which are nothing but their marginal valuation vectors. Therefore, the bids submitted by bidders 1 and 2 will be $(x, \min\{(\alpha - 1)x, \omega\})$ and $(y, \min\{(\gamma - 1)y, \omega\})$ respectively. As will be elaborated later, one can infer that for bidder 1, the necessary and sufficient condition for winning both the units does not depend on the bid for the second unit. Similarly, winning

---

[3] This assumption ensures that there is no risk of an exposure problem.

at least one unit is ensured by bidding ω for the second unit. So, in either case, the bidder has no incentive to bid more than ω for the second unit. The same logic holds true for bidder 2. When $\alpha, \gamma > 2$, we have a situation where both the bidders have positive synergy. In the auction, either bidder 1 wins both the units or bidder 2 wins both the units or each bidder wins a single unit. Bidder 1 wins both the units when $(\gamma - 1) y < x$, and similarly, bidder 2 wins both the units when $(\alpha - 1)x < y$. So the probability that bidder 1 wins both the units is the probability of the event $(\gamma - 1) y < x$, which is the same as the probability of the event $y < \frac{x}{\gamma-1}$, which is simply $F(\frac{x}{\gamma-1})$. Similarly, we can check that the probability that bidder 2 wins both the units is simply $F(\frac{y}{\alpha-1})$. The situation where each bidder wins a single unit arises when $\omega \geq (\alpha - 1)x > y$ and $\omega \geq (\gamma - 1) y > x$. In this situation, we basically have $\frac{x}{\gamma-1} < y < \min\{(\alpha - 1)x, \omega\}$ from bidder 1's perspective and $\frac{y}{\alpha-1} < x < \min\{(\gamma - 1) y, \omega\}$ from bidder 2's perspective (since both x and y are private information, bidders 1 and 2 do not know the values of y and x respectively with certainty). The probability that each bidder wins one unit from bidder 1's perspective will be $(F(\min\{(\alpha - 1)x, \omega\}) - F(\frac{x}{\gamma-1}))$, and this probability from bidder 2's perspective will be $\left(F\left(\min\left\{(\gamma - 1) y, \omega\right\}\right) - F\left(\frac{y}{\alpha-1}\right)\right)$.

The expected payment of bidder 1 when she wins both the units will be

$$F\left(\frac{x}{\gamma - 1}\right) \left[E\left((\gamma - 1) y\mid (\gamma - 1) y < x\right) + E\left(y\mid (\gamma - 1) y < x\right)\right].$$

The expected payment when she wins a single unit will be

$$\left(F\left(\min\left\{(\alpha - 1)x, \omega\right\}\right) - F\left(\frac{x}{\gamma - 1}\right)\right)$$

$$E\left[y\mid \frac{x}{\gamma - 1} < y < \min\{(\alpha - 1)x, \omega\}\right].$$

Similarly, the expected payment of bidder 2 when she wins both the units will be

$$F\left(\frac{y}{\alpha - 1}\right) \left[E\left((\alpha - 1)x\mid (\alpha - 1)x < y\right) + E\left(x\mid (\alpha - 1)x < y\right)\right].$$

The expected payment when she wins a single unit will be

$$\left(F \left(\min \left\{ (\gamma - 1)\, y, \omega \right\} \right) - F \left(\frac{y}{\alpha - 1} \right) \right)$$

$$E \left(x \big| \frac{y}{\alpha - 1} < x < \min \left\{ (\gamma - 1)\, y, \omega \right\} \right).$$

Therefore, the total expected payment for the whole auction can be written for bidder 1, after simplifying the terms, as

$$E\,[P_1] = F \left(\frac{x}{\gamma - 1} \right) \left[E \left((\gamma - 1)\, y \big| (\gamma - 1)\, y < x \right) + E \left(y \big| (\gamma - 1)\, y < x \right) \right]$$

$$+ \left(F \left(\min \{ (\alpha - 1)\, x, \omega \} \right) - F \left(\frac{x}{\gamma - 1} \right) \right)$$

$$E \left[y \big| \frac{x}{\gamma - 1} < y < \min \{ (\alpha - 1)\, x, \omega \} \right]$$

$$= \gamma \int\limits_{0}^{\frac{x}{\gamma-1}} y f\,(y)\,dy + \int_{\frac{x}{\gamma-1}}^{\min\{(\alpha-1)x,\omega\}} y f\,(y)\,dy.$$

Similarly, the total expected payment for bidder 2 for the whole auction can, after simplifying the terms, be written as

$$E\,[P_2] = F \left(\frac{y}{\alpha - 1} \right) \left[E \left((\alpha - 1)\, x \big| (\alpha - 1)\, x < y \right) + E \left(x \big| (\alpha - 1)\, x < y \right) \right]$$

$$+ \left(F \left(\min \left\{ (\gamma - 1)\, y, \omega \right\} \right) - F \left(\frac{y}{\alpha - 1} \right) \right)$$

$$E \left(x \big| \frac{y}{\alpha - 1} < x < \min \left\{ (\gamma - 1)\, y, \omega \right\} \right)$$

$$= \alpha \int\limits_{0}^{\frac{y}{\alpha-1}} x f\,(x)\,dx + \int_{\frac{y}{\alpha-1}}^{\min\{(\gamma-1)y,\omega\}} x f\,(x)\,dx.$$

Therefore, the total expected revenue for the seller from this auction will be

$$E\,[R_P] = \int\limits_{0}^{\omega} \left\{ \gamma \int\limits_{0}^{\frac{x}{\gamma-1}} y f\,(y)\,dy + \int_{\frac{x}{\gamma-1}}^{\min\{(\alpha-1)x,\omega\}} y f\,(y)\,dy \right\} f\,(x)\,dx$$

$$+ \int\limits_{0}^{\omega} \left\{ \alpha \int\limits_{0}^{\frac{y}{\alpha-1}} x f\,(x)\,dx + \int_{\frac{y}{\alpha-1}}^{\min\{(\gamma-1)y,\omega\}} x f\,(x)\,dx \right\} f\,(y)\,dy.$$

Case of Negative Synergy

When we consider negative synergy for both the bidders, we will have $\alpha, \gamma < 2$. Here also, just like the previous section, either bidder 1 wins both the units or bidder 2 wins both the units or each bidder wins one unit of the object. The bids are again the true demand functions

$(x, (\alpha - 1)x)$ and $(y, (\gamma - 1)y)$ submitted by bidders 1 and 2 respectively. In this case, very evidently $(\alpha - 1), (\gamma - 1) < 1$ and, therefore, the bid for the second unit is lower than that for the first unit for each bidder. Thus, bidder 1 wins both the units $(\alpha - 1)x > y$, while bidder 2 wins both the units when $(\gamma - 1)y > x$. Each bidder wins a single unit when $(\alpha - 1)x < y$ and $(\gamma - 1)y < x$, which effectively means $(\alpha - 1)x < y < \frac{x}{\gamma - 1}$ or $(\gamma - 1)y < x < \frac{y}{\alpha - 1}$. Proceeding exactly as was done in the previous section, we can say that the probability that bidder 1 wins both the units from the perspective of bidder 1 is $F(\min\{(\alpha - 1)x, \omega\})$, and the probability that she wins one unit will be $(F(\frac{x}{\gamma - 1}) - F(\min\{(\alpha - 1)x, \omega\}))$. Similarly, the probability that bidder 2 will win both the units from bidder 2's perspective will be $F(\min\{(\gamma - 1)y, \omega\})$, and the probability that she wins one unit will be $(F(\frac{y}{\alpha - 1}) - F(\min\{(\gamma - 1)y, \omega\}))$.

Therefore, the expected payment of bidder 1 when she wins both the units will be

$$F(\min\{(\alpha - 1)x, \omega\}) \left[E\left(y \middle| \frac{y}{\alpha - 1} < x\right) + E\left((\gamma - 1)y \middle| \frac{y}{\alpha - 1} < x\right) \right].$$

The expected payment when she wins a single unit will be

$$\left(F\left(\frac{x}{\gamma - 1}\right) - F(\min\{(\alpha - 1)x, \omega\}) \right)$$

$$E\left[(\gamma - 1)y \middle| (\alpha - 1)x < y < \frac{x}{\gamma - 1} \right].$$

Similarly, the expected payment of bidder 2, when she wins both the units will be

$$F((\gamma - 1)y) \left[E\left(x \middle| x < (\gamma - 1)y\right) + E\left((\alpha - 1)x \middle| x < x < (\gamma - 1)y\right) \right].$$

The expected payment when she wins a single unit will be

$$\left(F\left(\frac{y}{\alpha - 1}\right) - F((\gamma - 1)y) \right) E\left((\alpha - 1)x \middle| (\gamma - 1)y < x < \frac{y}{\alpha - 1} \right).$$

Therefore, the total expected payment for the whole auction can be written for bidder 1, after simplifying the terms, as

$$E[P_1] = F\left((\alpha-1)x\right)\left[E\left(x|x < (\gamma-1)y\right) + E\left((\alpha-1)x|x < (\gamma-1)y\right)\right]$$
$$+ \left(F\left(\frac{x}{\gamma-1}\right) - F\left((\alpha-1)x\right)\right)$$
$$E\left[(\gamma-1)y|(\alpha-1)x < y < \frac{x}{\gamma-1}\right]$$
$$= \gamma \int_0^{(\alpha-1)x} yf(y)\,dy + (\gamma-1)\int_{(\alpha-1)x}^{min\left\{\frac{x}{\gamma-1},\omega\right\}} yf(y)\,dy.$$

Similarly, the total expected payment for bidder 2 for the whole auction can, after simplifying the terms, be written as

$$E[P_2] = F\left((\gamma-1)y\right)\left[E\left(x|x< (\gamma-1)y\right) + E\left((\alpha-1)x| <x< (\gamma-1)y\right)\right]$$
$$+ \left(F\left(\frac{y}{\alpha-1}\right) - F\left((\gamma-1)y\right)\right)$$
$$E\left((\alpha-1)x|(\gamma-1)y < x < \frac{y}{\alpha-1}\right)$$
$$= \alpha \int_0^{(\gamma-1)y} xf(x)\,dx + \int_{(\gamma-1)y}^{min\left\{\frac{y}{\alpha-1},\omega\right\}} xf(x)\,dx.$$

Therefore, the total expected revenue for the seller from this auction will be

$$E[R_N] = \int_0^{\omega} \left\{ \gamma \int_0^{(\alpha-1)x} yf(y)\,dy + (\gamma-1)\int_{(\alpha-1)x}^{min\left\{\frac{x}{\gamma-1},\omega\right\}} yf(y)\,dy \right\} f(x)\,dx$$
$$+ \int_0^{\omega} \left\{ \alpha \int_0^{(\gamma-1)y} xf(x)\,dx + (\alpha-1)\int_{(\gamma-1)y}^{min\left\{\frac{y}{\alpha-1},\omega\right\}} xf(x)\,dx \right\} f(y)\,dy.$$

Examples

In this section, we consider three examples to compare the expected revenue from the Vickrey auction to that from other formats when the valuation on each individual unit for each bidder is distributed uniformly over [0, 1]. The first and second examples make a comparison of expected revenue from a Vickrey auction, a discriminatory auction and a uniform price auction, when there is positive and negative synergy[4] respectively, and both the bidders have the same synergy parameters. The third example makes a comparison of expected revenue from a

---

[4] The expected revenue formula for discriminatory and uniform price auctions are taken from Menezes and Monteiro (2005).

second-price sealed-bid auction for the package consisting of both the commodities to that from a Vickrey auction when the bidders have different synergy parameters.

Example 1. We consider an example here for which both the bidders have the same synergy parameter γ and the valuations of the bidders are distributed uniformly over the closed interval [0, 1]. We calculate the expected revenues for three alternative formats, for example, the discriminatory auction, the uniform price auction and the Vickrey auction. We use the bid functions given by Menezes and Monteiro (2005) for the first two formats. Now, for both the discriminatory and the uniform price auctions, the bid functions have been calculated explicitly for positive synergies, which is not the case for negative synergies. So, here we concentrate on positive synergies only.

The bid function for every unit for a discriminatory auction format (when the valuations are distributed following a continuous distribution function F over an interval $[0, \omega]$) is

$$b_D(x) = \frac{\gamma}{2F(x)} \int_0^x yf(y)\, dy.$$

Therefore, the expected revenue from the discriminatory auction, for our specific example, is

$$\begin{aligned}
E[R_D] &= 2 \int_0^1 2 \left\{ \frac{\gamma}{2x} \int_0^x y\, dy \right\} dx \\
&= 2\gamma \int_0^1 \frac{x}{2}\, dx \\
&= \gamma \left(\frac{1}{2} \right) \\
&= \frac{\gamma}{2}.
\end{aligned}$$

The bid function for each unit for a uniform price auction format (when the valuations are distributed following a continuous distribution function F over an interval $[0, \omega]$) is

$$b_U(x) = \frac{\gamma x}{2}.$$

Therefore, the expected revenue from the uniform price auction, for our specific example, is

$$\begin{aligned}
E[R_U] &= 2 \int_0^1 2\gamma \left(\frac{x}{2} \right) dx \\
&= 2\gamma \left(\frac{1}{2} \right) \\
&= \gamma.
\end{aligned}$$

Now, from our formula, the expected revenue from the Vickrey auction is

$$E[R_V] = 2\left[\gamma \int_0^1 \left\{\int_0^{\frac{x}{\gamma-1}} y dy\right\} dx + \int_0^{\frac{1}{\gamma-1}} \left\{\int_{\frac{x}{\gamma-1}}^{(\gamma-1)x} y dy\right\} dx\right.$$

$$\left. + \int_{\frac{1}{\gamma-1}}^1 \left\{\int_{\frac{x}{\gamma-1}}^1 y dy\right\} dx\right]$$

$$= 2\left[\gamma \int_0^1 \frac{x^2}{2(\gamma-1)^2} dx + \int_0^{\frac{1}{\gamma-1}} \left\{\frac{(\gamma-1)^2 x^2}{2} - \frac{x^2}{2(\gamma-1)^2}\right\} dx\right.$$

$$\left. + \int_{\frac{1}{\gamma-1}}^1 \left\{\frac{1}{2} - \frac{x^2}{2(\gamma-1)^2}\right\} dx\right]$$

$$= \frac{\gamma}{(\gamma-1)^2}\left(\frac{1}{3}\right) + \frac{(\gamma-1)^2}{3}\left\{\frac{1}{(\gamma-1)^3}\right\} - \frac{1}{3(\gamma-1)^2}\left\{\frac{1}{(\gamma-1)^3}\right\} + \left[1 - \frac{1}{\gamma-1}\right]$$

$$- \left[\frac{1}{3} - \frac{1}{3(\gamma-1)^3}\right]\frac{1}{(\gamma-1)^2}$$

$$= \frac{\gamma}{3(\gamma-1)^2} + \frac{1}{3(\gamma-1)} - \frac{1}{3(\gamma-1)^5} + 1 - \frac{1}{(\gamma-1)} - \frac{1}{3(\gamma-1)^2} + \frac{1}{3(\gamma-1)^5}$$

$$= 1 + \frac{(\gamma-1)}{3(\gamma-1)^2} - \frac{2}{3(\gamma-1)}$$

$$= 1 + \frac{1}{3(\gamma-1)} - \frac{2}{3(\gamma-1)}$$

$$= 1 - \frac{1}{3(\gamma-1)}.$$

Since we have assumed positive synergy, therefore, $\gamma > 2$ is always true. From the expressions of expected revenue in terms of γ, it is clear that $E[R_U] > E[R_D] > E[R_V]$ for our specific example.

Next we provide a similar example for the case of negative synergy.

Example 2. In case of negative synergy proceeding in the same way as in the previous example, we have found that the expected revenue from the Vickrey auction is the highest among the three auction formats considered here.

Next we proceed to compare the expected revenues from a Vickrey auction to that from a second price combinatorial auction where the bidders bid for the two items together as a package, both for the cases where the bidders have different synergy parameters.

Example 3. In this example, we first consider the situation where both the bidders have to submit a single bid for the package consisting of the two objects. It follows from the standard results of auction theory that each bidder will bid her valuation for the package, that is, the bids submitted by the bidders will be nothing but αX and γY respectively.

We assume for our case $\alpha < \gamma$. We assume the valuation for a single unit to be distributed uniformly over the interval $[0, 1]$. So from this using the transformation formula provided by Mood et al. (1974) we can easily verify that αX will be distributed uniformly over $[0, \alpha]$ and γY will be distributed uniformly over $[0, \gamma]$. Following Krishna (2010) we can derive the distribution of the selling price p in this auction, which can be written as

$$F_p\left(p\right) = Prob\left[\min\left\{\alpha X, \gamma Y\right\} \leq p\right],$$

where $p \in [0, \alpha]$. We have

$$F_p\left(p\right) = F_\alpha\left(p\right) + F_\gamma\left(p\right) - F_\alpha\left(p\right)F_\gamma\left(p\right)$$
$$= \frac{p}{\alpha} + \frac{p}{\gamma} - \left(\frac{p}{\alpha}\right)\left(\frac{p}{\gamma}\right)$$
$$= \frac{(\alpha+\gamma)p - p^2}{\alpha\gamma}.$$

The corresponding density function is

$$f_p\left(p\right) = \frac{\alpha + \gamma - 2p}{\alpha\gamma}.$$

We now proceed to calculate the expected revenue from this auction, which is nothing but the expected price, and thus obtain

$$E\left[R_C\right] = \int_0^\alpha p f_p\left(p\right) dp$$
$$= \int_0^\alpha p\left(\frac{\alpha+\gamma-2p}{\alpha\gamma}\right) dp$$
$$= \frac{\alpha+\gamma}{\alpha\gamma}\int_0^\alpha p\,dp - \frac{2}{\alpha\gamma}\int_0^\alpha p^2\,dp$$
$$= \frac{\alpha+\gamma}{\alpha\gamma}\left(\frac{\alpha^2}{2}\right) - \frac{2}{\alpha\gamma}\left(\frac{\alpha^3}{3}\right)$$
$$= \frac{\alpha(\alpha+\gamma)}{2\gamma} - \frac{2\alpha^2}{3\gamma}$$
$$= \frac{3\alpha(\alpha+\gamma) - 4\alpha^2}{6\gamma}$$
$$= \frac{3\alpha^2 + 3\alpha\gamma - 4\alpha^2}{6\gamma}$$
$$= \frac{3\alpha\gamma - \alpha^2}{6\gamma}.$$

From the formula that we have calculated for a Vickrey auction with positive synergy, we can derive the formula for expected revenue when the valuations for a single unit is uniformly distributed over $[0, 1]$.

We thus obtain

$$
E[R_P] = \gamma \int_0^1 \left\{ \int_0^{\frac{x}{\gamma-1}} y\,dy \right\} dx + \int_0^{\frac{1}{\alpha-1}} \left\{ \int_{\frac{x}{\gamma-1}}^{(\alpha-1)x} y\,dy \right\} dx + \int_{\frac{1}{\alpha-1}}^1 \left\{ \int_{\frac{x}{\gamma-1}}^1 y\,dy \right\} dx
$$

$$
+\alpha \int_0^1 \left\{ \int_0^{\frac{y}{\alpha-1}} x\,dx \right\} dy + \int_0^{\frac{1}{\alpha-1}} \left\{ \int_{\frac{y}{\alpha-1}}^{(\gamma-1)y} x\,dx \right\} dy + \int_{\frac{1}{\gamma-1}}^1 \left\{ \int_{\frac{y}{\alpha-1}}^1 x\,dx \right\} dy
$$

$$
= \gamma \int_0^1 \frac{x^2}{2(\gamma-1)^2}\,dx + \int_0^{\frac{1}{\alpha-1}} \left\{ \frac{(\alpha-1)^2 x^2}{2} - \frac{x^2}{2(\gamma-1)^2} \right\} dx + \int_{\frac{1}{\alpha-1}}^1 \left\{ \frac{1}{2} - \frac{x^2}{2(\gamma-1)^2} \right\} dx
$$

$$
+\alpha \int_0^1 \frac{y^2}{2(\alpha-1)^2}\,dy + \int_0^{\frac{1}{\alpha-1}} \left\{ \frac{(\gamma-1)^2 y^2}{2} - \frac{y^2}{2(\alpha-1)^2} \right\} dy + \int_{\frac{1}{\gamma-1}}^1 \left\{ \frac{1}{2} - \frac{y^2}{2(\alpha-1)^2} \right\} dy
$$

$$
= \frac{\gamma}{2(\gamma-1)^2} \left[\frac{1}{3} \right] + \frac{(\alpha-1)^2}{2} \left(\frac{1}{3(\alpha-1)^3} \right) - \frac{1}{2(\gamma-1)^2} \left(\frac{1}{3(\alpha-1)^3} \right) + \frac{1}{2} - \frac{1}{\alpha-1}
$$

$$
- \frac{1}{2(\gamma-1)^2} \left[\frac{1}{3} \right] + \frac{1}{2(\gamma-1)^2} \left(\frac{1}{3(\alpha-1)^3} \right) + \frac{\alpha}{2(\alpha-1)^2} \left[\frac{1}{3} \right] + \frac{(\gamma-1)^2}{2} \left(\frac{1}{3(\gamma-1)^3} \right)
$$

$$
- \frac{1}{2(\alpha-1)^2} \left(\frac{1}{3(\gamma-1)^3} \right) + \frac{1}{2} - \frac{1}{\gamma-1} - \frac{1}{2(\alpha-1)^2} \left[\frac{1}{3} \right] + \frac{1}{2(\alpha-1)^2} \left(\frac{1}{3(\gamma-1)^3} \right)
$$

$$
= \frac{\gamma}{6(\gamma-1)^2} + \frac{1}{6(\alpha-1)} + \frac{1}{2} - \frac{1}{\alpha-1} - \frac{1}{6(\gamma-1)^2} + \frac{\alpha}{6(\alpha-1)^2} + \frac{1}{6(\gamma-1)} + \frac{1}{2} - \frac{1}{\gamma-1} - \frac{1}{6(\alpha-1)^2}
$$

$$
= \frac{1}{6(\gamma-1)} + \frac{1}{6(\alpha-1)} - \frac{5}{6(\gamma-1)} - \frac{5}{6(\alpha-1)} + 1
$$

$$
= 1 - \frac{2}{3(\alpha-1)} - \frac{2}{3(\gamma-1)}
$$

$$
= \frac{3\alpha\gamma - 3\alpha - 3\gamma + 3 - 2(\alpha-1) - 2(\gamma-1)}{3(\alpha-1)(\gamma-1)}
$$

$$
= \frac{3\alpha\gamma - 3\alpha - 3\gamma + 3 - 2\alpha + 2 - 2\gamma + 2}{3(\alpha-1)(\gamma-1)}
$$

$$
= \frac{3\alpha\gamma - 5\alpha - 5\gamma + 7}{3(\alpha-1)(\gamma-1)}.
$$

Next we proceed to compare the levels of expected revenues for these two auctions and thus obtain

$$
E[R_C] - E[R_P]
$$
$$
= \frac{3\alpha\gamma - \alpha^2}{6\gamma} - \frac{3\alpha\gamma - 5\alpha - 5\gamma + 7}{3(\alpha-1)(\gamma-1)}.
$$

When $\alpha, \gamma > 2$ and $\alpha < \gamma$, we will always have $E[R_C] > E[R_P]$. (The calculations and the explanations are provided in the Appendix.)

Next we calculate the formula for expected revenue with negative synergy so that $1 < \alpha, \gamma < 2$. We retain the assumption $\alpha < \gamma$. Therefore, the expected revenue formula for the package auction remains the same.

From the formula that we have calculated for a Vickrey auction with negative synergy, we can derive the formula for expected revenue when the valuations for a single unit is uniformly distributed over [0, 1].

We thus obtain

$$
E[R_N] = \gamma \int_0^1 \left\{ \int_0^{(\alpha-1)x} y\,dy \right\} dx + (\gamma-1) \int_0^{(\gamma-1)} \left\{ \int_{(\alpha-1)x}^{\frac{x}{\gamma-1}} y\,dy \right\} dx
$$

$$
+ \int_{(\gamma-1)}^1 \left\{ \int_{(\alpha-1)x}^1 y\,dy \right\} dx + \alpha \int_0^1 \left\{ \int_0^{(\gamma-1)y} x\,dx \right\} dy
$$

$$
+ (\alpha-1) \int_0^{(\alpha-1)} \left\{ \int_{(\alpha-1)y}^{\frac{y}{\alpha-1}} x\,dx \right\} dy + \int_{(\alpha-1)}^1 \left\{ \int_{(\alpha-1)y}^1 x\,dx \right\} dy
$$

$$
= \gamma \int_0^1 \frac{(\alpha-1)^2 x^2}{2} dx + (\gamma-1) \int_0^{(\gamma-1)} \left\{ \frac{x^2}{2(\gamma-1)^2} - \frac{(\alpha-1)^2 x^2}{2} \right\} dx
$$

$$
+ \int_{(\gamma-1)}^1 \left\{ \frac{1}{2} - \frac{(\alpha-1)^2 x^2}{2} \right\} dx + \alpha \int_0^1 \frac{(\gamma-1)^2 y^2}{2} dy
$$

$$
+ (\alpha-1) \int_0^{(\alpha-1)} \left\{ \frac{y^2}{2(\alpha-1)^2} - \frac{(\gamma-1)^2 y^2}{2} \right\} dy + \int_{(\alpha-1)}^1 \left\{ \frac{1}{2} - \frac{(\gamma-1)^2 y^2}{2} \right\} dy
$$

$$
= \frac{\gamma(\alpha-1)^2}{2} \left(\frac{1}{3} \right) + (\gamma-1) \left[\frac{1}{2(\gamma-1)^2} \left\{ \frac{(\gamma-1)^3}{3} \right\} - \frac{(\alpha-1)^2}{2} \left\{ \frac{(\gamma-1)^3}{3} \right\} \right]
$$

$$
+ \left[\frac{1}{2} - \frac{(\gamma-1)}{2} \right] - \frac{(\alpha-1)^2}{2} \left(\frac{1}{3} \right) + \frac{(\alpha-1)^2}{2} \left\{ \frac{(\gamma-1)^3}{3} \right\} + \frac{\alpha(\gamma-1)^2}{2} \left(\frac{1}{3} \right)
$$

$$
+ (\alpha-1) \left[\frac{1}{2(\alpha-1)^2} \left\{ \frac{(\alpha-1)^3}{3} \right\} - \frac{(\gamma-1)^2}{2} \left\{ \frac{(\alpha-1)^3}{3} \right\} \right]
$$

$$
+ \left[\frac{1}{2} - \frac{(\alpha-1)}{2} \right] - \frac{(\gamma-1)^2}{2} \left(\frac{1}{3} \right) + \frac{(\gamma-1)^2}{2} \left\{ \frac{(\alpha-1)^3}{3} \right\}
$$

$$
= \frac{\gamma(\alpha-1)^2}{6} + \frac{(\gamma-1)^2}{2} - \frac{(\alpha-1)^2(\gamma-1)^4}{6} + \frac{1}{2} - \frac{(\gamma-1)}{2} - \frac{(\alpha-1)^2}{6} + \frac{(\alpha-1)^2(\gamma-1)^3}{6}
$$

$$
+ \frac{\alpha(\gamma-1)^2}{6} + \frac{(\alpha-1)^2}{2} - \frac{(\gamma-1)^2(\alpha-1)^4}{6} + \frac{1}{2} - \frac{(\alpha-1)}{2} - \frac{(\gamma-1)^2}{6} + \frac{(\gamma-1)^2(\alpha-1)^3}{6}
$$

$$
= \frac{(\alpha-1)^2}{6} \left[\gamma - (\gamma-1)^4 + (\gamma-1)^3 - 1 \right] - \frac{(\gamma-1)^2}{6} - \frac{(\gamma-1)}{2} + \frac{1}{2}
$$

$$
+ \frac{(\gamma-1)^2}{6} \left[\alpha - (\alpha-1)^4 + (\alpha-1)^3 - 1 \right] - \frac{(\alpha-1)^2}{6} - \frac{(\alpha-1)}{2} + \frac{1}{2}
$$

$$
= \frac{(\alpha-1)^2}{6} \left[(\gamma-1) - (\gamma-1)^3 (\gamma-1-1) \right] - \frac{(\gamma-1)}{2} \left\{ \frac{(\gamma-1)}{3} + 1 \right\} + 1
$$

$$
+ \frac{(\gamma-1)^2}{6} \left[(\alpha-1) - (\alpha-1)^3 (\alpha-1-1) \right] - \frac{(\alpha-1)}{2} \left\{ \frac{(\alpha-1)}{3} + 1 \right\}
$$

$$
= \frac{(\alpha-1)^2}{6} \left[(\gamma-1) - (\gamma-1)^3 (\gamma-2) \right] - \frac{(\gamma-1)}{2} \left\{ \frac{(\gamma+2)}{3} \right\} + 1
$$

$$
+ \frac{(\gamma-1)^2}{6} \left[(\alpha-1) - (\alpha-1)^3 (\alpha-2) \right] - \frac{(\alpha-1)}{2} \left\{ \frac{(\alpha+2)}{3} \right\}
$$

$$
= \frac{(\alpha-1)^2(\gamma-1)}{6} \left[1 - (\gamma-1)^2 (\gamma-2) \right] - \frac{(\gamma-1)(\gamma+2)}{6} + 1
$$

$$
+ \frac{(\gamma-1)^2(\alpha-1)}{6} \left[1 - (\alpha-1)^2 (\alpha-2) \right] - \frac{(\alpha-1)(\alpha+2)}{6}.
$$

Next we proceed to compare the expected revenues as follows

$$
E[R_C] - E[R_N]
$$

$$
= \frac{3\alpha\gamma - \alpha^2}{6\gamma} - \frac{(\alpha-1)^2(\gamma-1)}{6} \left[1 - (\gamma-1)^2 (\gamma-2) \right] + \frac{(\gamma-1)(\gamma+2)}{6}
$$

$$
- \frac{(\gamma-1)^2(\alpha-1)}{6} \left[1 - (\alpha-1)^2 (\alpha-2) \right] + \frac{(\alpha-1)(\alpha+2)}{6} - 1
$$

For negative synergy, we mostly obtain $E[R_C] > E[R_N]$. But for the values of the synergy parameters very close to 1, we get the opposite result (the calculations and explanations are provided in the Appendix).

Conclusion

This essay is an attempt to analyse some properties of auctions with synergy. First, it explicitly calculates the formula for expected revenue from a Vickrey auction involving two bidders and two homogeneous, indivisible objects separately for positive and negative synergies, with different synergy parameters. Then in an example the expected revenues from discriminatory auction, uniform price auction and Vickrey auction are compared when the valuations of each bidder for a single object is distributed uniformly over [0, 1], the synergy parameters are the same and there is positive synergy. The expected revenue from a discriminatory auction lies above that from a Vickrey auction and below that from a uniform price auction. In case of negative synergy, the Vickrey auction yields the highest expected revenue. Next, in another example, the expected revenues from a combined second-price auction of the two objects as a package and that from a Vickrey auction when the valuations of each bidder for a single object is distributed uniformly over [0, 1], and the synergy parameters are different for the two bidders are compared separately for positive and negative synergies.

The results derived suggest that the expected revenue from a combined second-price sealed-bid auction is higher than that from the Vickrey auction for positive synergy. When the degree of the negative synergy is very high, then the expected revenue from a Vickrey auction exceeds that from a combined second-price auction, otherwise always the reverse is true. Further scope of research lies in analysing all these situations mentioned here in a general context.

Appendix

The calculations have been conducted in a free mathematical software Maxima. The outputs are shown subsequently.

For negative synergy, we obtain a point in the interior, a point $\left(\alpha = 1.5, \gamma = 1.6\right)$ for which $E[R_C] > E[R_N]$ and another point $\left(\alpha = 1.0000001, \gamma = 1.00001\right)$ for which $E[R_C] < E[R_N]$.

In case of positive synergy, first, let us define $R(x, y) \equiv E[R_C] - E[R_P]$. Since for positive synergy, $\alpha, \gamma > 2$, therefore, α and γ are both lying in the open interval $(2, \infty)$. In our Maxima output, x represents α and y represents γ. We are interested in showing that in the above interval $R(x, y)$ is always positive.[5] For this, our objective is to show that no interior extremum and no corner points exist for which $R(x, y) < 0$.

To verify the first claim, we first check in the interior for the existence of local extrema in which $R(x, y)$ is negative. Maxima shows that there are two points in the interior where local extrema exist (we have not checked the second-order conditions here and, thus, cannot comment on the nature of the extremum). For each of these points, $R\left(x, y\right)$ is positive. Therefore, if the function has any local minima, then at that minima, $R(x, y)$ is positive. This proves the first claim.

For the second claim, let us first define the boundary points of this problem. Although the domain of $R\left(x, y\right)$ is an open interval, the boundary points of $R\left(x, y\right)$ is given by $\left(x = 2, y \geq 2\right)$ and $\left(x > 2, y \to \infty\right)$. We want to check the sign of $R\left(x, y\right)$ in the ϵ-neighbourhood of this boundary point because $R\left(x, y\right)$ is a continuous function. Therefore, if the value of $R\left(x, y\right)$ is positive at the boundary points $\left(x = 2, y \geq 2\right)$, then $R\left(x, y\right)$ will either be positive elsewhere or it will have a local extrema at the ϵ-neighbourhood of $\left(x = 2, y \geq 2\right)$. We obtain $R\left(x, y\right) > 0$ for $\left(x = 2, y \geq 2\right)$. Finally, note that $lim_{y \to \infty} R(x, y) = 3x^2 - 9x + 10$, which is always positive for all $x > 2$. So, $R\left(x, y\right) > 0$ for $\left(x > 2, y \to \infty\right)$. Since we have already checked for the existence of extreme points in the interior and no such point in the ϵ-neighbourhood of $\left(x = 2, y \geq 2\right)$ has been found, and the function is always positive for extremely large y, therefore, we can conclude that $R\left(x, y\right) > 0$ in the framework concerned.

Maxima Output

i1:   *R(x,y):=((3*(x*y)-(x^2))/(6*y))-((3*(x*y)-(5*x)-(5*y)+7)/(3*((x-1)**
(y-1))));
o1: R(x,y):=(3*(x*y)-x^2)/(6*y)-(7-5*y-5*x+3*(x*y))/(3*((x-1)*(y-1)))

i2: factor(diff(R(x,y),x));
o2: (3*x^2*y-6*x*y-y-2*x^3+4*x^2-2*x)/(6*(x-1)^2*y)

i3: factor(diff(R(x,y),y));
o3: (x*y-2*y-x)*(x*y+2*y-x)/(6*(y-1)^2*y^2)

i4: R_x(x,y):=((3*((x^2)*y)-6*(x*y)-y-2*(x^3)+4*(x^2)-2*x))/(6*
((x-1)^2)*y);

---

[5] Note that $x < y$.

o4: R_x(x,y):=(-2*x+4*x^2-2*x^3-y-6*(x*y)+3*(x^2*y))/(6*(x-1)^2*y)

i5: R_y(x, y):=((x*y-2*y-x)*(x*y+2*y-x))/(6*((y-1)^2)*y^2);
o5: R_y(x,y):=(-x-2*y+x*y)*(-x+2*y+x*y)/(6*(y-1)^2*y^2)

i6: solve([R_x(x, y)=0,R_y(x, y)=0],[x,y]);
o6: [[x=-1,y=-1],
[x=-(2*sqrt(3)*sqrt(5)*%i-20)/(sqrt(3)*sqrt(5)*%i+13),
y=-(sqrt(15)*%i-10)/23],
[x=-(2*sqrt(3)*sqrt(5)*%i+20)/(sqrt(3)*sqrt(5)*%i-13),
y=(sqrt(15)*%i+10)/23],
[x=0,y=0],
[x=3,y=3],
[x=(2*sqrt(17)-8)/(sqrt(17)-\ 3),y=4-sqrt(17)],
[x=(2*sqrt(17)+8)/(sqrt(17)+3),y=sqrt(17)+4]]

i7: R(2,y);
o7: (6*y-4)/(6*y)-(y-3)/(3*(y-1))

i8: factor((6*y-4)/(6*y)-(y-3)/(3*(y-1)));
o8: 2*(y^2-y+1)/(3*(y-1)*y)

i9:   R_N(x,y):=((3*(x*y)-(x^2))/(6*y))-(((x-1)^2*(y-1))*(1-((y-1)^2*(y-2))))/6-(((y-1)^2*(x-1))*(1-((x-1)^2*(x-2))))/6+((y-1)*(y+2))/6+((x-1)*(x+2))/6-1;
o9:   R_N(x,y):=-1+(x-1)*(2+x)/6+(y-1)*(2+y)/6+(-(y-1)^2*(x-1)*(1-(x-1)^2*(x-2)))/6-(x-1)^2*(y-1)*(1-(y-1)^2*(y-2))/6+(3*(x*y)-x^2)/(6*y)

i10: R_N(1.5,1.6);
o10: .10494166666666671

i11: R_N(1.0000001,1.00001);
o11: -.6666599333329997

References

Hendricks, K. and R. Porter. 1988. 'An Empirical Study of an Auction with Asymmetric Information', *American Economic Review*, 78(5):865–83.

Krishna, V. 2010. *Auction Theory*. San Diego: Academic Press.

Krishna, V. and R. W. Rosenthal. 1996. 'Simultaneous Auctions with Synergies', *Games and Economic Behaviour*, 17(1):1–31.

Leufkens, K., R. Peeters and D. Vermeulen. 2010. 'Sequential Auctions with Synergies: The Paradox of Positive Synergies', *Economics Letters*, 109(3):139–41.

Menezes, F. M. and P. K. Monteiro. 2004. 'Auctions with Synergies and Asymmetric Buyers', *Economics Letters*, 85(2):287–94.

———. 2005. *An Introduction to Auction Theory*. Oxford: Oxford University Press.

Milgorm, P. 2004. *Putting Auction Theory to Work*. New York: Cambridge University Press.

Mood, A. M., F. A. Graybill and D. C. Boes. 1974. *Introduction to the Theory of Statistics*. New York: McGraw-Hill.

Rosenthal, R. W. and R. Wang. 1996. 'Simultaneous Auctions with Synergies and Common Values', *Games and Economic Behaviour*, 17(1):32–55.

Xu, X., D. Levin and L. Ye. 2010. 'Auctions with Synergy and Resale', *International Journal of Game Theory*, 41(2):397–426.

CHAPTER 9

Negligence as Existence of a Cost-Justified Untaken Precaution and the Efficiency of Liability Rules

Satish K. Jain

A study of actual court judgments makes it clear that the courts employ the notion of negligence in at least two different senses. At times the courts hold a party to be negligent because its care level falls short of what the courts deem to be the due care for that party; and at times, they hold a party to be negligent on account of its failure to take some cost-justified precaution. Thus, one way to define the idea of negligence is to declare a party to be negligent if and only if its care level is less than the due care specified by the courts for the party in question; and non-negligent otherwise. Another way to define negligence is to deem a party to be negligent if and only if there exists a precaution which the party could have taken but did not and which would have cost less than the reduction in expected loss that it would have brought about.[1] These two different ways of defining negligence have very different implications for the efficiency of liability rules.

In the mainstream law and economics literature, the notion of negligence is usually defined as shortfall from the due care and

---

[1] The notion of negligence as existence of a cost-justified untaken precaution has been extensively discussed in Grady (1983, 1984, 1989).

the efficiency of liability rules—rules for apportioning accident loss between the injurer and the victim—is considered within a framework which can be termed as the standard tort model.[2] The standard tort model is concerned with two-party interactions and assumes that the probability of accident as well as the quantum of harm in case of accident depend on the care levels taken by the two parties. Both parties are assumed to be risk-neutral; and to prefer alternatives involving lower expected costs to alternatives involving higher expected costs, and to be indifferent between alternatives with equal expected costs.

A liability rule apportions the accident loss between the injurer and the victim as a function of the parties' proportions of non-negligence. A liability rule is efficient if and only if its structure is such that both parties to the interaction are invariably induced to act in ways so that total social costs of interaction are minimized. If negligence is defined as failure to take at least the due care then, within the framework of the standard tort model, efficient liability rules are characterized by the condition of negligence liability.[3] However, if negligence is defined as existence of a cost-justified untaken precaution then, within the framework of the standard tort model, there is no liability rule which is efficient.[4]

The structure of the proof of the theorem showing that there are no efficient liability rules when negligence is defined as existence of a cost-justified untaken precaution is such that the applications in which there is complementarity in cares of the two parties seem to play a crucial role. Now, from the definition of an efficient liability rule it is clear that a liability rule is inefficient if it fails to yield efficient outcome in at least one case. If instead of considering all possible applications, we consider only a subset of them, then it is clear that a liability rule which is inefficient might turn out to be efficient with respect to the subset of applications under consideration.

As mentioned earlier, the way the proof of the impossibility theorem has been constructed, complementarity in the care levels of the two parties seems to play an important role in rendering liability rules ineffi-

---

[2] What is being termed here as the standard tort model was formulated by Brown (1973); and is discussed and elaborated upon in Landes and Posner (1987) Shavell (1987) and Jain and Singh (2002), among others.

[3] A liability rule satisfies the condition of negligence liability if its structure is such that whenever one party is negligent and the other non-negligent the entire loss in case of accident is borne by the negligent party. See Jain and Singh (2002).

[4] See Jain (2006).

cient when the notion of negligence is defined in terms of cost-justified untaken precautions. Thus, an interesting question that arises is whether there are any liability rules which are efficient if we rule out complementarity in care levels. Although in actual cases complementarity in care levels cannot always be ruled out, it is also true that in most cases of interaction care levels are likely to be substitutes, even if imperfectly. Then the use of a liability rule which is efficient with respect to the subset of applications without complementarity in care levels can be expected to result in efficient outcomes in most cases likely to arise. Thus, it is important to determine whether there are any liability rules which are efficient with respect to applications in which care levels do not display complementarity. It is shown in the essay that even when complementarities are ruled out there are no liability rules which are efficient, given that negligence is defined as existence of a cost-justified untaken precaution.

Thus, the impossibility theorem regarding efficient liability rules when negligence is defined as existence of a cost-justified untaken precaution is quite robust. The proof of the theorem, apart from conclusively demonstrating that the impossibility theorem is in no way related to complementarity or otherwise in care levels of the parties, is also much simpler than in Jain (2006). It is of course immediate that the impossibility theorem with respect to all applications follows as a corollary of the theorem proved for the subset of applications without complementarity in care levels.

The essay, apart from this introduction, has three sections. The first section spells out the framework of analysis and contains, among other things, the definitions and assumptions. The proof of the theorem that there are no efficient liability rules even if complementarities in care levels are ruled out, given that negligence is defined as existence of a cost-justified untaken precaution, is provided in the second section. The last section concludes with some remarks.

Definitions and Assumptions

We consider accidents resulting from interaction of two parties, assumed to be strangers to each other, in which, to begin with, the entire loss falls on one party to be called the victim. The other party would be referred to as the injurer. We denote by $c \geq 0$ the cost of care taken by the victim; and by $d \geq 0$ the cost of care taken by the injurer. Costs of care would be assumed to be strictly increasing functions of indices of care, i.e., care levels; consequently, costs of care themselves can be taken to be indices of care.

Let

$C = \{c \mid c \geq 0$ is the cost of some feasible level of care which can be taken by the victim$\}$, and

$D = \{d \mid d \geq 0$ is the cost of some feasible level of care which can be taken by the injurer$\}$.

We will identify $c = 0$ with the victim taking no care; and $d = 0$ with the injurer taking no care.

We assume $0 \in C \wedge 0 \in D$.   (A1)

Assumption (A1) merely says that taking no care is always a feasible option for both parties.

Let π denote the probability of occurrence of accident and $H \geq 0$ the loss in case of occurrence of accident. Both π and H will be assumed to be functions of c and d; $\pi = \pi(c, d), H = H(c, d)$. Let $L = \pi H$. L is, thus, the expected loss due to accident.

We assume:

$$(\forall c, c' \in C)(\forall d, d' \in D)[[c > c' \rightarrow \pi(c, d) \leq \pi(c', d)] \wedge [d > d' \rightarrow \pi(c, d) \leq \pi(c, d')]]$$ (A2)

and

$$(\forall c, c' \in C)(\forall d, d' \in D)[[c > c' \rightarrow H(c, d) \leq H(c', d)] \wedge [d > d' \rightarrow H(c, d) \leq H(c, d')]].$$ (A3)

In other words, it is assumed that a larger expenditure on care by either party, given the expenditure on care by the other party, does not result in a higher probability of occurrence of accident or in larger accident loss.

From (A2) and (A3) it follows that:

$(\forall c, c' \in C)(\forall d, d' \in D)[[c > c' \rightarrow L(c, d) \leq L(c', d)] \wedge [d > d' \rightarrow L(c, d) \leq L(c, d')]].$

That is to say, a larger expenditure on care by either party, given the expenditure on care by the other party, results in lesser or equal expected accident loss.

Total social costs (TSC) are defined to be the sum of cost of care by the victim, cost of care by the injurer, and the expected loss due to accident; $TSC = c + d + L(c, d)$. Let $M = \{(c', d') \in C \times D \mid c' + d' + L(c', d')$ is minimum of $\{c + d + L(c, d) \mid c \in C \wedge d \in D\}\}$. Thus, M is the set of all costs of care configurations (c', d') which are TSC minimizing. It will be assumed that:

C, D and L are such that M is non-empty.   (A4)

Corresponding to each $(c, d) \in C \times D$, we define:
$C^u(c, d) = \{c^u \in C \mid c^u > c \wedge L(c, d) - L(c^u, d) > c^u - c\}$
$D^u(c, d) = \{d^u \in D \mid d^u > d \wedge L(c, d) - L(c, d^u) > d^u - d\}$.

Thus, $C^u(c, d)$ is the set of all cost-justified untaken precautions at (c, d) which the victim could have taken; and $D^u(c, d)$ is the set of all cost-justified untaken precautions at (c, d) which the injurer could have taken.

We define:

$$\hat{c}(c, d) = \sup C^u(c, d) \quad \text{if } C^u(c, d) \neq \emptyset$$
$$= c \qquad\qquad\quad \text{if } C^u(c, d) = \emptyset$$

and

$$\hat{d}(c, d) = \sup D^u(c, d) \quad \text{if } D^u(c, d) \neq \emptyset$$
$$= d \qquad\qquad\quad \text{if } D^u(c, d) = \emptyset.$$

Let I denote the closed unit interval $[0, 1]$.[5] Given C, D, π and H, we define functions p and q as follows:

$$p : C \times D \mapsto I \text{ by} : p(c, d) = \tfrac{c}{\hat{c}(c, d)} \quad \text{if } \hat{c}(c, d) \neq 0$$
$$= 1 \quad \text{if } \hat{c}(c, d) = 0$$
$$q : C \times D \mapsto I \text{ by} : q(c, d) = \tfrac{d}{\hat{d}(c, d)} \quad \text{if } \hat{d}(c, d) \neq 0$$
$$= 1 \quad \text{if } \hat{d}(c, d) = 0.$$

p and q would be interpreted as proportions of non-negligence of the victim and the injurer respectively. Consequently, $(1 - p)$ and $(1 - q)$ would denote the proportions of negligence of the victim and the injurer respectively.

---

[5] Let a and b be real numbers such that $a < b$. We use the following standard notation to denote:
by $[a, b]$ the set $\{x \mid a \leq x \leq b\}$,
by $[a, b)$ the set $\{x \mid a \leq x < b\}$,
by $(a, b]$ the set $\{x \mid a < x \leq b\}$, and
by (a, b) the set $\{x \mid a < x < b\}$.

A liability rule is a rule which specifies the proportions in which the two parties are to bear the loss in case of occurrence of accident as a function of proportions of two parties' non-negligence. Formally, a liability rule is a function f from I^2 to I^2, $f : I^2 \mapsto I^2$, such that: $f(p, q) = (x, y)$, where $x + y = 1$.

Let C, D, π and H be given. If accident takes place and loss of $H(c, d)$ materializes, then $xH(c, d)$ will be borne by the victim and $yH(c, d)$ by the injurer. As, to begin with, in case of occurrence of accident, the entire loss falls upon the victim, $yH(c, d)$ represents the liability payment by the injurer to the victim. The expected costs of the victim and the injurer, to be denoted by EC_1 and EC_2 respectively, therefore, are $[c + xL(c, d)]$ and $[d + yL(c, d)]$ respectively. Both parties are assumed to prefer smaller expected costs to larger expected costs and be indifferent between alternatives with equal expected costs.

Let f be a liability rule. An application of f consists of specification of C, D, π and H satisfying (A1)–(A4). The class of all applications satisfying (A1)–(A4) will be denoted by $\mathcal{A}$.

An application is S-restricted if $(\forall c, c' \in C)(\forall d, d' \in D)[c > c' \land d > d' \rightarrow [L(c', d) - L(c, d) \le L(c', d') - L(c, d')] \land [L(c, d') - L(c, d) \le L(c', d') - L(c', d)]]$.

We denote the class of all S-restricted applications satisfying (A1)–(A4) by $\mathcal{A}_S$.

f is defined to be efficient for a given application $< C, D, \pi, H >$ satisfying (A1)–(A4) if $(\forall(\bar{c}, \bar{d}) \in C \times D)[(\bar{c}, \bar{d})$ is a Nash equilibrium $\rightarrow (\bar{c}, \bar{d}) \in M]$ and $(\exists(\bar{c}, \bar{d}) \in C \times D)[(\bar{c}, \bar{d})$ is a Nash equilibrium]. In other words, a liability rule is efficient for a given application $< C, D, \pi, H >$ satisfying (A1)–(A4) if (a) every $(\bar{c}, \bar{d}) \in C \times D$ which is a Nash equilibrium is TSC minimizing, and (b) there exists at least one $(\bar{c}, \bar{d}) \in C \times D$ which is a Nash equilibrium. f is defined to be efficient with respect to a class of applications if it is efficient for every application belonging to that class.

The following example illustrates some of the above ideas.

Example

Let liability rule f be the rule of strict liability with the defence of contributory negligence defined by: $(\forall q \in [0, 1])(\forall p \in [0, 1])[f(p, q) = (1, 0)] \land (\forall q \in [0, 1])[f(1, q) = (0, 1)]$.

Consider the following application of f.
$C = D = \{0, 1, 2\}$.

For $(c, d) \in C \times D$, let $L(c, d)$ be as given in the following array:

		d		
		0	1	2
	0	9.0	7.0	6.5
c	1	7.0	5.0	4.5
	2	6.5	4.5	3.4

The following array gives TSC (c, d) for $(c, d) \in C \times D$.

		d		
		0	1	2
	0	9.0	8.0	8.5
c	1	8.0	7.0	7.5
	2	8.5	7.5	7.4

Thus, $(1, 1)$ is the unique TSC-minimizing configuration of costs of care.

For $(c, d) \in C \times D$, we have $C^u(c, d)$ as given in the following array:

		d		
		0	1	2
	0	$\{1, 2\}$	$\{1, 2\}$	$\{1, 2\}$
c	1	$\emptyset$	$\emptyset$	$\{2\}$
	2	$\emptyset$	$\emptyset$	$\emptyset$

And the following array gives $D^u(c, d)$ for $(c, d) \in C \times D$:

		d		
		0	1	2
	0	$\{1, 2\}$	$\emptyset$	$\emptyset$
c	1	$\{1, 2\}$	$\emptyset$	$\emptyset$
	2	$\{1, 2\}$	$\{2\}$	$\emptyset$

Therefore, the following array gives $\hat{c}(c, d)$ for $(c, d) \in C \times D$:

		d		
		0	1	2
	0	2	2	2
c	1	1	1	2
	2	2	2	2

And the following array gives $\hat{d}(c, d)$ for $(c, d) \in C \times D$:

		d		
		0	1	2
	0	2	1	2
c	1	2	1	2
	2	2	2	2

The following array gives, for $(c, d) \in C \times D$, $EC(c, d) = (EC_1(c, d), EC_2(c, d))$:

		d		
		0	1	2
	0	$(9, \underline{0})$	$(7, 1)$	$(6.5, 2)$
c	1	$(\underline{1}, 7)$	$(\underline{1}, 6)$	$(5.5, \underline{2})$
	2	$(2, 6.5)$	$(2, 5.5)$	$(\underline{2}, \underline{5.4})$

Therefore, $(2, 2)$ is the only Nash equilibrium. Thus, f is inefficient for this application.

This application violates the S-restriction as we have: $L(1, 1) - L(2, 1) = 5 - 4.5 = .5$ and $L(1, 2) - L(2, 2) = 4.5 - 3.4 = 1.1$.

S-Restricted Applications and the Efficiency of Liability Rules

Theorem 1 *There is no liability rule which is efficient for every application belonging to $\mathcal{A}_S$.*

Proof: Let f be any liability rule.

Take any $0 < p_0 < 1$ and $0 < q_0 < 1$. Denote $f(p_0, q_0)$ by (x_0, y_0); and $f(1, 1)$ by (x^*, y^*).
Suppose $x_0 < 1$.
Choose positive numbers $c_0, d_0, \epsilon_1, \epsilon_2, \epsilon_3, \epsilon_4$ such that:
1. $\epsilon_3 < \epsilon_1$

2. $\epsilon_4 < min\{(\epsilon_1 - \epsilon_3), (\frac{1}{q_0} - 1)d_0\}$

3. $\epsilon_4 < \epsilon_2$

4. $\frac{(\epsilon_1 + \frac{d_0}{q_0})x_0}{(1-p_0)(1-x_0)} < c_0.$[6]

Now consider the following application.

$C = \{0, p_0c_0, c_0\}, D = \{0, d_0, \frac{d_0}{q_0}\}.$

For $(c, d) \in C \times D$, let $L(c, d)$ be as given in the following array:

		d	
	0	d_0	$\frac{d_0}{q_0}$
0	$c_0+\epsilon_1+\frac{d_0}{q_0}+\epsilon_2$	$c_0+\epsilon_1+(\frac{1}{q_0}-1)d_0$	$c_0+\epsilon_1-\epsilon_3$
c p_0c_0	$(1-p_0)c_0+\epsilon_1+\frac{d_0}{q_0}+\epsilon_2$	$(1-p_0)c_0+\epsilon_1+(\frac{1}{q_0}-1)d_0$	$(1-p_0)c_0+\epsilon_1-\epsilon_3$
c_0	$\frac{d_0}{q_0}+\epsilon_2$	$(\frac{1}{q_0}-1)d_0$	ϵ_4

This application belongs to $\mathcal{A}_S$ as we have: $[L(0, d_0) - L(0, \frac{d_0}{q_0}) = L(p_0c_0, d_0) - L(p_0c_0, \frac{d_0}{q_0}) = (\frac{1}{q_0} - 1)d_0 + \epsilon_3 > L(c_0, d_0) - L(c_0, \frac{d_0}{q_0}) = (\frac{1}{q_0} - 1)d_0 - \epsilon_4] \wedge [L(0, 0) - L(0, d_0) = L(p_0c_0, 0) - L(p_0c_0, d_0) = L(c_0, 0) - L(c_0, d_0) = d_0 + \epsilon_2] \wedge [L(p_0c_0, 0) - L(c_0, 0) = L(p_0c_0, d_0) - L(c_0, d_0) = (1 - p_0)c_0 + \epsilon_1 > L(p_0c_0, \frac{d_0}{q_0}) - L(c_0, \frac{d_0}{q_0}) = (1 - p_0)c_0 + \epsilon_1 - \epsilon_3 - \epsilon_4] \wedge [L(0, 0) - L(p_0c_0, 0) = L(0, d_0) - L(p_0c_0, d_0) = L(0, \frac{d_0}{q_0}) - L(p_0c_0, \frac{d_0}{q_0}) = p_0c_0].$

The following array gives TSC(c, d) for $(c, d) \in C \times D$:

		d	
	0	d_0	$\frac{d_0}{q_0}$
0	$c_0 + \epsilon_1 + \frac{d_0}{q_0} + \epsilon_2$	$c_0 + \epsilon_1 + \frac{d_0}{q_0}$	$c_0 + \epsilon_1 + \frac{d_0}{q_0} - \epsilon_3$
c p_0c_0	$c_0 + \epsilon_1 + \frac{d_0}{q_0} + \epsilon_2$	$c_0 + \epsilon_1 + \frac{d_0}{q_0}$	$c_0 + \epsilon_1 + \frac{d_0}{q_0} - \epsilon_3$
c_0	$c_0 + \frac{d_0}{q_0} + \epsilon_2$	$c_0 + \frac{d_0}{q_0}$	$c_0 + \frac{d_0}{q_0} + \epsilon_4$

---

[6] This can always be done. First choose $\epsilon_3 > 0$. Next choose ϵ_1 such that it is greater than ϵ_3. Next choose $d_0 > 0$. Now, both $\epsilon_1 - \epsilon_3$ and $(\frac{1}{q_0} - 1)d_0$ are positive numbers; therefore, one can choose $\epsilon_4 > 0$ to be less than both $\epsilon_1 - \epsilon_3$ and $(\frac{1}{q_0} - 1)d_0$. Next choose ϵ_2 to be greater than ϵ_4. Finally, one chooses $c_0 > 0$ so that is greater than $\frac{(\epsilon_1 + \frac{d_0}{q_0})x_0}{(1-p_0)(1-x_0)}$.

(c_0, d_0), therefore, is the unique TSC-minimizing configuration.

We obtain $C^u(c, d)$, $(c, d) \in C \times D$, as given in the following array:

		d	
	0	d_0	$\frac{d_0}{q_0}$
0	$\{c_0\}$	$\{c_0\}$	$\{c_0\}$
$c \quad p_0 c_0$	$\{c_0\}$	$\{c_0\}$	$\{c_0\}$
c_0	$\emptyset$	$\emptyset$	$\emptyset$

And $D^u(c, d)$, $(c, d) \in C \times D$, as given in the following array:

		d	
	0	d_0	$\frac{d_0}{q_0}$
0	$\{d_0, \frac{d_0}{q_0}\}$	$\{\frac{d_0}{q_0}\}$	$\emptyset$
$c \quad p_0 c_0$	$\{d_0, \frac{d_0}{q_0}\}$	$\{\frac{d_0}{q_0}\}$	$\emptyset$
c_0	$\{d_0, \frac{d_0}{q_0}\}$	$\emptyset$	$\emptyset$

Therefore, we obtain $(\forall(c, d) \in C \times D)[\hat{c}(c, d) = c_0]$.

And $\hat{d}(c, d)$, $(c, d) \in C \times D$, as given in the following array:

		d	
	0	d_0	$\frac{d_0}{q_0}$
0	$\frac{d_0}{q_0}$	$\frac{d_0}{q_0}$	$\frac{d_0}{q_0}$
$c \quad p_0 c_0$	$\frac{d_0}{q_0}$	$\frac{d_0}{q_0}$	$\frac{d_0}{q_0}$
c_0	$\frac{d_0}{q_0}$	d_0	$\frac{d_0}{q_0}$

Now, expected costs of the victim at $(c_0, d_0) = EC_1(c_0, d_0)$
$= c_0 + x^* L(c_0, d_0)$
$= c_0 + x^*[(\frac{1}{q_0} - 1)d_0]$.
$EC_1(p_0 c_0, d_0)$
$= p_0 c_0 + x(p_0, q_0)L(p_0 c_0, d_0)$
$= p_0 c_0 + x_0[(1 - p_0)c_0 + \epsilon_1 + (\frac{1}{q_0} - 1)d_0]$.
$EC_1(c_0, d_0) - EC_1(p_0 c_0, d_0)$
$= c_0 + x^*[(\frac{1}{q_0} - 1)d_0] - p_0 c_0 - x_0[(1 - p_0)c_0 + \epsilon_1 + (\frac{1}{q_0} - 1)d_0]$

$$\geq (1 - x_0)(1 - p_0)c_0 - x_0[\epsilon_1 + (\tfrac{1}{q_0} - 1)d_0]$$
$$= (1 - x_0)(1 - p_0)c_0 - x_0[\epsilon_1 + \tfrac{d_0}{q_0}] + x_0 d_0$$
$$\geq (1 - x_0)(1 - p_0)c_0 - x_0[\epsilon_1 + \tfrac{d_0}{q_0}]$$
$$> 0, \text{ as } \frac{(\epsilon_1 + \frac{d_0}{q_0})x_0}{(1 - p_0)(1 - x_0)} < c_0.$$

Therefore, it follows that (c_0, d_0) is not a Nash equilibrium. Consequently, f is not an efficient liability rule for every application belonging to $\mathcal{A}_S$. By an analogous argument it can be shown that if $y_0 < 1$ then f is not an efficient rule for every application belonging to $\mathcal{A}_S$. As we must have $x_0 < 1 \vee y_0 < 1$, the theorem is established.

Concluding Remarks

This essay has considered one important case of restricted domain. Another important case of restricted domain is that of unilateral care. An application is a unilateral care application if the optimal care by the victim or the injurer is zero. When negligence is defined as shortfall from due care, then the set of efficient liability rules with unilateral care is a proper superset of the set of efficient liability rules with bilateral care. It is of considerable interest to investigate whether an analogous proposition is true when negligence is defined in terms of cost-justified untaken precautions.

References

Brown, John Prather. 1973. 'Toward an Economic Theory of Liability', *Journal of Legal Studies*, 2(2):323–50.

Grady, Mark F. 1983. 'A New Positive Economic Theory of Negligence', *Yale Law Journal*, 92(5):799–829.

——— 1984. 'Proximate Cause and the Law of Negligence', *Iowa Law Review*, 69(2):363–449.

——— 1989. 'Untaken Precautions', *Journal of Legal Studies*, 18(1):139–56.

Jain, Satish K. 2006. 'Efficiency of Liability Rules: A Reconsideration', *Journal of International Trade & Economic Development*, 15(3): 359–73.

Jain, Satish K. and Ram Singh. 2002. 'Efficient Liability Rules: Complete Characterization', *Journal of Economics* (*Zeitschrift für Nationalökonomie*), 75(2):105–24.

Landes, William M. and Richard A. Posner. 1987. *The Economic Structure of Tort Law.* Cambridge (MA): Harvard University Press.

Shavell, Steven. 1987. *Economic Analysis of Accident Law.* Cambridge (MA): Harvard University Press.

CHAPTER 10

The 11–20 Money Request Game and the Level-k Model: Some Experimental Results

Sugato Dasgupta, Sanmitra Ghosh and
Rajendra P. Kundu*

In an important recent paper, Arad and Rubinstein (2012) (henceforth AR) consider the following simultaneous-move two-player game. Each player requests an amount of money, where the amount is restricted to be an integer between 11 and 20 shekel. A player receives the amount that she requests; furthermore, a bonus of 20 shekel is received if she asks for exactly one shekel less than the other player. Assuming players are risk neutral and maximize the expected payoff, it is easy to check that the '11–20 money request' (henceforth 11–20) game has a unique Nash equilibrium. The first row of Table 10.1 shows the Nash equilibrium distribution. In equilibrium, players randomize over the numbers 15 to 20, with probability weights that are weakly decreasing as the numbers increase.

Using 108 undergraduate economics students from Tel Aviv University, AR experimentally study the 11–20 game. The distribution of subjects' choices in the experiment is shown in the second row of Table 10.1. A comparison of the two rows of Table 10.1 suggests, and

* The authors would like to thank Satish Jain for his advice and steadfast support. Of course, the usual disclaimer applies.

TABLE 10.1 Nash Distribution and Subjects' Choices in the AR Experiment

	Choices/Money request amounts									
	11	12	13	14	15	16	17	18	19	20
Distribution of choices in the Nash equilibrium	0%	0%	0%	0%	25%	25%	20%	15%	10%	5%
Distribution of choices in the AR experiment	4%	0%	3%	6%	1%	6%	32%	30%	12%	6%

Notes: In the 11–20 game, a player's money request amount is an integer between 11 and 20. Row 1 shows the chance of choosing each integer in the 11–20 range in the unique Nash equilibrium of the game. 108 subjects participated in the experimental test of the 11–20 game reported in AR. For this experiment, row 2 shows the percentage of subjects that chose each integer in the 11–20 range.

formal statistical tests confirm, that the Nash equilibrium fails to explain experimental findings. The main discrepancies are twofold. First, the Nash equilibrium predicts that a request of 15 or 16 shekel would be observed 50 per cent of the time; in the experiment, such a request is chosen by only 6 per cent of the subjects. Second, the Nash equilibrium predicts that a request in the 17–19 shekel range would be observed less than 50 per cent of the time; in the experiment, 74 per cent of subjects' requests are bunched on 17 to 19 shekel.[1]

Since subjects in the AR experiment play a one-shot game without precedent or communication, it is hardly surprising that their behaviour deviates *systematically* from Nash equilibrium. AR rationalize subjects' behaviour by an appeal to the level-k model,[2] which features prominently in the behavioural economics literature. Most subjects in

---

[1] The experimental results in AR generalize to non-standard subject pools (that is, non-students). Arad and Rubinstein (2009) report that in the Passover 2009 supplement of the newspaper *Calcalist* and on the newspaper's website, a modified 11–20 game with hypothetical payoffs was posted wherein (*a*) the amount requested by a player was required to be an integer between 91 and 100 shekel and (*b*) the bonus from requesting one shekel less than the other player was set at 100 shekel. Contrary to the Nash predictions, *Calcalist* readers who participated in the game made requests that were concentrated on 97, 98 and 99 shekel.

[2] See, for instance, Nagel (1995) and Stahl and Wilson (1995).

the experiment, according to the level-k model, are rational and ask for money amounts that maximize the expected payoff, given beliefs about what their opponents will do. But beliefs vary across subjects and reflect the different steps of iterative thinking that subjects perform. More specifically, a level-0 subject is deemed to be non-strategic and acts *instinctively* without forming beliefs about others' behaviour. In the 11–20 game, AR argue persuasively that it is instinctive to ask for the maximal amount, that is, 20 shekel. The choice of level-0 subjects triggers the process of iterative reasoning. A level-1 subject engages in one round of iterative thinking: she mistakenly believes that all other subjects are level-0 types. Given such beliefs, a level-1 subject maximizes her payoff in the 11–20 game by asking for 19 shekel. A level-2 subject performs two rounds of iterative thinking: since she maintains that all other subjects are level-1 types, she maximizes her payoff with a request for 18 shekel. Similarly, a level-3 subject does three rounds of iterative thinking, believes that all other subjects are level-2 types, and views a 17-shekel request as her optimal choice. For $k = 0, 1, 2, \ldots$, notice that the algorithm inductively assigns a *unique* money request amount to a level-k subject. With the distribution of types in the subject pool left unspecified, the level-k model easily accounts for patterns in the AR data, for example, subjects' money request amounts are bunched on 17 to 19 shekel because the proportion of subjects in the category 'level-1 to level-3' is high; a request for 15 or 16 shekel is rarely observed in the experiment because few subjects are level-4 or level-5 types; and so on.

This paper builds on AR and experimentally studies the 11–20 game. We establish that the principal finding in AR is robust. Despite differences in the subject pool and experimental protocol, subjects' choices in our experiment are *not* drawn from the Nash equilibrium distribution. But the central question of our paper is: Should the level-k model be used to explain subjects' behaviour? Our answer, which is mixed, consists of two parts.

First, observe that a level-k' subject, by assumption, performs more steps of thinking than a level-k'' subject, for k'' less than k'. But whilst participating in the same game, why would one subject do more steps of thinking than another? Camerer et al. (2004: 877) speculate that a model endogenizing thinking steps would end up 'comparing benefits of thinking further with thinking costs (constrained by working memory, and permitting individual differences)'. The level-k model, supplemented with the plausible insight of Camerer et al. (2004), therefore, yields an immediate prediction: subjects with high cognitive abilities and low costs of thinking do more steps of thinking than subjects who are less able; this, in turn, finds reflection in the choices subjects make in an experiment. Does our data provide support for this prediction? All our subjects took the three-item Cognitive Reflection Test (henceforth CRT), devised by Frederick (2005). Each question in the CRT is specifically devised to invite a spontaneous and intuitive answer that is demonstrably incorrect. Thus, a subject obtains a high CRT score only when she has the ability to suppress immediate responses and engage in critical deliberation. We find that a subject's CRT score, viewed as a measure of cognitive ability, predicts her behaviour in our experiment. Specifically, subjects with high CRT scores ask for less money and are classified as higher level-k types than subjects with low CRT scores.[3] This then provides an *independent* justification for using the level-k model to rationalize subjects' behaviour in the 11–20 game.

Second, Rubinstein (2007) argues that when subjects respond to game situations, their choices can be categorized as cognitive (involving a reasoning process), instinctive (based on an emotion) or reasonless (the outcome of a random process with little reasoning in the decision process). Experimental data in Rubinstein (2007) show that decision makers' response time can be used to distinguish an instinctive choice from a cognitive one. Simply put, an instinctive choice is made more swiftly than a cognitive choice. The level-k model

---

[3] There is a small and recent literature that links cognitive ability of individuals and behaviour in *decision* environments. Two types of links are usually considered. First, among others, Oechssler et al. (2009) and Hoppe and Kusterer (2011) demonstrate that cognitively able individuals are less susceptible to various biases (for example, the base rate fallacy) that are emphasized in the behavioural economics and finance literatures. Second, among others, Frederick (2005), Dohmen et al. (2010) and Chen et al. (2013) show that cognitive ability is related to subjects' time preferences, risk attitudes and even social preferences. Our paper—which documents the connection between a subject's CRT score and her choice in the 11–20 game—contributes directly to a nascent literature that links cognitive ability of individuals and choices made in *game* situations. Burnham et al. (2009), Rydval et al. (2009) and Branas-Garza et al. (2012) study the guessing game introduced in Nagel (1995). The guessing game is dominance solvable and the Nash equilibrium has all players choosing the number zero. The aforementioned papers demonstrate that subjects who perform well on a cognitive ability test tend to choose small numbers in the guessing game (that is, exhibit behaviour that is close to the Nash equilibrium). We show that the predictive power of cognitive ability extends to a game for which the Nash equilibrium is difficult to compute and which is *not* dominance solvable.

applied to the 11–20 game unambiguously ranks the various choices in terms of the steps of thinking involved: a request of 20 money units is deemed to be an instinctive choice made by a non-strategic level-0 player, a request for 19 money units requires one round of iterative reasoning and, hence, entails some cognitive activity, and so on. The level-*k* model, supplemented with the insight of Rubinstein (2007), therefore, yields an immediate prediction: subjects' mean response time should increase as the money request amount in the 11–20 game decreases.[4] Does our data provide support for this prediction?

For each subject participating in our experiment, we record both her money request amount and the time (in seconds) it takes to submit her request. Surprisingly, we discover that subjects asking for the maximal amount, 20 rupees (deemed to be the *most* instinctive action according to the level-*k* model), have higher mean and median response time than subjects with money requests in the 17–19 rupees range. If we attach *some* weight to Rubinstein (2007), then the level-*k* model *fails* a decisive test. Our experiment advocates caution in using the level-*k* model to interpret subjects' behaviour in the 11–20 game.

The remainder of this paper is organized as follows. The next section describes our experiment, while the findings are reported in the third section. The fourth concludes.

The Experiment

The experiment used a total of 238 subjects and was conducted at the Centre for Experiments in Social and Behavioural Sciences at Jadavpur University, a well-known public university located in Kolkata, India. All of our subjects had expressed a prior interest to participate in experiments and were enrolled at the university. About 58 per cent of the subject pool was male and approximately 48 per cent comprised economics students.

---

[4] There is a small literature (see, for instance, Branas-Garza et al. 2007; Lotito et al. 2011; and Piovesan and Wengstrom 2008) that uses mean response time to decide whether it is instinctive for subjects to be fair. The idea is to check whether fair decisions are taken more quickly than decisions that are plainly egoistic. Our paper, on the other hand, uses the Rubinstein (2007) insight in a context that is plausibly unaffected by fairness considerations. Notice that when a subject manages to successfully undercut her opponent in the 11–20 game, she raises her own earnings, but leaves the earnings of her opponent unaffected.

The experiment was run on networked personal computers and was programmed using the z-Tree software (Fischbacher 2007). We conducted 17 sessions, each consisting of 14 subjects. A session was split in two halves. The first half took an hour to complete, and subjects participated in an experiment that explored the effects of incentives on group decision-making. The details of this experiment varied across the 17 sessions.[5] The second half of a session—the results of which this paper reports—was shorter in duration and lasted barely 10 minutes. Subjects participated in the one-question 11–20 game and completed the three-item CRT. We believe that the experiment conducted in the first half of a session did not affect subjects' decision-making later on. At a minimum, the reader may be assured that variations in the structure of the first experiment did not induce changes in either the distribution of subjects' choices in the 11–20 game or the distribution of subjects' CRT scores (results available upon request).

The 11–20 Money Request Game

At the outset, an experimenter read aloud the following instructions, which were projected on a screen visible to all subjects:

> You are randomly matched to play a game against one of the persons in this room. In this game, each of you requests an amount of money (an integer) between 11 rupees and 20 rupees. Each participant will receive the amount she requests. A participant will receive an additional 20 rupees if she asks for exactly one rupee less than the other player. You will receive your payment at the end of the session without knowing against whom you played. What amount of money do you request?

Subjects were permitted to ask for clarification if the instructions were found to be confusing or ambiguous. The questions were answered by an experimenter in public and for all to hear.

Upon receiving a prompt from the subject, our experimental program generated a computer screen that displayed (once again) the instructions for the 11–20 game, read out previously in the instruction phase and noted above. Some subjects reread the instructions, while

---

[5] The group decision-making experiments in the 17 sessions were major and minor variants of Van Huyck et al.'s (1990) minimum-effort game. The details are available upon request.

most did not. In a specific location on the computer screen, a subject had to input her money request amount and confirm her choice. For each subject, the experimental program recorded her response time, measured as the time (in seconds) between the moment that the 11–20 game screen appeared for the subject and the moment that the subject confirmed her choice in the game. As in Rubinstein (2007), subjects were not informed that response time was being recorded.

After the experimental program had received the money request information from all 14 subjects, it paired subjects randomly and determined each subject's earnings from the 11–20 game. A subject's earnings for the entire session was her earnings from the 11–20 game added to that obtained from the earlier and unreported experiment.

We conclude this subsection with the following two observations about our implementation of the 11–20 game. First, we recognize that subjects' response time is, at best, a noisy measure of the time spent thinking about an answer to the posed question. This is because a part of the variation in response time derives from the fact that some subjects reread the 11–20 game instructions on the computer screen while others did not. Furthermore, even within the set of subjects who reread the instructions, reading time is likely to vary substantially. Second, we acknowledge that the monetary incentive in our experiment is small— the maximum that a subject can earn in the 11–20 game is 39 rupees (approximately 0.80 US dollars at the current exchange rate). We anticipate that as the monetary incentive is raised, subjects would engage in additional rounds of cognitively costly introspection. As a result, the distribution of subjects' choices might change.[6]

The Cognitive Reflection Test

As the final task in the experiment, subjects took the three-item CRT. No verbal instructions were given. Each subject's computer screen displayed the following three questions:

1. A bat and a ball cost $1.10 in total. The bat costs $1.00 more than the ball. How much does the ball cost? _____ cents
2. If it takes 5 machines 5 minutes to make 5 widgets, how long would it take 100 machines to make 100 widgets? _____ minutes
3. In a lake, there is a patch of lily pads. Every day, the patch doubles in size. If it takes 48 days for the patch to cover the entire lake,

---

[6] See Alaoui and Penta (2012) for evidence of this incentive effect.

how long would it take for the patch to cover half of the lake? _____ days

We permitted subjects to use pencil and paper to do calculations if required. The test was not time bound and ended when subjects inputed their answers on the computer screen. No payment was made to subjects for taking the CRT.

Frederick (2005) observes that each question in the CRT is so constructed that an intuitive answer immediately comes to mind (10 cents, 100 minutes and 24 days for questions 1, 2 and 3 respectively). But the intuitive answer is incorrect. Minimal reflection suffices to spot the error in the intuitive answer, at which point the right answer (5 cents, 5 minutes and 47 days for questions 1, 2 and 3 respectively) becomes transparent. Subjects with low CRT scores are, therefore, cognitively impulsive; they stick with intuitive answers and do not expend the effort required to ascertain their validity. By contrast, subjects with high CRT scores engage in cognitive reflection; they are capable of critically examining and suppressing spontaneous responses that are plainly compelling as well.

In our sample of 238 subjects, the distribution of the CRT score is as follows: 26 subjects (10.9 per cent) scored 3 (all questions answered correctly), 51 subjects (21.4 per cent) scored 2 and 68 subjects (28.6 per cent) scored 1, while the remaining 93 subjects (39.1 per cent) scored 0. The mean CRT score in our sample is 1.04, which is comparable to that reported in Frederick (2005).[7] Table 10.2 shows the distribution of answers for each CRT question. Table 10.2 elicits two observations. First, the 'bat and ball' question proved the hardest to answer correctly and created the most confusion, as measured by the proportion of our subjects who gave an answer that was neither correct nor intuitive. We suspect that framing this question in terms of dollars and cents was inappropriate for subjects used to a *different* currency. Second, when incorrect answers were given by subjects, the chance that the intuitive answer was selected ranges from 47 per cent in question 1 to 62 per cent in question 3. Clearly, within the set of all incorrect answers, the intuitive answer receives disproportionate attention. Our subjects' behaviour, therefore, reflects the underlying logic of the CRT:

---

[7] Frederick (2005) reports that the CRT was administered to 3,428 respondents, mostly undergraduates at various US universities, over a 26-month period beginning in January 2003. The mean CRT score was 1.24.

TABLE 10.2 Subjects' Responses in the Cognitive Reflection Test

	Subjects providing the correct answer	Subjects providing an incorrect answer	
		Intuitive answer	Other answer
(1) Bat and ball	26.5%	34.5%	39.0%
(2) Machines and widgets	43.7%	32.8%	23.5%
(3) Lily pad and pond	34.5%	40.3%	25.2%

Notes: 238 subjects took the CRT. The 'correct answer' for questions 1, 2 and 3 of the CRT are 5 cents, 5 minutes and 47 days respectively. The 'intuitive answer' for questions 1, 2 and 3 of the CRT are 10 cents, 100 minutes and 24 days respectively. 'Other answer' for a question refers to an answer that is neither the correct answer nor the intuitive answer.

to a first approximation, subjects were 'choosing' between the wrong but intuitive answer and the correct but cognitively demanding answer.

Experimental Results

We present the experimental results in three parts. The first contrasts the Nash predictions of the 11–20 game with the distribution of subjects' choices in our experiment. The second tests whether a subject's CRT score predicts the amount of money requested in the experiment. Finally, the third links the mean response time of subjects to the number of steps of iterative reasoning implicit in a choice.

Distribution of Subjects' Choices

Row 1 of Table 10.3 shows the Nash equilibrium distribution for the 11–20 game, while row 2 shows the distribution of subjects' choices in our experiment. Consistent with the findings in AR, it is immediate that the Nash equilibrium does not explain our experimental data. Indeed, the Pearson's chi-squared test rejects at the 1 per cent significance level the null hypothesis that money request amounts in our experiment are drawn from the Nash equilibrium distribution. The Nash equilibrium predictions fail on two counts. First, the occurrence of a money request for either 15 or 16 rupees is overpredicted (10 per cent of our subjects make such a request in contrast to the prediction of 50 per cent). Second, the occurrence of a money request in the 17–19 rupees range

TABLE 10.3 Nash Distribution and Subjects' Choices in Our Experiment

	Choices/Money request amounts									
	11	12	13	14	15	16	17	18	19	20
Distribution of choices in the Nash equilibrium	0%	0%	0%	0%	25%	25%	20%	15%	10%	5%
Distribution of choices in our experiment	3%	3%	3%	4%	5%	5%	9%	29%	29%	10%

Notes: In the 11–20 game, a player's money request amount is an integer between 11 and 20. Row 1 shows the chance of choosing each integer in the 11–20 range in the unique Nash equilibrium of the game. 238 subjects from Jadavpur University, Kolkata, participated in our experimental test of the 11–20 game. For this experiment, row 2 shows the percentage of subjects that chose each integer in the 11–20 range.

is underpredicted (67 per cent of our subjects make such a request in contrast to the prediction of 50 per cent).

The distribution of subjects' choices in our experiment is also distinct from that in AR, shown in row 2 of Table 10.1. At the 5 percent significance level, the Pearson's chi-squared test rejects the null hypothesis that the distributions of subjects' choices in the two experiments share a common data generating process. The main difference between the two distributions centres on the relative use of the level-1 strategy (that is, 19) and the level-3 strategy (that is, 17). In the AR experiment, money requests of 17 shekel and 19 shekel were made by 32 per cent and 12 per cent of the subjects respectively; in our experiment, the corresponding numbers are 9 per cent and 29 per cent. In other words, AR subjects did more rounds of iterative thinking than our subjects. We are unsurprised that the distribution of level-k strategies varies with the subject pool.[8] Conclusion 1 summarizes the preceding discussion.

Conclusion 1: Consistent with the findings in AR, the Nash equilibrium of the 11–20 game does not explain our experimental data. Relative to the Nash equilibrium predictions, too many of our subjects ask for

---

[8] There are several procedural differences as well between our experiment and that reported in AR (for example, computerized versus hand-run). But we view these procedural differences as minor and, therefore, unlikely to account for the disparities in the distributions of subjects' choices in the two experiments.

money in the 17–19 rupees range and too few submit a request for either 15 or 16 rupees.

CRT Score and Depth of Iterative Reasoning

We have argued in the beginning that the structure of the level-*k* model, augmented by the cost–benefit argument in Camerer et al. (2004), suggests a *direct* link between the cognitive ability of a person and the number of steps of iterative reasoning that she uses when placed in a game situation. We provide a test of this link. The question we pose is as follows: In our experiment, do subjects with high CRT scores ask for less money (thereby implicitly displaying more steps of level-*k* thinking) than subjects with low CRT scores?

Before addressing the question, a preliminary remark is necessary. Notice that when the level-*k* model is applied mechanically to the 11–20 game, every money request amount can be rationalized as the action taken by *some* level-*k* player (for example, a 12-rupee request is made by a level-8 player, a 11-rupee request is made by a level-9 player, and so on). But carefully conducted experiments confirm that subjects in the laboratory rarely engage in more than a few steps of iterative reasoning. Crawford et al. (2013) survey applications of the level-*k* model in economics and observe, 'The type distribution is fairly stable across settings, with most weight on *L1*, *L2*, and perhaps *L3*.'[9] Camerer et al. (2003) develop a closely related cognitive hierarchy model and show that except in two analytically skilled and outlier groups (computer scientists and game theorists), the average number of steps of iterative thinking never exceeds three. These findings have a bearing on how we interpret subjects' choices in our experiment. We maintain that a money request in the 11–16 rupees range *cannot* come from a subject engaged in level-*k* thinking since this would involve too many steps of iterative reasoning;[10] by contrast, when a subject asks for money in the 17–20 rupees range, we assume that level-*k* thinking *may* apply.

In the empirical analysis that follows, attention is restricted to the 182 subjects with money requests in the 17–20 rupees range. We

---

[9] In Crawford et al. (2013), *L1*, *L2* and *L3* are shorthands for level-1, level-2 and level-3 respectively.

[10] To make matters concrete, 10 per cent of our subjects submitted a request for either 15 or 16 rupees (refer to Table 10.3). Perhaps such subjects were using the simple heuristic of picking a money request amount close to the mid-point of the two extreme requests, 11 rupees and 20 rupees.

partition these subjects into two roughly equal-sized groups: group I comprises subjects with CRT scores equal to zero, while subjects in group II answered at least one CRT question correctly. Splitting the sample this way is of course arbitrary, but the results we report are qualitatively unchanged for other reasonable ways of grouping our subjects (results available upon request). Consider Figure 10.1. On the x-axis are marked four numbers: 17, 18, 19 and 20. Fix attention on any *one* of the four numbers. The height of the associated black bar shows the proportion of subjects in group I whose money request amounts in our experiment were less than or equal to the chosen number; the height of the grey bar shows the corresponding proportion for group II subjects.[11] Notice that in the 17–19 rupees range, the height of the grey bar strictly exceeds that of the black bar, that is, in our experiment, the empirical cumulative distribution function of money request amounts for group I subjects first-order stochastically dominates the corresponding empirical cumulative distribution function for group II subjects. Put simply, Figure 10.1 demonstrates that on an average, subjects with CRT scores equal to zero ask for more money than subjects with CRT scores exceeding zero.

Does a formal regression analysis confirm the message of Figure 10.1? We proceed in three steps. First, we construct the dependent variable *Level* as follows. On the basis of her money request amount in the 11–20 game, $Level_i$ is the k-level assigned to subject i (for example, a 20-rupee request classifies the subject as 0-level, a 19-rupee request classifies the subject as 1-level, and so on). *Level* is, therefore, a discrete and ordinal variable that takes four integer values, 0 to 3. Second, we construct three binary explanatory variables—*Genderdum*, *Econdum* and *CRTdum*—as follows. $Genderdum_i$ is equal to 1 if subject i is male and is 0 otherwise. $Econdum_i$ is equal to 1 if subject i is enrolled in an economics programme and is 0 otherwise. $CRTdum_i$ is equal to 1 if subject i answered correctly at least one question in the CRT and is 0 otherwise. Third, to determine whether a subject's CRT score predicts her assigned k-level in the 11–20 game, we ran ordered probit regressions. Table 10.4 shows the results.

Column 1 of Table 10.4 explains the variation in *Level* using a single regressor: *CRTdum*. The coefficient on this regressor is statistically

---

[11] Consider the number 18. The height of the black (grey) bar shows that approximately 33 per cent (61 per cent) of the subjects in group I (II) ask for either 17 or 18 rupees in our experiment.

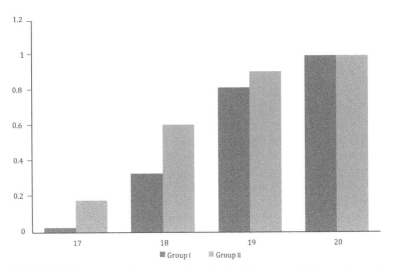

FIGURE 10.1 Empirical Cumulative Distribution Functions of Money Request Amounts

significant and positive. On average, therefore, subjects with *CRTdum* equal to one ask for smaller money amounts and are deemed to be higher level-k types than subjects with *CRTdum* equal to zero.[12] This, of course, is also the central message of Figure 10.1. Column 2 includes *Genderdum* and *Econdum* as additional regressors. Relative to column 1, the coefficient on *CRTdum* decreases in magnitude, but remains positive and statistically significant. On the other hand, the variables *Genderdum* and *Econdum* do not achieve statistical significance. To test the robustness of the results in columns 1 and 2, we replace *CRTdum* with the variable *CRTscore*, which is simply the

---

[12] The ordered probit model posits three cut-point parameters, α_j, $j = 0, 1, 2$ that are strictly increasing in j. For $j = 0, 1, 2$, let $Pr(Level_i \leq j | CRTdum_i = 1)$ and $Pr(Level_i \leq j | CRTdum_i = 0)$ denote the probability that the level assigned to subject i is less than or equal to j given that her CRT score is non-zero and zero respectively. The ordered probit model says that $Pr(Level_i \leq j | CRTdum_i = 1)$ is equal to $\Phi(\alpha_j - \beta)$, while $Pr(Level_i \leq j | CRTdum_i = 0)$ is equal to $\Phi(\alpha_j)$, where $\Phi(.)$ is the standard normal cumulative distribution function and β is the coefficient on *CRTdum*. Since β is estimated to be positive in Table 10.4, the distribution of *Level* for subjects with *CRTdum* equal to one first-order stochastically dominates the distribution of *Level* for subjects with *CRTdum* equal to zero.

TABLE 10.4 Ordered Probit Model of Subjects' Levels

	[1]	[2]	[3]	[4]
CRTdum	0.75**	0.68**		
	(0.18)	(0.18)		
Econdum		−0.14		−0.09
		(0.22)		(0.24)
Genderdum		0.25		0.21
		(0.20)		(0.20)
CRTscore			0.41**	0.37**
			(0.10)	(0.10)
Cut-point α_1	−0.67	−0.47	−0.64	−0.69
	(0.50)	(0.54)	(0.48)	(0.63)
Cut-point α_2	0.59	0.80	0.63	0.59
	(0.49)	(0.53)	(0.47)	(0.64)
Cut-point α_3	1.91**	2.14**	1.95**	1.92**
	(0.50)	(0.53)	(0.48)	(0.67)
Pseudo R-squared	0.08	0.08	0.08	0.08
No. of obs.	182	182	182	182

Notes: The dependent variable is *Level*, which takes four values: 0, 1, 2 and 3. The four independent variables—*CRTdum*, *Econdum*, *Genderdum* and *CRTscore*—are defined in the text. All four regressions included session dummies as independent variables, and many of these dummies are statistically significant (results available upon request). For each estimated coefficient, the robust standard errors are shown in parentheses. ** denotes significance at the 0.01 level (two-tailed).

score received by subjects in the CRT.[13] The findings of columns 3 and 4 are identical to that of the first two columns: the CRT score of subject i predicts her behaviour in the 11–20 game, but gender and field of study (economics versus non-economics) have no explanatory power. Conclusion 2 notes the main result of this subsection.

Conclusion 2: A subject's CRT score predicts her behaviour in our experiment. Specifically, subjects with high CRT scores ask for less money and are classified as higher level-k types than subjects with low CRT scores.

---

[13] Since there are three questions in the CRT, *CRTscore* takes four values: 0, 1, 2 and 3.

TABLE 10.5 Distribution of Subjects' Response Time

Money request amount (rupees) [1]	No. of subjects [2]	Min. response time (seconds) [3]	Max. response time (seconds) [4]	Mean response time (seconds) [5]	Median response time (seconds) [6]
17	22	3	85	29.9	22.5
18	69	4	164	29.0	18.0
19	68	4	173	38.3	22.0
20	23	6	134	44.7	40.0

Notes: In our experiment, 182 subjects chose money request amounts in the 17–20 rupees range. For each money request amount, column 2 shows the number of subjects making that choice. Given the empirical distribution of response times for each money request amount, columns 3–6 show the minimum response time, the maximum response time, the mean of the response times and the median of the response times respectively.

Response Time and Depth of Iterative Reasoning

We have argued in the beginning that the level-*k* model, supplemented with the insight of Rubinstein (2007), yields the following a priori expectation: the mean response time of subjects should increase as the money request amount in the 11–20 game decreases. What do the data say?

As in the previous section, we restrict attention to the 182 subjects with money requests in the 17–20 rupees range. For *each* money request amount in this range, we examined the empirical distribution of subjects' response time and report summary statistics of this distribution in columns 3–6 of Table 10.5. Our findings do *not* comport with our prior expectation. Two observations make this point starkly. First, consider column 5. When the money requested is in the 17–19 rupees range, the means of subjects' response time range from 29.0 seconds to 38.3 seconds. By contrast, the mean response time for subjects requesting 20 rupees is a significantly higher 44.7 seconds. Second, consider column 6. When the money requested is in the 17–19 rupees range, the medians of subjects' response time range from 18 seconds to 22.5 seconds. By contrast, the median response time jumps to 40 seconds for subjects requesting 20 rupees.

We buttress the message of Table 10.5 with regression results. The dependent variable *ResponseTime* is constructed as follows.

TABLE 10.6 Regression Analysis of Subjects' Response Time

	[1]	[2]
20dum	10.05*	10.05*
	(5.01)	(5.03)
Econdum		−3.02
		(3.40)
Genderdum		0.79
		(3.22)
R-squared	0.81	0.81
No. of obs.	182	182

Notes: The results in columns 1 and 2 are for ordinary least squares regressions. The dependent variable is *ResponseTime*, which is the time taken by a subject to submit her money request amount in the 11–20 game. *Response Time* is measured in seconds. *20dum* is a binary variable that is equal to 1 if the subject makes a 20-rupees request in the 11–20 game and is 0 otherwise. *Econdum* and *Genderdum* are defined previously in the text. The regressions include session dummies as independent variables, and many of these dummies are statistically significant (results available upon request). For each estimated coefficient, the robust standard errors are shown in parentheses. *denotes significance at the 0.05 level (two-tailed).

$ResponseTime_i$ measures the time (in seconds) taken by subject i to make her money request in the 11–20 game. The critical explanatory variable *20dum* is constructed as follows: $20dum_i$ is equal to 1 if subject i requests 20 rupees and is 0 otherwise. Column 1 of Table 10.6 explains the variation in *ResponseTime* by running an ordinary least squares regression with a single regressor: *20dum*. Column 2 of Table 10.6 includes *Genderdum* and *Econdum* as additional regressors. Our conclusions are twofold. First, the coefficient on *20dum* is statistically significant, positive and remarkably stable across the two columns of Table 10.6. On average, subjects making 20-rupee requests take 10 seconds more to respond in the 11–20 game relative to subjects asking for less than 20 rupees. Second, the variables *Genderdum* and *Econdum* are not statistically significant. So, a subject's gender and field of study have no bearing on her response time. Conclusion 3 highlights the main finding of this subsection.

Conclusion 3: In our experiment, a subject's money request amount predicts her response time. Subjects asking for 20 rupees have higher mean and median response time than subjects with money requests in the 17–19 rupees range.

Conclusion 3 can be interpreted in two ways. First, if we insist that subjects' response time successfully discriminates between instinctive and cognitive choices a la Rubinstein (2007), then the level-k model *fails* a decisive test. In the specific context of the 11–20 game, the level-k model argues that the 20-rupee request constitutes the most instinctive choice for subjects; yet the mean response time criterion identifies this choice as cognitively demanding. Second, consistent with Chong et al. (2005), we could insist that the level-k model stands unscathed whilst suggesting that the Rubinstein (2007) intuition be modified. The argument is as follows. A request for 17 rupees entails several steps of iterative thinking unlike the instinctive 20-rupee request. But subjects making the 17–rupee request are intrinsically smarter than those asking for 20 rupees. If smart subjects are fast thinkers to boot, the mean response time for the 17–rupee request could well be smaller than that corresponding to the 20-rupee request. We do not have the data to take a firm stance on the relative merits of the two interpretations. But the latter interpretation, based on the endogenous sorting of subjects, is unlikely to be *entirely* correct. It turns out that if we regress *ResponseTime* on *20dum* and a control for the smartness of the subject (for example, *CRTdum*), the coefficient on *20dum* remains positive and statistically significant (results omitted for brevity but available upon request).

Conclusion

The 11–20 game has a simple structure that is easy to understand. Yet, when AR study the 11–20 game experimentally, the unique Nash equilibrium of the game does not explain subjects' behaviour. AR rationalize subjects' behaviour by appealing to the level-k model.

This paper builds on AR. We establish that the main finding in AR is robust. Despite differences in subject pool and experimental protocol, our experiment with the 11–20 game also shows that subjects' choices are not drawn from the Nash equilibrium distribution. But does the level-k model *rationalize* subjects' behaviour? We provide two perspectives. First, if depth of reasoning in the level-k model reflects the cognitive ability of subjects, then an independent measure of cognitive ability should predict choices in the 11–20 game. Indeed, in our experiment, a subject's CRT score predicts her money request amount. Second, if instinctive choices are made more swiftly than cognitive choices, then a 20-rupee money request—identified by the level-k model as the most instinctive action in the 11–20 game—should take less time to make than a request in the 17–19 rupees range. Surprisingly, in our experiment, subjects asking for 20 rupees have higher mean and median response times than subjects with money requests in the 17–19 rupees range. In the context of the 11–20 game, we advocate caution in using the level-k model to interpret experimental data.

References

Alaoui, Larbi and Antonio Penta. 2012. 'Level-k Reasoning and Incentives: An Experiment (Summary)', Mimeo.

Arad, Ayala and Ariel Rubinstein. 2009. 'Let Game Theory Be?' *Calcalist*, 11 May.

————. 2012. 'The 11–20 Money Request Game: A Level-k Reasoning Study', *American Economic Review*, 102(7):3561–73.

Branas-Garza, Pablo, Teresa Garcia-Munoz and Roberto Hernan. 2012. 'Cognitive Effort in the Beauty Contest Game', *Journal of Economic Behavior and Organization*, 83(2):254–60.

Branas-Garza, Pablo, Ana Leon-Mejia and Luis Miller. 2007. 'Response Time under Monetary Incentives: The Ultimatum Game', Mimeo.

Burnham, Terence, David Cesarini, Magnus Johannesson, Paul Lichtenstein and Bjorn Wallace. 2009. 'Higher Cognitive Ability Is Associated with Lower Entries in a p-beauty Contest', *Journal of Economic Behavior and Organization*, 72(1):171–75.

Camerer, Colin, Teck-Hua Ho and Juin-Kuan Chong. 2003. 'Models of Thinking, Learning, and Teaching in Games', *American Economic Review*, 93(2):192–95.

————. 2004. 'A Cognitive Hierarchy Model of Behavior in Games', *Quarterly Journal of Economics*, 119(3):861–98.

Chen, Chia-Ching, I-Ming Chiu, John Smith and Tetsuji Yamada. 2013. 'Too Smart to Be Selfish? Measures of Cognitive Ability, Social Preferences, and Consistency', Mimeo.

Chong, Juin-Kuan, Colin Camerer and Teck-Hua Ho. 2005. 'Cognitive Hierarchy: A Limited Thinking Theory in Games', in Rami Zwick and Amnon Rapoport (eds), *Experimental Business Research*, Vol. III. Netherlands: Springer, pp. 203–28.

Crawford, Vincent, Miguel Costa-Gomes and Nagore Iriberri. 2013. 'Structural Models of Nonequilibrium Thinking: Theory,

Evidence, and Applications', *Journal of Economic Literature*, 51(1): 5–62.

Dohmen, Thomas, Armin Falk, David Huffman and Uwe Sunde. 2010. 'Are Risk Aversion and Impatience Related to Cognitive Ability?' *American Economic Review*, 100(3):1238–60.

Fischbacher, Urs. 2007. 'z-Tree: Zurich Toolbox for Ready-Made Economic Experiments', *Experimental Economics*, 10(2):171–78.

Frederick, Shane. 2005. 'Cognitive Reflection and Decision Making', *Journal of Economic Perspectives*, 19(4):25–42.

Hoppe, Eva and David Kusterer. 2011. 'Behavioral Biases and Cognitive Reflection', *Economics Letters*, 110(2):97–100.

Lotito, Gianna, Matteo Migheli and Guido Ortona. 2011. 'Is Cooperation Instinctive? Evidence from the Response Times in a Public Goods Game', Mimeo.

Nagel, Rosemarie. 1995. 'Unraveling in Guessing Games: An Experimental Study', *American Economic Review*, 85(5):1313–26.

Oechssler, Jorg, Andreas Roider and Patrick Schmitz. 2009. 'Cognitive Abilities and Behavioral Biases', *Journal of Economic Behavior and Organization*, 72(1):147–52.

Piovesan, Marco and Erik Wengstrom. 2008. 'Fast or Fair? A Study of Response Times', Mimeo.

Rubinstein, Ariel. 2007. 'Instinctive and Cognitive Reasoning: A Study of Response Times', *Economic Journal*, 117(523):1243–59.

Rydval, Ondrej, Andreas Ortmann and Michal Ostatnicky. 2009. 'Three Very Simple Games and What It Takes to Solve Them', *Journal of Economic Behavior and Organization*, 72(1):589–601.

Stahl, Dale and Paul Wilson. 1995. 'On Players' Models of Other Players: Theory and Experimental Evidence', *Games and Economic Behavior*, 10(1):218–54.

Van Huyck, John, Raymond Battalio and Richard Beil. 1990. 'Tacit Coordination Games, Strategic Uncertainty, and Coordination Failure', *American Economic Review*, 80(1):234–48.

For Product Safety Concerns and Information please contact our EU
representative GPSR@taylorandfrancis.com Taylor & Francis Verlag GmbH,
Kaufingerstraße 24, 80331 München, Germany

Printed and bound by CPI Group (UK) Ltd, Croydon, CR0 4YY
08/05/2025
01864327-0001